Christians and Muslims in Early Medieval Italy

In the early Middle Ages, Italy became the target of Muslim expansionist campaigns. The Muslims conquered Sicily, ruling there for more than two centuries, and conducted many raids against the Italian Peninsula. During this period, however, Christians and Muslims were not always at war – trade flourished, and travel to the territories of the 'other' was not uncommon. By examining how Muslims and Christians perceived each other and how they communicated, this book brings the relationship between Muslims and Christians in early medieval Italy into clearer focus, showing that the followers of the Cross and those of the Crescent were in reality not as ignorant of one another as is commonly believed.

Luigi Andrea Berto is Professor of Medieval History at Western Michigan University, USA. His research focuses on medieval Italy and the Mediterranean, with a special interest in the use of the past and the relationships between Christians and Muslims.

Studies in Medieval History and Culture

Recent titles include

Christians and Muslims in Early Medieval Italy

Perceptions, Encounters, and Clashes

Luigi Andrea Berto

Routledge
Taylor & Francis Group

LONDON AND NEW YORK

First published 2020
by Routledge
2 Park Square, Milton Park, Abingdon, Oxon OX14 4RN

and by Routledge
52 Vanderbilt Avenue, New York, NY 10017

Routledge is an imprint of the Taylor & Francis Group, an informa business

© 2020 Luigi Andrea Berto

British Library Cataloguing-in-Publication Data
A catalogue record for this book is available from the British Library

Library of Congress Cataloging-in-Publication Data
A catalog record for this title has been requested

ISBN: 978-0-367-41472-6 (hbk)
ISBN: 978-0-367-81464-9 (ebk)

Typeset in Times
by Deanta Global Publishing Services, Chennai, India

Published in Italian in a different version as *Cristiani e musulmani
nell'Italia dei primi secoli del Medioevo. Percezioni, scontri e incontri*
(Milan: Jouvence, 2018).

Contents

Maps

Abbreviations

BAS   *Biblioteca Arabo-Sicula*, Italian translation by M. Amari, 2 vols. (Turin and Rome, 1880–1881)

MGH   *Monumenta Germaniae Historica*

Acknowledgments

I wish to thank Michael Greenwood for agreeing to publish this volume and the staff at Routledge, Delphine, Stefano Trovato, and Matthew Trojacek, for their help. I also thank the Burnham–MacMillan History Department Endowment of Western Michigan University for covering a part of the copy-editing costs.

Introduction

Introduction

Muslim expansion into the western Mediterranean in the early Middle Ages had a great influence on Italy. Indeed, Muslims conquered Sicily, created some independent dominions in southern Italy, and frequently raided some parts of the Peninsula. Most of the primary sources about this period are narrative sources that focus above all on the events of war (war and violence have always been popular news), and therefore the image of adversaries portrayed in them is, unsurprisingly, negative. The idea of an unceasing state of belligerence between Muslims and Christians is, however, inaccurate. Without minimizing the extent of the destruction that occurred in these centuries, this study primarily intends to contextualize the features of those images, considering the existence of some nuances. To have a better understanding of the history of this period, besides examining the effects of wars and raids, this book will also analyze what was known about the 'other' as well as the relationships between them during peaceful times. The epoch here examined is very broad, and Italy in these centuries was diverse economically, politically, and culturally. Consequently, I will not make any grand generalizations. What emerges for a specific context will not be considered valid for every part of Italy and for all the early Middle Ages. I hope this book will demonstrate the existence of a panorama of life and interaction more diversified than that usually depicted between Christians and Muslims.

The chronological period under examination ranges from the first part of the ninth century to the late eleventh century, thus completing a cycle that begins with the Muslim conquest of Sicily and ends with the return of the island to Christian hands. Because the analysis will be comparative and the Muslim primary sources about the Norman conquest of Sicily are very brief, I will also examine Muslim works about Sicily and North Africa in the twelfth century, as they provide more detail. In this way, it will be possible to make comparisons with texts in which the Muslims were those who suffered the attacks of Italian Christians.

This book is addressed to a non-specialist audience and therefore issues related to sources, hypotheses, and historiographical debates will not be discussed here in order not to weigh down the text and the endnotes. Some information about the sources and bibliographical references are mentioned in the appendix. An overview of the main events will guide those unfamiliar with early medieval Italian history through this volume. As for terminology, the word 'Arab' will not be used, because most of the Muslims of the centuries examined here did not descend from the warriors who came from the Arabian Peninsula. They were, in fact, inhabitants of northwestern Africa and Sicily converted to Islam. To avoid too many repetitions, the word 'Saracen', which is the most common term for Muslims in the Christian sources, will be utilized as a synonym for Muslim. The dates will be indicated according to the Christian era, but when mentioning chronological references recorded in Muslim works, the dating quoted there will be reported as well. Keep in mind that 'year zero' of the Muslim era corresponds to AD 622 and that the Muslims follow the lunar calendar, which has 355 days.

The events

The Muslims' arrival to Sicily in 827 was nothing new to the western Mediterranean. They had conquered easily almost all the Middle and Near East by taking advantage of the poor resistance of the local peoples and of the weakening of the Persian and Byzantine Empires (the latter being the heir of the Eastern Roman Empire); Mohammed's (d. 632) successors, however, could not overcome the powerful defenses of Constantinople. Instead, they met greater success moving westward. The Muslim warriors arrived on the Atlantic coast of northwestern Africa near the end of the seventh century, and at the beginning of the next century easily conquered almost all the Iberian Peninsula. From these lands, they launched several incursions against Sicily and, above all, Sardinia. A famous precedent to these raids occurred shortly after 663, when, taking advantage of some conflicts among the Byzantines in Sicily, a Saracen fleet sailed from Alexandria and sacked Syracuse.

Upon the Muslims' arrival in Sicily in 827, the political situation in Italy was stable. The earthquake had taken place in the previous century, when the king of the Franks Charlemagne conquered the northern area of the kingdom of the Lombards, who had settled in Italy at the end of the sixth century.

During the eighth century, Rome and some parts of central Italy became independent of Constantinople's authority. In the South, the Lombards of the Duchy of Benevento (consisting of the hinterland of Campania, Salerno, and some areas of Apulia, Basilicata, and Calabria) created an independent principality, while, on the Tyrrhenian coast, Naples became autonomous from the Byzantines. The remaining areas of southern Italy and Sicily belonged to Constantinople.

As in other cases, in the Muslim campaign of 827, the faithful of Islam benefited from the dissensions among the Byzantines; on that occasion, a rebel imperial officer invited them to join him in fighting the Byzantines. The lack of a strong cohesion among the Christians on the island and the failure to send a large army from Constantinople, too busy on the eastern front, led the invaders to stay and conquer Sicily. It was not a quick war. Unlike the subjects of the southeastern provinces of the Byzantine Empire, most of the Sicilians did not have a strong grudge against the authorities of Constantinople, did not perceive the Muslims as liberators, and therefore decided to resist the invaders. They did not face them in the open field, however, but preferred to lock themselves in their well-fortified cities. The Saracens had to besiege them, sometimes for many months, and conquer these cities one by one. Palermo fell in 831 and northwestern Sicily was subjugated in the following ten years. From there, the followers of Islam moved eastwards along the coast and took Messina in 842/843; six years later they occupied the southwestern part of the island and Ragusa. Thanks to the conquest of Castrogiovanni (present-day Enna), gained in 859 after several attempts, the Muslims controlled the central area of Sicily. The powerful defenses of the cities on the eastern coast, several insurrections, the help of the imperial fleet, and disagreements among the Muslims slowed the completion of the conquest of the island. After repeated attacks, Syracuse fell only in 878; Taormina in 902 (the latter subsequently returned to imperial control and was finally taken around 964).

In the same period, the Muslims' presence grew stronger in other areas of Italy as well. The quarrelsome Christian rulers of the South of the Peninsula often employed Saracen mercenaries in their struggles against each other. The further fragmentation of the power in that region, the near complete disappearance of the Byzantines from that territory, and the wars among Charlemagne's grandchildren favored some enterprising Muslim military leaders. As soon as they discovered how weak their Christian employers were, they did not hesitate to create independent dominions in Apulia. They also established some strongholds on the coasts of Campania and Calabria.

The most famous domains were those of Bari and Taranto, created in the 840s. The settlement at the mouth of the Garigliano River between Latium and Campania, on the other hand, was founded forty years later. Contacts between these centers and the Saracens in Sicily likely took place, but their leaders acted independently from the Muslim authorities of the island, who were still engaged with the conquest of Sicily. Moreover, they only created small dominions from which no attempts were made to seize other areas. Their formation and survival were due more to the Christians' weakness than to the Muslims' power in those territories. The faithful of Islam used these bases to carry out raids along the coasts as well as throughout southern Italy. The victims of the Muslim raids were not exclusively the inhabitants of southern Italy. In the 840s, Allah's followers carried out two expeditions through the Adriatic Sea: they pillaged several coastal cities and defeated the Venetian fleet twice. Thirty years later, they conducted another raid in the northern Adriatic Sea, then entered the Po River delta and set Comacchio on fire. The most spectacular incursion in these years was, however, the one carried out in 846 against Rome. The city was not taken, but the assailants looted the St. Peter and St. Paul basilicas, which were located outside the city walls. This raid against the heart of western Christianity had a great resonance in western Europe. The Frankish emperor Lothar, who until then had been engaged in defending his dominions beyond the Alps, arranged an expedition led by his son Louis II against the Muslims of southern Italy. The only result, however, was the reconquest of Benevento from the Saracens' control. Louis II, king of Italy since 844 and emperor since 855, had always lived in the Peninsula and demonstrated a great commitment to fighting the Muslims, but the lack of a large army and the ineffective collaboration on the part of the suspicious Christian rulers of the South prevented him from intervening effectively for several years. Only in 871 did he succeed in ending the Muslims' control over Bari, thanks to the help provided by the Byzantine fleet and the southern Lombards. There were no further successes because, fearing that Louis II would demand his submission, the prince of Benevento imprisoned him shortly afterwards; he released the emperor only after extorting from him the promise that he would never enter those regions again unless invited. The Muslims took advantage of the Christian front's disintegration to launch a large-scale attack against Salerno, an event that previously had never happened. The city was saved only because the Lombards managed to persuade Louis II to help them against such a powerful enemy. The death of the sovereign in 875 without an heir began the struggle for the crown, and, after Louis II, no king of Italy had the interest or strength needed to deal with the Saracens in the South.

The strengthening of Byzantine power in these years allowed them to regain Apulia, Basilicata, and Calabria and to prevent the creation of other Muslim dominions in the Lower Adriatic. The weakness of and the conflicts between the Lombards and the duchies of the Tyrrhenian coast, as well as the need for the Campanian city-states to enjoy peaceful relationships with the followers of Islam to ensure a certain degree of safety for their trade activities in the Tyrrhenian Sea, permitted the Saracens to continue their incursions in this region as well as in Latium. It was in this chaotic period that the great monasteries of Saint Vincent at Volturno and Montecassino, which until then had been kept safe by giving tributes to the faithful of Islam, were plundered and burned by the Muslims in 881 and 883 respectively.

In 915, during an unusual moment of cohesion, the pope and the main Christian powers of southern Italy formed an alliance and, with the help of a Byzantine fleet, managed to eliminate the Muslims' base on the Garigliano, thus ending their raids in that area. The Saracens from Sicily kept attacking the Campanian coast, but more sporadically. The last serious assault occurred in 1016 against Salerno. The most frequent and destructive raids were those carried out in Apulia and especially in nearby Calabria; the latter region was even the subject of attempted conquest. After taking Taormina in August 902, Emir Ibrāhīm II crossed the Strait of Messina and conquered Reggio Calabria, causing great apprehension in the South. His death by natural causes in the autumn of that year, during the siege of Cosenza, however, put an end to the campaign. Starting in 976, Abū al-Qasim led several attacks into the South of the Peninsula, resulting in the intervention of the German emperor Otto II, who was eager to enlarge his influence in that area. His disastrous defeat in Calabria in 982, however, ended his ambitions. Though defeated, this battle was not a total loss for the Christians, as the death of the Muslim commander persuaded his coreligionists to end their campaigns.

In the tenth and early eleventh centuries, Allah's followers made their presence felt even further north. Sardinia was repeatedly assaulted and some areas of the island were occupied for several years. Raids from Sardinia, Spain, and Sicily struck the coasts of Tuscany and Liguria. Genoa and Pisa were pillaged twice. Thanks to their base at Fraxinetum in Provence, the Saracens managed to attack some points of the northwestern Alps and western Po Valley. The famous abbey of Novalesa, located in northwestern Piedmont, was abandoned by its monks for fear of the Muslims, who pillaged and burned it. On one occasion, they came within sixty kilometers of

Pavia. As was the case for the Garigliano base, the stronghold of Fraxinetum could survive only thanks to the political fragmentation and rowdiness of the Christian rulers of southern France and northern Italy. When these dissensions were temporarily set aside, the base was easily eliminated in 973.

During the eleventh century, however, the tide had changed. The end of the political unity of the Muslims in the Iberian Peninsula and in Sicily was accompanied by the economic and military growth of Pisa and Genoa, who started attacking effectively throughout the Tyrrhenian Sea and in Sardinia. A clear sign of the change was the raid they carried out in 1087 against al-Mahdīya, one of the most important cities in Tunisia. Venice proved her power in the Adriatic Sea by stopping the Muslim siege of Bari in 1002. In the 960s, Constantinople tried unsuccessfully to regain Sicily. In 1041–1042 the Byzantines, hoping to profit from the political instability of the island, made a new attempt. Led by the skillful general Maniakes, the imperial army easily conquered several cities. The commander, however, fell into disgrace shortly afterwards and was recalled to the capital. His achievements were thus wiped out and the army withdrew. Troubles for the Muslims, however, did not end there. Among Maniakes's troops were some Norman mercenaries, captained by William of Hauteville. They had come in small groups from Normandy and soon became the new protagonists of the political scene in the South. After providing their services to the various rulers of the area, they managed to create their own dominions by using both weapons and marriages with members of the families ruling that area. The numerous members of the Hauteville family were the most successful of these Norman mercenaries. Driven by the impossibility of acquiring new territories in the South of the Peninsula, the youngest among them, Roger, invaded Sicily. In 1061 what had already happened in 827 took place again. The roles, however, were reversed. The Norman leader accepted the invitation of the Sicilian emir Ibn al-Thumma to move to the island to fight his opponents, but the Muslim ruler had few supporters and Roger took care of his own interests. His conquest of Sicily was slightly quicker than that accomplished by the Saracens in the ninth century. A faster occupation of the island was prevented by interference from the Muslims of northwestern Africa and, especially, the small number of troops in his service. Except for a couple of large-scale battles, raids and sieges characterized this war. A vital turning point took place in 1072 with the occupation of Palermo, gained through the help provided by Robert Guiscard, Roger's brother. Further conquests followed: Trapani (1077), Syracuse (1085), Castrogiovanni (1086), and Agrigento (1087). The last area of resistance, located near Syracuse, was defeated in 1091. Unlike his brother Robert,

Roger preferred to consolidate what he had acquired, refusing to undertake campaigns outside of Italy. He rejected the summons of the First Crusade, and he did not attack the Muslims in northwest Africa, with whom he had established peaceful relations. On the contrary, his son Roger II and his grandson William tried to conquer that area.

1 References, definitions, and circulation of news

References

The Apulian historical texts, which briefly report the main events in southern Italy year by year between the ninth and eleventh centuries, well emphasize how dangerous the Muslims were to that area. At the same time, these works indicate that large Saracen raids did not constantly hit the region, that they took place over a long chronological period, and that they occurred in different parts of the South. For example, the *Annals of Bari* mentions attacks against Calabria (902), Taranto (927, 972, 991), Oria (924, 977), Matera (994), and Bari (988, 1003).[1] In a similar text, perhaps written in Calabria, an area more exposed to Saracen incursions than Apulia, the number of attacks is greater, and minor raids are recorded as well. For example, this text mentions a large expedition from Africa against Calabria in 915 and the conquest of important cities – Taormina (902) and Taranto (928) – of medium-sized towns – Sant'Agata (922) and Oria (926) – and of small centers such as Bruzzano (924) and Tiriolo (930).[2]

Without minimizing the Muslim threat to the South, it is important to emphasize that most Christian writers did not want to create the idea of an obsessive Saracen presence in those territories. The biographies of the saints and the chronicles are divided into sections of different length, and calculating how many times the Muslims appear in them therefore only has an indicative value.[3] In the *Life of Saint Elias the Younger* (ca. 823–ca. 903) they are mentioned very often (in twenty-nine chapters out of seventy-six).[4] This work is, however, exceptional because Elias lived in one the 'hottest' periods for Muslim incursions into Sicily and Calabria and dwelt for a few years in North Africa and the Near East. This kind of percentage drastically decreases in the biographies of the other saints of those regions: Neilos (eleven chapters out of one hundred),[5] Philaretos of Seminara (four pages out of fifty-five)[6], Nicodemus of Kellarana (three chapters out of twenty-one),[7] Vitalis of Castronovo (two chapters out of twenty-five),[8] Luke of Demenna (three chapters out of sixteen),[9] Gregory of Cassano (one chapter out of thirteen),[10] and Bartholomew of Simeri (one out of thirty-one).[11] The Muslims are never mentioned in the life of Saint Phantinus the Younger (d. ca. 974), who spent most of his life in the South.[12] Another exception is the omnipresence of the Muslims in a Cassinese chronicle about the period from 839 to ca. 863 (nineteen chapters out of thirty-two)[13] because that work is specifically devoted to explaining why the Saracens were in southern Italy. The number of references to them is much smaller in the other chronicles, especially in those that were not written in the South.[14]

The text about Saint Constantius's deeds is a very rare exception for a couple of reasons. Not only does it mention the name of the Muslim leader and the year in which the incursion took place (991), but it also includes all the sites along the Amalfi Coast and the Gulf of Naples affected by these marauders, even including little towns and small islands. This work accurately explains what they did in each place (including how many Christians were taken prisoners or killed). It also illustrates how a small raid took place. The aforesaid Muslims were part of a larger expedition that a strong wind scattered between Sicily and Sardinia. This group was pushed to the coasts of Basilicata and from there moved to the Amalfi Coast and the Gulf of Naples. In such areas, the raiders only attacked small-sized centers, abandoning assaults when the inhabitants resisted them. The duke of Amalfi, instead of fighting, preferred to offer the Saracens gifts and food. The Muslims, however, kept away from Naples and its surroundings because of the presence of Neapolitan soldiers in that area. They subsequently planned to attack Capri, but a storm caused by Saint Constantius pushed them back south.[15]

Widespread distant echoes

The horizons of the narrative works of this period mirror the interests of their authors and their audiences and are essentially regional. These horizons, however, become larger in the case of events believed to be particularly relevant; such cases include episodes related to the Muslim campaigns throughout Italy. First, the reference to these events shows how news circulated across the Italian Peninsula and sometimes outside of it. These references also indicate that people were interested in what was happening in other areas, because those events could also be relevant for their home region. In addition, the existence of different versions of the same episodes sometimes provides valuable information about the authors and the contexts in which those texts were produced.

The Italian chroniclers do not mention the various phases of the conquest of Sicily by the Muslims, perhaps because little information was available or because of the lack of interest towards an area that was under Byzantine rule. They, however, did not neglect to record the beginning of that invasion (827), which brought far-reaching consequences for the history of all southern Italy. By comparing them to a bee-swarm, the monk of Montecassino Erchempert (second half of the ninth century) briefly describes the devastation the Muslims caused on the island and points out that almost all the inhabitants suffered under their rule.[16] The Neapolitan John the Deacon (late ninth century/early tenth century), on the other hand, states that they arrived on the invitation of a Syracusan named Euthymius, who fled to Africa following the failure of his uprising against the Byzantine authorities.

> The Syracusans, together with the faction of a certain Euthymius, rebelled against this Michael and killed Patrician Gregory. For this reason, the emperor sent a large army against them and the Syracusans were forced to flee because of the considerable number of soldiers. Also Euthymius went to Africa with his wife and children and led the ruler of the Saracens, Arcarius, against the Greeks with numerous ships. Since the Greeks could not resist, they retreated into the city walls of Syracuse and, after a hard siege, gave him fifty thousand solidi as a tribute. From that day, the Saracens plundered and devastated Sicily without fear. Eventually, they conquered the province of Palermo and took all their inhabitants into captivity.[17]

Other sources mention that a Sicilian rebel was responsible for the Muslims' arrival. The version circulating in Constantinople, however, had details perhaps created with the intention of ridiculing the subject who had tried to become emperor. According to a ninth-century anonymous Byzantine author, Euphemius fell in love with a nun and married her. To escape the punishment imposed on him, the Sicilian fled to the Saracens in Africa and promised them a considerable sum of money if they helped him to take Sicily and to support his election as emperor, to which they agreed.[18]

The tenth-century anonymous Salernitan chronicler, on the other hand, uses that episode to blame an officer of the Byzantines, who are often criticized by this Lombard author, for that catastrophic event for southern Italy. The author reports that, in exchange for money, the Sicilian commander – called disdainfully *Graeculus* (little Greek) – kidnapped Euphemius's wife and gave her to another man. In revenge, the disgraced husband promised that the wives of many others would also suffer the same fate. The

Muslims immediately accepted his invitation to attack Sicily, sowing death and destruction. 'Because of a single young woman,' the writer comments, 'many others were made widows. And those who once had banquets and parties had to pour out a lot of tears because of just one little Greek.'[19] A vague echo of the Muslims' military activities in Sicily emerges from the work of the Venetian chronicler John the Deacon (late tenth century – early eleventh century), who reports that in those years the Venetian fleet intervened twice in Sicilian waters at the request of Constantinople, but this author does not explain against whom.[20]

In 846 the Muslims attacked Rome. The city was not taken, but the assailants looted the basilicas of St. Peter and St. Paul, located outside the city walls. The fact that, in addition to those of central Italy,[21] authors from other areas of the Peninsula and beyond the Alps remembered this event marks its especial relevance. The assault upon the heart of western Christianity did not, however, inspire them to make any comment, and that episode was reported with the detachment of a modern press agency. The authors probably felt torn between a wish to record the extraordinary news and a desire not to linger too much on an event that was a painful blow for Christianity.

For example, the *Annals of St. Bertin* (France) record that in 846, 'in August the Saracens and the Moors got to Rome up to the Tiber, laid waste the basilica of St. Peter Prince of the Apostles, and along with the very altar which had been placed over his tomb, they carried off all ornaments and treasures'.[22] The *Annals of Fulda* (Germany) and the ninth-century chronicle of Montecassino are even more laconic.[23] The same tone can be found in the *History of the Venetians* by John the Deacon. In this case it is noteworthy that the author inserts this information in a section where the Muslims beat the Venetians in the Adriatic in that same period. John the Deacon thus seems to suggest that those defeats were justifiable because his compatriots confronted an adversary powerful enough to pillage even Rome.

> In this period, Patrician Theodosius came to Venice from Constantinople and bestowed the investiture of the office of spatharius to Duke Peter. He remained in Venice for an entire year and insistently asked the duke on behalf of the emperor not to refuse to give him an army in order to defeat the Saracens, which the duke did not refuse to do with pleasure. He then had sixty war-ships prepared quickly and sent them to Taranto where the Prince of the Saracens, Saba, stayed with a very big army. But almost all the Venetians were captured and killed by a multitude of Saracens. Seeing that they had obtained a victory against

the Christians, the Saracens did not hesitate to go as far as the city of Ossero, which they destroyed with fire. They then went to the city of Ancona and set fire to it in the same way, taking away many captives with them. Then, navigating here and there through the vast sea, they arrived in the port of Adria, which is near Venice. Having foreseen that they would not have obtained any booty from that place, they returned home. After arriving at the exit of the Adriatic gulf, they seized all the ships of the Venetians that were returning from both Sicily and other locations. In the following year, again, the above-mentioned Saracens arrived with a very big army in the gulf of Quarnaro. The Venetians went towards them with a fleet and fiercely attacked them near a place called Sansego, but eventually the Venetians turned their backs and withdrew defeated. The Saracens also dared to go to Rome and sack the church of St. Peter, but, as they arrived at the church of St. Paul, they were almost all killed by the Roman citizens.[24]

Concerning the shipwreck of the same Muslim fleet, Christian authors do not simply mention it, but rather paint an elaborate picture of divine retribution. Immediately after the Saracens had cursed God, Jesus, and the apostles, narrates the annalist of St. Bertin, 'suddenly there arose a terrible storm from which they could not escape, their ships were dashed against each other, and all were lost. The sea tossed up some of the corpses of the drowned Saracens on the shore, still clutching treasures to their breasts. When these treasures were found, they were taken back to the tomb of the Blessed Apostle Peter'.[25] According to a ninth-century Cassinese chronicler, at the very moment when the Muslims celebrated the appearance of their country's mountains on the horizon, a violent storm broke out, leading to the shipwreck of the Saracen fleet and the death of all the Muslims. Thus, none of them could recount their deeds to their compatriots.[26]

In 871 a coalition led by Emperor Louis II conquered Bari, which had been in Muslim hands for about 30 years. Even though this victory was undoubtedly a major success, it did not solve the problem of the Saracen presence in the South; rather it was primarily important from a psychological perspective, since it was the first major victory against the Muslims. On this occasion, the Christians also demonstrated their unity and eliminated a dangerous Saracen settlement that had been a cause of suffering for the peoples between Apulia and Campania. The authors of that period are, however, very concise in describing the event.

The late-ninth-century Cassinese chronicler Erchempert stated that 'with the help of God's right hand, Louis had sent an army and taken Bari, where he captured the cruel king Sawdān and some of his men'.[27] According to the late-ninth-century northern Italian author Andreas of Bergamo, 'having passed the fifth year since the siege of Bari, the lord emperor captured the *soldanus* and killed the Saracens who remained there.'[28] Even more laconic is the tenth-century anonymous Salernitan chronicler: 'And after having besieged Bari for a long time, the city was eventually taken by the Franks and the Lombards'.[29]

This attitude can be explained by the fact that the Christian victory was immediately followed by the scandalous imprisonment of Louis II by the Lombards of Benevento, who feared that the emperor would conquer all of southern Italy. The lack of cohesion among the Christians therefore re-emerged and the Muslims took advantage of it to counterattack. Moreover, Louis II died in 875 and his successors were too busy defending their dominions in northern Italy to display any interest in fighting the Muslims in the South. There was therefore very little to celebrate. Nearly 140 years later, however, the Venetian chronicler John the Deacon described that episode with a little more enthusiasm.

> Meanwhile, the city of Bari was conquered by his lordship the King of the Franks and the Lombards, Louis. Thanks to the gastald of that city, Bando, the people of the Saracens held Bari for nearly thirty years. In the thirty-first year, with the favor of the divine grace, the impiety that they (the Saracens) had previously brought onto the Christian citizens was given back to them. It was taken on February 2, on the day the purification of the holy virgin and mother of God, Mary, is celebrated.[30]

It is not known what sources John the Deacon had at his disposal. His interest in that episode about non-Venetian history, however, can be explained by the fact that the presence of the Muslims in Bari represented a serious threat to the Venetians' commercial activities, on which most of Venice's wealth was based. Any deed that strove to keep the sea-lanes free therefore had to be praised.

The German Emperor Otto II (d. 983) tried to expand his sphere of influence to southern Italy and decided to confront the Muslims that landed in Calabria in 982. The heavy defeat he suffered on that occasion, however, put an end to his plans over that area. Several German sources mention this episode and the most accurate description of it can be found in the chronicle of Thietmar of Merseburg (975–1018); an uncle of his mother died in that battle and that event therefore was also a part of his family history. Although Calabria was a part of the Byzantine Empire, the German author describes Otto II's intervention in that region as an expedition to defend his dominions from the destructive incursions of the Saracens. According to Thietmar, Otto II managed to drive the Saracens from one city after defeating them, and he believed they had been annihilated; the Muslims regrouped, however, and attacked the German army by surprise, completely defeating it. The emperor avoided capture by boarding a Byzantine ship from which he later escaped.[31] This episode was also recorded by two early medieval northern Italian chroniclers. At the end of the eleventh century, Arnulf of Milan narrated how Otto II had gone to Calabria to protect it from those invaders and justified the defeat by citing the numerical superiority of the Muslim army; despite being outnumbered, the Germans fought to the last man. Otto II, added the Milanese author, had been captured by the Saracens but was able to escape.[32]

At the beginning of the eleventh century, the Venetian John the Deacon, on the contrary, emphasized that this route had been due to Otto's lack of tactical skill. According to him, the German ruler ordered his forces to engage the threatening Muslim host without considering the possibility that the Saracens held troops in reserve. His soldiers easily dispersed the overt enemy forces, but a huge Muslim army came down from the hills and overwhelmed the German troops as they were returning to their camp, forcing the emperor into a narrow escape.

> Then, passing through Ravenna, Otto quickly went to Rome, where he learned that the terrible people of the Saracens had invaded Calabria. He went to Apulia and tried to attack the Saracens. However, while he was incautiously approaching the nearest places where a multitude of Saracens resided, a dreadful cohort suddenly tried to challenge the Christian army to battle. The emperor, unaware that most of the Saracens were hidden in the mountains, thought he could easily defeat those he saw. He audaciously attacked them in battle, and, with the help of Christ, overcame them with great courage. While the Christian troops were returning to their tents with the glory of triumph, a multitude of pagans came down from the mountains, burst upon them suddenly, and began to massacre them without mercy, so that those, to whom any escape was denied, fell cruelly hit. The emperor then reached the coast passing through the barbarian ranks with great difficulty, and, frightened by the cruelty of the enemy, entered the waving sea. There, two ships of the Greeks, called *chelandria* in their language, had anchored not far from land. He was picked up by them along with two of his servants.[33]

John the Deacon probably added those embarrassing details about Otto II's behavior in order to put in a bad light a person who had been a fierce enemy of the Venetians.

Definitions

According to some medieval Christian authors, the Muslims used to call themselves Saracens, claiming to be descendants of Sarah, Abraham's wife. Other writers believed that the Muslims descended from Ishmael, the son whom Abraham had by Agar, Sarah's handmaid, and therefore called them Agarenes and Ishmaelites. Italian writers are not an exception and employ these words as well (especially the term Saracens). Only in some cases do they mention the biblical account from which these terms come. While describing an incursion, the biographer of Saint Vitalis points out how a paradox was created when the children of the 'slave', that is Agar, reduced the children of the 'free woman', namely Sarah, into slavery.[34] The author refers to the fact that Sarah subsequently gave birth to Isaac from whom the Jews and then the Christians would descend. In the biography of Saint Philaretos, the Muslims are called 'descendants of Agar',[35] while Pope John VIII (872–882) defines them as 'false children of Sarah' and 'children of the fornication', that is the fruit of the relationship between Abraham and Agar.[36]

The word 'Arabs', which indicates the knowledge that Islam originated in Arabia, was used very rarely.[37] Even rarer are the terms *Mauri*[38] (from which the word Moors comes) and *Fusci*,[39] that is, 'dark', which probably refers to the dark color of the skin of some Muslims. In this regard, two authors use the term Ethiopians for some warriors in the Muslim armies, thus indicating individuals probably coming from sub-Saharan Africa;[40] Muslim sources confirm this presence.[41] The word 'Africans' appears in some Christian texts, but it is used for the raiders coming from the coasts of northern Africa,[42] which is called Ifrīqiya (Africa) in Muslim works.[43] A chronicler maintains that some Muslims were Libyans.[44] To point out that among the Saracen soldiers used by the Christian rulers there were some men coming from the Iberian Peninsula, the term *Ispani* (Spanish) was utilized.[45] The well-educated Liudprand of Cremona (d. 972) called the Muslims of Mediterranean Africa 'Phoenicians' and those from the Middle East 'Assyrians', probably because he wanted to create parallels with the enemies of the ancient Romans and of the Jews of the Bible,[46] while Pope John VIII called them Edomites (traditional opponents of the ancient Jews).[47] The Italian writers derogatorily defined the Muslims as *barbari* (barbarians),[48] but in the medieval translation into French of the chronicle by Amatus of Montecassino (second half of the eleventh century) (the original Latin text went missing) this word seems to be used as an ethnic definition; he narrates how 'li Arabi et li Barbare' went to Palermo to help its inhabitants who were besieged by the Normans.[49] It is therefore possible that the author wanted to refer to the northeastern African people of the Berbers. In a work composed in Greek the word *Βέρβερος*, that is Berbers, is used.[50]

In the Middle Ages, Muslim writers named the Byzantines 'Rūm' (Romans) and used that same term for the Italian peoples, including those who were not subject to the Byzantines anymore.[51] Aware that a part of the South had been occupied by a non-Latin population, they called a part of that area Longobardia and its inhabitants Lombards.[52] The remaining Europeans were named Franks. Muslim authors adopted this term to identify the Norman conquerors of Sicily, thus demonstrating that they knew that they were not natives of southern Italy.[53]

Information about the other

Among the very few texts composed by the western European pilgrims who visited the Holy Land in the early Middle Ages, none were written in Italy. Christian authors from this area did not write ethnographic descriptions (not only about the Muslims) in their works either. A few Italian texts, however, contain brief information about the Muslims, thus proving that the Christians were not completely ignorant about these dangerous opponents and suggesting that further information about them might have been known.[54]

In the account of the transfer of Saint Mark's relics from Alexandria in Egypt to Venice (ca. 828), the anonymous author emphasizes that the Venetian merchants went to the Egyptian city only by chance (trade with the Saracens was forbidden).[55] The Venetians, however, demonstrated their familiarity with Muslim habits by hiding the precious remains under pork, a food forbidden by the Koran. In that anecdote, written in Latin, even the Arabic word *canzir* is quoted, explaining that it means pig and that the horrified Saracens said it as soon as they saw what the Venetians were carrying to their ship.

> Then the Venetians... took Saint Mark's body and put it into a basket, covering it with leaves, such as cabbage and other vegetables, and above it put pig meat. As they rushed to the ship, some Saracens approached them to see what they were carrying. But as soon as they saw pig meat, which was a dirty thing for them, they started screaming: 'Canzir! Canzir!', that is: 'Pig! Pig!', and they moved away spitting.[56]

Although it is a hypothesis that cannot be demonstrated, it is not entirely absurd to assume that the commentary, mentioned in the proceedings of two English Councils of 786, concerning the ban forbidding clergy to eat during the fasting periods, 'because it would be a hypocritical action of the Saracens'—a clear reference to the Ramadan, the fasting yearly period of the Muslims—had been added by the papal representatives present on that occasion.[57]

Most of the Christian authors describe events that took place in Italy or in nearby areas; sometimes, their horizons widened to include the rest of the Mediterranean, and these writers prove to have some information about the Muslim world. The biographer of Pope Gregory II (715–731) narrates how the Saracens invaded Spain, leaving from Ceuta (Morocco) and subsequently clashing with the Franks in southern France.[58] A coeval Neapolitan anonymous author also narrates how at the beginning of the tenth century, the Neapolitan authorities, fearing a Muslim attack, decided to transfer the relics of a saint into the city. This account presents a correct brief overview of what was happening during that period in the dominions of the Muslim dynasty of the Aghlabids (northern Africa and Sicily). In this way his readers could understand how a Saracen leader threatened to conquer all of southern Italy.[59]

Benedict of St. Andreas of Soratte (second half of the tenth century) correctly identifies Cordoba, the capital of Muslim Iberia, as one of the main centers of Muslim power in the western Mediterranean,[60] while Liudprand of Cremona specifies that the Spanish city is the place where the ruler of Iberian Muslims resided.[61] Thanks to his activity as ambassador of the German ruler Otto, this author could receive some information about several areas of the Mediterranean. In the description of a solar eclipse he specifies that it took place on the day in which the Christian king of Galitia (Spain) defeated the caliph of Cordoba (the names of the two rulers are correctly mentioned).[62] The Pisan author of the work about the Christian expedition against al-Mahdīya (Tunisia) in 1087 does the same for the governor of that city.[63]

Several chroniclers mention this type of information for some Muslim leaders who were active in southern Italy. The names were probably written as they were pronounced: for example, Massar, Cincimo, Calfon, Ferraci, Abdila, Abemelec. These names constitute important information because most of them were either local leaders or had a low rank and the Muslim sources therefore did not mention them. Some Christian sources also recorded the names of the very few important rulers who led expeditions in the South: they are *Boulambès*, that is Abû al'Abbâs, and his father, *Brachimos*, i.e., the Aghlabid Emir Ibrāhīm II (d. 902).[64] In one case the consonance between two words induced an author to consider an office as a name. Andreas of Bergamo, in fact, calls Sawdān the emir of Bari, *soldanus*, that is sultan ('ruler' in Arabic).[65] The well-informed biographer of Roger of Hauteville did not make this type of mistake, correctly reporting the Latinization of both Muslim titles emir (*admiraldus*) and Ka'id (*gaytus*) as well as the names of Saracen leaders: Betumen (Ibn al-Thumna), Belcamedus (Ibn al-Ḥawwās), Benneclerus (Ibn al-Maklātī).[66] Other southern Italian authors mention the offices of emir and *ka'id* as well.[67] The Sicilian Saint Elias the Younger spent some years in northern Africa and in the Near East both as a slave and a freeman. In his biography, there is no reference either to the lands he visited or to the habits and customs of the peoples in those regions. The absence of this information is, however, due to the fact that they were not considered relevant to that text, since it focused on the life of the saint. A Muslim ruler is however referred to with the proper title of 'Prince of the Believers'.[68]

Arabic was not completely unknown either. According to Amatus of Montecassino, a churchman at the service of Robert Guiscard spoke like the Saracens,[69] while Geoffrey Malaterra narrates how the crew of a ship in the Norman fleet was fluent in Arabic.[70] A Pisan author, on the other hand, mentions the Latinization of the Arabic words for mosque (*meschita*) and fortified place (*cassarum*; this word derives from *qasr*);[71] as has been already emphasized, a Venetian wrote in his Latin work the Arabic term for pig.[72] The fact that the monk Theodosius (second half of the ninth century) recounts how a Muslim addressed the archbishop of Syracuse in Greek indicates that the languages of their adversaries were not completely unknown to the Saracens either.[73]

Benedict of St. Andreas knew a legend that became well known during the Middle Ages. From Charlemagne's biography written by Einhard in the 820s, he verbatim copied the information of the friendly relationships between the Franks' ruler and the Caliph Hārūn al-Rashīd (786-809); Benedict also reported that the former had been granted the jurisdiction over the church of the Holy Sepulcher in Jerusalem. The chronicler, however, added that the two rulers had met in Alexandria, pointing out that the joy for that event had been so great among both the Franks and the Saracens that they seemed almost like relatives.[74] The fact that in 1023 the abbot of Montecassino had a work titled *Historia Sarracenorum (History of the Saracens)* copied suggests that in Italy in those years a text dedicated to the Muslims existed. Unfortunately, except for the reference to that title, nothing else is known about this work.[75]

In the Muslim world, geographic and encyclopedic works were quite popular genres, and some authors did not fail to include some information about the Italian Peninsula. The Iraqi traveler and geographer Ibn Ḥawqal (tenth century), who visited Sicily in the 970s, reports a map of the Islamic West in his work. This map shows that he was well informed as to the names of the cities of the 'Calabrian land', which is described as separated from the 'Longobardia' (i.e., the land of the southern Italian Lombards) by a narrow strait, which in reality does not exist.[76] The Italian Peninsula ends with a mountain range, probably depicting the Apennines. Rome is located beyond it, near France.[77] The port city of Genoa is, on the other hand, incorrectly depicted as an island.[78] In his work, Ibn Ḥawqal shows Calabria and the land of the Lombards of the South as two different entities, ignoring, however, that the duchies of the Campanian coast did not belong to the second area. In fact, he considers Amalfi the most prosperous city of the Lombard region and includes Naples in the same region. This city is considered less important than Amalfi, but the author praises its linen fabrics of unrivaled quality.[79]

The chronicler 'Ibn 'al 'Atir (1160–1230) mentions Bari, which the Muslims conquered in the 840s and held for thirty years, and demonstrates his knowledge that in that period the city was no longer under the rule of the Byzantines but under the Lombards.

> On the west, there is a province called the Great Land....Here, by the sea, there is a city called Barah; its population is Christian but does not belong to the Rūm.[80]

Although there are some approximations and exaggerations, the remarks by al-Mas'ūdī (ca. 896–956) are noteworthy; he records the ancient title of duke used by the rulers of southern Longobardia, indicates the role of Benevento as the capital of that area, and explains how the Muslims had been expelled from that territory in his time.

> The territories of the Lombards are adjacent to Maghrib and their settlements are located in the north. They own many peninsulas in which different populations live; the Lombards are characterized by great courage and defense capabilities; they rule many cities and are reunited in one kingdom. The titles of their kings are always dukes. The largest of their cities, their capital, is Benevento. A large river crosses that city and divides it into two parts. This river is one of the waterways in the world that are famous for their flow and wonders; it is called Sabato... Their neighboring Muslims, coming from the lands of al-Andalus and Maghrib, conquered many of their towns, such as the cities of Bari, Taranto, and the city of Sardinia and many other great cities; the Muslims settled there for

a certain time. Later the Lombards grew braver and attacked the Muslims who lived there and drove them out after several long wars. At present, that is in the year 336 (947), the cities that we mentioned earlier are in the hands of the Lombards.[81]

On the other hand, an anonymous text refers to the situation before Charlemagne's conquest of the northern and central part of the Lombard kingdom in 774. In fact, it locates the Lombard dominions between those of the Rūm (that is the Byzantines) and those of the Franks. Moreover, this author explains that they had to fight against the Slavs and the Franks, who 'surrounded and oppressed them'.[82] The Lombards, however, are not only remembered for their geographical position and their warrior qualities. In one case, they are also mentioned in a cultural context. In a chapter dedicated to diverse types of writing, Ibn-al Nadīm (second half of the tenth century) states the following observations.

> The writing of the Lombards and the Saxons…Their writing is called epistulic and includes twenty-two letters. They start writing from left to right, but the reason for this is different from that of the Rūm. They say that this happens because the writing should start from the heartbeat and not in opposition to it.[83]

Ibn Ḥawqal acknowledges the emerging role of Venice in the Adriatic Sea during the early Middle Ages by calling the Adriatic the 'Gulf of the Venetians'.[84] Venice is also mentioned in the account of the journey from Constantinople to Rome by Hārūn b. Yaḥya (late ninth century through the beginning of the tenth century), but his comments are very synthetic and stereotypical. In fact, he uses the same words to describe both the area inhabited by the Venetians and the territory between that region and Rome. The lifestyle of those who resided in the latter region is also reported with the same sentence used to describe the Balkan area.

> They (the Venetians) live in a large plain, but do not have villages or towns and their houses are made of wood cut into planks… they (the inhabitants of the area between Venice and Rome) live in the Kurdish way, since they live in tents throughout the plain.[85]

More accurate, instead, is the description of Verona mentioned in al-Turtusi's account of his trip to central and western Europe (around 960/965). He praises the wealth and buildings of that city, especially the Roman arena, and compares it to the Spanish city of Tarragona; he also remembers the presence of a river (that is the Adige River) and its distance from the sea.

> Verona, one of the Lombard cities, is built with good stone blocks arranged with a building technique which resembles that of Tarragona. Its buildings are all beautiful and impressive, and there is a considerably large amphitheater with a remarkable structure. The city of Verona has a wide territory, with numerous fortifications and copious resources. It is located on a river whose mouth is in the sea at a site which is two days away.[86]

This author mentions another unidentified urban center in a very flattering tone (some scholars suggest it might be Pavia, while others believe that it is Benevento). Among the reasons for the splendor of that city, however, he inserts clearly false information with the probable intent of exalting the superiority of Muslim civilization. According to this writer, in the city the Lombards asked 300 Muslim judges to resolve cases for them.[87] One cannot exclude the presence of Muslim merchants in that center, but the number he provides is probably exaggerated.

> There are rich Muslim merchants in this city, I would add more than four hundred, who own wonderful buildings and have a flourishing trading activity.[88]

There are numerous descriptions of Rome, which, however, is often confused with Constantinople, 'the second Rome'.[89] For example, the account by Ibn Khurrādhbih (ninth century) is one of the earliest and most copied. The details he quotes clearly indicate that the place he describes is the capital of the Byzantine Empire.

> It has three sides (the eastern one, the southern one, and the western one) on the sea. The northern side is connected to the mainland... It is surrounded by a double stone wall with walls separated by a space which is sixty arms long.[90]

On the contrary, it is certainly Rome the city a Muslim merchant described to the geographer of Damascus al-Walīd (d. 810). Noteworthy is the account of the visitors' reaction to the view of the very numerous rooftops of Rome.

> One of the merchants told me: 'We went on a sea voyage and the ship dropped us on the shore of Rome. And we sent to them: 'We have intended

[to deal with] you and so send us an escort.' After this we went out with him. We climbed a mountain on our way and, lo and behold, there was something green like the sea. So we said: 'God is great!' The escort said to us: 'Why did you say 'God is great'?' We said, 'This is the sea, and it is our custom to say 'God is great' when we see the sea.' So he laughed. And he said: 'These are the roofs of Rome, and all of them are made of lead.'"[91]

To explain that the pope was the leader of the inhabitants of Rome, an author adopts a terminology that could be easily understood by his readers: thus, he calls him the 'Christians' caliph'.[92] According to Yaḥya, the pontiff was a king.[93] The Andalusian writer al-Bakrī (d. 1094), on the other hand, mentions a bishop of Rome named 'Yuwānish', narrating how he ordered the construction of a new city beyond the Tiber river,[94] likely a reference to Pope John VIII (872–882), who had the area around the basilica of St. Paul fortified.

As for the Christian leaders, Muslim writers record this kind of information very rarely; for example, they mention Roger of Hauteville, the Norman conqueror of Sicily.[95] The German Emperor Otto II, who was defeated by the Saracens in 982, was the subject of an interesting mistake in a text written in the fourteenth century. He is, in fact, called Baldwin,[96] a name five Christian kings of Jerusalem bore in the twelfth century. In the memories of the period when the Christians had occupied some Muslim territories, different characters and episodes were evidently mixed up.

Notes

1 *Annales Barenses*, ed. G. Pertz, in MGH, *Scriptores*, vol. 5 (Hanover, 1844), pp. 52–56.
2 P. Schreiner, *Die byzantinischen Kleinchroniken* (Vienna, 1975), pp. 336–38.
3 As I already emphasized, the Muslim chroniclers who describe their co-religionists' campaigns in Italy were not from Italy and did not live in the early Middle Ages. Moreover, those episodes are mentioned in works that cover several centuries of the history of Muslim world. This type of analysis for those texts would therefore be meaningless.
4 *Vita di Sant'Elia il Giovane*, ed. G. Rossi Taibbi (Palermo, 1962), chapters 3–9, 15–17, 22–26, 28, 32, 38, 39, 41, 43–44, 49-50, 53, 55, 57, 64, 68.
5 *Vita di san Nilo fondatore e patrono di Grottaferrata*, ed. G. Giovannelli (Badia di Grottaferrata, 1973), chapters 2, 6, 14, 24, 29–31, 36, 68, 70, 72.
6 Neilos, *Vita di san Filareto di Seminara*, ed. U. Martino (Reggio Calabria, 2014, second edition), pp. 32, 42, 44, 48. This text is not divided into chapters.
7 *Vita di s. Nicodemo di Kellarana*, ed. M. Arco Magri (Rome, 1969), chapters 6, 18, 19.
8 *Vita Vitalis*, in *Acta Sanctorum, Martii*, II (Antverp, 1668), chapters 14, 23.
9 *Vita s. Lucae abbatis Armenti*, in *Acta Sanctorum, Octobris*, VI (Paris-Rome, 1868), chapters 5, 10, 11.
10 *Vita S. Gregorii abbatis Porcetensis prior*, ed. O. Holder-Egger, in MGH, *Scriptores*, vol. 15, 2 (Hanover, 1888), chapter 9. I could not consult the other editions of this

text. *Gregor von Kalabrien. Die beiden mittelalterlichen Lebensbeschreibungen des Gründers der Abtei Burtscheid. Vitae Gregorii abbatis Porcetensis prior et posterior. Lateinisch-Deutsch*, ed. H. Deutz (Aachen, 1997); and *San Gregorio da Cerchiara*, ed. P. Damiano Franzese (Castrovillari, 2010).

11 *Vita e fatti del nostro padre Bartolomeo*, in G. Zaccagni, 'Il Bios di san Bartolomeo da Simeri', *Rivista di studi bizantini e neoellenici*, n.s. 33 (1996), chapter 24.

12 This could however be due to the fact that, since the biographer was a monk of Thessaloniki, he was not well informed about all the details of the life of Saint Phantinus.

13 *Cronicae Sancti Benedicti Casinensis*, ed. L. A. Berto (Florence, 2006), II, 1–8, 10, 13–15, 17, 22, 25–26, 28, 30, 32.

14 For example, twenty-seven chapters out of eighty-one in Erchempert, *Piccola Storia dei Longobardi di Benevento / Ystoriola Longobardorum Beneventum degentium*, ed. L. A. Berto (Naples, 2013), chapters 11, 16–18, 20, 29, 33–35, 38–39, 44, 47–49, 51, 54–58, 61, 65–66, 73–77, 79, 81; seven chapters out of twenty-five in John the Deacon, *Gesta episcoporum Neapolitanorum*, in *Storia dei vescovi napoletani (I secolo – 876) / Gesta Episcoporum Neapolitanorum*, ed. L. A. Berto (Pisa, 2018), chapters 54, 57, 60, 61, 64–66; five chapters out of twenty-four in Andreas of Bergamo, *Historia*, in *Italian Carolingian Historical and Poetic Texts*, edition and English translation by L. A. Berto (Pisa, 2016), chapters 15, 17–19, 22; nine chapters out of one hundred and eighty-five in John the Deacon, *Istoria Veneticorum*, ed. L. A. Berto (Bologna, 1999), II, 50–51, III, 7, 8, 12, 15, IV, 1, 22, 66–68.

15 *Sermo de virtute Sancti Constantii*, ed. A. Hofmeister, in MGH, *Scriptores*, vol. 30, 2 (Leipzig, 1934), chapters 10–11.

16 Erchempert, *Piccola Storia dei Longobardi di Benevento / Ystoriola Longobardorum Beneventum degentium*, chapter 11.

17 John the Deacon, *Gesta episcoporum Neapolitanorum*, chapter 54.

18 Theophanes Continuatus, *Chronographia*, in *Theophanes Continuatus, Joannes Cameniata, Symeon magister, Georgius Monachus*, ed. J. Bekker (Bonn, 1838), pp. 81–82.

19 *Chronicon Salernitanum: A critical edition with Studies on Literary and Historical Sources and on Language*, ed. U. Westerbergh (Stockholm, 1956), chapter 60.

20 John the Deacon, *Istoria Veneticorum*, II, 38.

21 *Liber pontificalis*, ed. L. Duchesne, 2 vols. (Paris, 1886-1892), vol. 2, pp. 98–101; Benedict of St. Andreas, *Chronicon*, in *Il Chronicon di Benedetto, monaco di S. Andrea del Soratte e il Libellus de imperatoria potestate in urbe Roma*, ed. G. Zucchetti (Rome, 1920), pp. 148–49.

22 *The Annals of St Bertin*, trans. J. Nelson (Manchester, 1991), p. 63. For the Latin text, see *Les Annales de Saint Bertin*, eds. F. Grat, J. Vielliard, S. Clémencet (Paris, 1964), year 846.

23 *Annales Fuldenses*, eds. G. Pertz and F. Kurze, MGH, *Scriptores rerum Germanicarum in usum scholarum separatim editi* (Hanover, 1891), p. 36, year 846; *Cronicae Sancti Benedicti Casinensis*, II, 3.

24 John the Deacon, *Istoria Veneticorum*, II, 50–51.

25 *Annals of St Bertin*, pp. 64–65.

26 *Cronicae Sancti Benedicti Casinensis*, II, 6.

27 Erchempert, *Ystoriola*, chapter 33.

28 Andreas of Bergamo, *Historia*, chapter 19.

29 *Chronicon Salernitanum*, chapter 108. The conquest of Bari is also very briefly described in Lupus Protospatarius, *Annales*, ed. G. Pertz, in MGH. *Scriptores*, vol. 5 (Hanover, 1844), p. 52.

30 John the Deacon, *Istoria Veneticorum*, III, 6.

31 Thietmar of Merseburg, *Chronicon*, ed. R. Holtzmann, MGH, *Scriptores rerum Germanicarum in usum scholarum*, n. s. 9 (Berlin, 1935), III, 2.

32 Arnulf of Milan, *Liber gestorum recentium*, ed. I. Scaravelli (Bologna, 1996), I, 9. The northern Italian chronicler of the abbey of Novalesa (mid-eleventh century) incorrectly wrote that on that occasion Otto II had fought against the Byzantines. *Cronaca di Novalesa*, ed. G. C. Alessio (Turin, 1982), pp. 342–47.

33 John the Deacon, *Istoria Veneticorum*, IV, 22–23. A very brief reference to Otto II's defeat and to the fact that the emperor managed to escape with great difficulty can be found in the chronicle of the Cassinese monk Leo (early twelfth century). *Chronica Monasterii Casinensis*, ed. H. Hoffmann, MGH, *Scriptores*, vol. 34 (Hanover, 1980), II, 9, pp. 186–87.

34 *Vita Vitalis*, chapter 23.

35 Neilos, *Vita di san Filareto di Seminara*, p. 33.

36 John VIII, *Registrum*, ed. E. Caspar, in MGH, *Epistolae*, vol. 7 (Berlin, 1928), number 32, p. 31. The pontiff also calls them children of Ishmael and of the handmaid. John VIII, *Registrum*, numbers 22, 279, pp. 20, 246.

37 *Vita S. Eliae Spelaeotae*, in *Acta Sanctorum, Septembris*, III (Venice, 1761), chapter 69; John VIII, *Registrum*, number 47, p. 45; *Carmen in victoriam Pisanorum*, in G. Scalia, 'Il carme pisano sull'impresa contro i Saraceni del 1087', in *Studi di filologia romanza offerti a Silvio Pellegrini* (Padua, 1971), stanzas 61 and 65; Amatus of Montecassino, *Ystoire de li Normant*, ed. V. de Bartholomeis (Rome, 1935), V, 23, VII, 1; Geoffrey Malaterra, *De rebus gestis Rogerii Calabriae et Siciliae Comitis et Roberti Guiscardi ducis fratris eius*, ed. E. Pontieri, *Rerum Italicarum Scriptores, Series Secunda*, vol. 5, 1 (Bologna, 1925-1928), II, 32, 33, 35, 46.

38 *Historia Langobardorum codicis Gothani*, in *Italian Carolingian Historical and Poetic Texts*, edition and English translation by L. A. Berto (Pisa, 2016), chapter 11; *Vita Walfredi und Kloster Monteverdi: Toskanisches Mönchtum Zwischen Langobardischer und Fränkischer Herrschaft*, ed. K. Schmid (Tübingen, 1991), pp. 60, 62.

39 *Cronaca di Novalesa*, V, 18. As far as I know, this is the only early medieval Italian text to use this term.

40 *Epistola Theodosii monachi ad Leonem Archidiaconum de expugnatione Syracusarum*, in *Vitae Sanctorum Siculorum*, ed. O. Caietani, vol. 2 (Palermo, 1657), p. 276; *Sermo de virtute Sancti Constantii*, chapter 10, p. 1018.

41 BAS, vol. 1, p. 443.

42 For example, John the Deacon, *Gesta episcoporum Neapolitanorum*, chapter 60; *Translatio sancti Severini auctore Iohanne Diacono*, ed. G. Waitz, in MGH, *Scriptores rerum Langobardicarum et Italicarum saec. VI-IX* (Hanover, 1878), p. 452; Liudprand of Cremona, *Antapodosis*, in Id., *Opera omnia*, ed. P. Chiesa, *Corpus Christianorum, Continuatio Mediaevalis*, vol. 156 (Turnhout, 1998), II, 44, 50, 51; Geoffrey Malaterra, *De rebus gestis Rogerii*, II, 17, 32, 33, 35.

43 For example, BAS, vol. 1, pp. 448, 450, 452.

44 Erchempert, *Piccola Storia dei Longobardi di Benevento / Ystoriola Longobardorum Beneventum*, chapter 17.

45 Erchempert, *Piccola Storia dei Longobardi di Benevento / Ystoriola Longobardorum Beneventum*, chapter 17.

46 Liudprand of Cremona, *Antapodosis*, IV, 5; Liudprand of Cremona, *Historia Ottonis*, chapters 39, 44, 45; Liudprand of Cremona, *Relatio*, chapters 39, 44, 45.

47 John VIII, *Registrum*, number 32, p. 31.

48 For example, *Vita di Sant'Elia il Giovane*, chapters 22, 24, 57; *Vita Vitalis*, chapter 14; *Cronaca di Novalesa*, V, 2, 9; John the Deacon, *Istoria Veneticorum*, IV, 23.

49 Amatus of Montecassino, *Ystoire de li Normant*, VII, 1.

50 Schreiner, *Die byzantinischen Kleinchroniken*, pp. 336–38, chapters 27, 32.

51 For example, BAS, vol. 1, pp. 11, 412, 420, 423, 440.

52 G. Mandalà, 'La Longobardia, i Longobardi e Pavia nei geografi arabo-islamici del Medioevo', *Aevum* 88 (2014), pp. 331–86.
53 BAS, vol. 1, pp. 442, 447.
54 What was known about Mohammed and Islam will be examined in chapter 2.
55 *Translatio Marci Evangelistae Venetias [BHL 5283–5284]*, in E. Colombi, *Storie di cronache e reliquie nella 'Venetia' altomedievale* (Trieste, 2012), chapter 8.
56 *Translatio Marci Evangelistae Venetias*, chapters 13–14.
57 Hypothesis suggested by B. Z. Kedar, *Crusade and Mission: European Approaches Toward the Muslims* (Princeton, 1984), p. 30.
58 *Liber pontificalis*, vol. 1, p. 401.
59 *Translatio sancti Severini*, p. 452, chapter 1.
60 Benedict of St. Andreas, *Chronicon*, p. 147.
61 Liudprand of Cremona, *Antapodosis*, V, 19.
62 Liudprand of Cremona, *Antapodosis*, V, 2.
63 *Carmen in victoriam Pisanorum*, line 17.
64 *Vita di Sant'Elia il Giovane*, chapters 41, 49, pp. 62, 74; Schreiner, *Die byzantinischen Kleinchroniken*, p. 336.
65 Andreas of Bergamo, *Historia*, chapters 18–19.
66 Geoffrey Malaterra, *De rebus gestis Rogerii*, II, 3, 4, 16, 18, 20, 22, IV, 16.
67 Amatus of Montecassino, *Ystoire de li Normant*, IV, 20, V, 8, 9, 13, 16, 18, 22–24, VI, 19; *Annales Barenses*, p. 53, year 1003; Lupus Protospatarius, *Annales*, pp. 55–57, years 972, 998, 1002, 1009.
68 *Vita di Sant'Elia il Giovane*, chapters 16–17, pp. 24–27.
69 Geoffrey Malaterra, *De rebus gestis Rogerii*, IV, 2.
70 Amatus of Montecassino, *Ystoire de li Normant*, V, 24.
71 *Carmen in victoriam Pisanorum*, lines 205, 225. *Muscheta* in William of Apulia, *La Geste de Robert Guiscard*, ed. M. Mathieu (Palermo, 1961), III, line 333.
72 *Translatio Marci Evangelistae Venetias*, chapter 14.
73 *Epistola Theodosii monachi*, pp. 275–76.
74 Benedict of St. Andreas, *Chronicon*, pp. 113–14.
75 G. Becker, *Catalogi bibliothecarum antiqui* (Bonn, 1885), p. 133.
76 Calabria is a region located at the tip of the Italian Peninsula. The Muslim writer probably made a mistake, but, since Calabria was then under the Byzantines, that strait could have been added to symbolize the difference between the land of the Lombards and an area under the rule of Constantinople.
77 Perhaps Rome was located near France because of the connection between this city and the Carolingian world. Charlemagne and some of his heirs were crowned as emperors in Rome.
78 Mandalà, 'La Longobardia, i Longobardi e Pavia', pp. 336–37.
79 BAS, vol. 1, pp. 24–25.
80 BAS, vol. 1, p. 390.
81 Italian translation in Mandalà, 'La Longobardia, i Longobardi e Pavia', p. 344.
82 Italian translation in Mandalà, 'La Longobardia, i Longobardi e Pavia', p. 347.
83 This writer worked in Baghdad. Mandalà, 'La Longobardia, i Longobardi e Pavia', p. 350.
84 Italian translation in Mandalà, 'La Longobardia, i Longobardi e Pavia', p. 336.
85 Italian translation in Mandalà, 'La Longobardia, i Longobardi e Pavia', p. 344.
86 Italian translation in Mandalà, 'La Longobardia, i Longobardi e Pavia', p. 356. This author also mentions the Garda lake and the town of Rocca di Garda. Mandalà, 'La Longobardia, i Longobardi e Pavia', p. 356. In reality this work is mentioned in a fourteenth-century text that took this information from a text that went missing. Mandalà, 'La Longobardia, i Longobardi e Pavia', pp. 354–55.
87 Mandalà, 'La Longobardia, i Longobardi e Pavia', p. 356.

88 Italian translation in Mandalà, 'La Longobardia, i Longobardi e Pavia', p. 356.
89 A. De Simone – G. Mandalà, *L'immagine araba di Roma. I geografi del Medioevo (secoli IX–XIV)* (Bologna, 2002), p. 73.
90 Italian translation in De Simone – Mandalà, *L'immagine araba di Roma*, p. 65.
91 M. McCormick, *Origins of the European Economy: Communications and Commerce AD 300–900* (Cambridge, 2002), pp. 622-23.
92 Italian translation in De Simone – Mandalà, *L'immagine araba di Roma*, p. 58.
93 Italian translation in De Simone – Mandalà, *L'immagine araba di Roma*, p. 67.
94 D. G. König, *Arabic-Islamic Views of the Latin West. Tracing the Emergence of Medieval Europe* (Oxford, 2015), p. 241.
95 BAS, vol. 1, pp. 447, 449, 451. His son, Roger II of Hauteville, who became king of Sicily and fought against the Muslims in northwestern Africa, is mentioned more often.
96 BAS, vol. 2, p. 198.

2   Religious otherness

Muslims in Christian texts

Anti-Muslim treatises were not composed in Italy during the early Middle Ages, and there are no ethnographic overviews about them in the narrative Italian works. This does not mean, however, that all the Christians of the Peninsula ignored the religious otherness of the Saracens. It is obviously impossible to determine what the average person and rulers of that period knew of these dangerous neighbors, but it is likely that they had at least some simple notions about the religious differences of the Muslims (a situation not unlike today). Christian authors demonstrate that they recognized this diversity and that they were, therefore, aware that Muslims were 'special' adversaries. This knowledge is underlined, above all, by the widespread use of the term 'pagans' for the Muslims, a term probably used to compare these new persecutors to those of Christianity's first centuries. More rare, but extremely significant are other appellations such as infidels,[1] unbelievers,[2] gentiles,[3] impious,[4] godless,[5] God haters,[6] people rebellious to God[7] and ignorant of God,[8] and enemies of God.[9] In the biography of Elias the Younger (ca. 823–ca. 903), the Muslim faith is called a vain religion and superstition.[10] According to a Cassinese chronicler, in 1087 Christians went to northern Africa to fight 'infidelity.'[11] It is not clear what the 'profane books' that a Bulgarian ruler had taken from the Muslims were – they are mentioned in a query about the appropriate behavior for good Christians that the sovereign sent to Pope Nicholas (858–867). By calling them 'harmful and blasphemous' and suggesting that they be burned, the pontiff probably believed that they were texts about the Muslim religion and therefore unsuitable for Christian neophytes.[12]

At the beginning of the tenth century, a Neapolitan author explains that he wants to recount all that a Muslim sovereign committed against 'the people of our religion.' According to the same writer, that Saracen promised to annihilate the Christians because they had rebelled against God (of course, the God of the Muslims).[13] Moreover, this ruler also tried to convince the bishop of Taormina to convert to Islam.[14] The young Leo Luke of Corleone (ca. 810–ca.

910), wishing to become a monk, was advised to abandon Sicily because, due to the violent Muslim attacks, the island had been left without Christians.[15] The *Life of Luke of Isola of Capo Rizzuto* recounts how he went to Sicily in ca. 1105 to re-evangelize the island, emphasizing that Sicily had remained without the 'word' of Christ during the prior two centuries of Muslim rule.[16] The biographer of Pope Leo IV (847–855) explains that, in the Muslim raid against Rome in 846, many sacred objects were taken away from the church of St. Peter by the 'impious hands' of the Saracens,[17] while the tenth-century anonymous Salernitan chronicler, writing about a similar situation, utilizes the term 'sin' to refer to the help the Neapolitans gave to the Muslims.[18]

At the end of the eleventh century, the Norman chroniclers glorify and at the same time justify the deeds of Roger of Hauteville and his brother Robert Guiscard by emphasizing that the Sicilian Muslims are enemies of God, ignorant of the divine cult, idol-worshippers, and subjects of demons.[19] According to William of Apulia, the main mosque of Palermo was the temple of the iniquitous, of superstition, and the see of Mohammed and the demon.[20] The texts on which the Muslims swore their oaths are called 'the books of their superstitious law' (in this case law means religion).[21] Islam is also defined as the 'detestable madness of the Saracens'.[22]

William's chronicle is not the only Christian source mentioning Mohammed. An ecclesiastical council, which was probably held at Benevento between 840 and 880, forbade clerics to use slaves as concubines, claiming that this was a practice allowed by Muslims and their 'pseudo-prophet called Machameta.'[23] The Sicilian monk Theodosius recounts how a Christian soldier insulted Mohammed every day during the siege of Syracuse (878). This writer's knowledge of Islam's prophet is also made evident by his mention of a dialogue between the archbishop of Syracuse and the emir of Palermo.

> The attendants made the bishop stand forth, and through an interpreter the emir asked: 'Hast thou our manner of praying to God?' Our most wise superior would not admit that. 'Why in that manner?' asked the bishop; 'since I am the high priest of Christ and the leader of the mysteries of the servants of Christ, of whom the prophets and the righteous prophesied of old.' 'They are not prophets to you, in truth,' answered the emir, 'but only in name, since by them you would not be led away to your false doctrines, nor turned from the right path. For why do you assail our prophet with blasphemies?' 'We do not blaspheme the prophets at all,' returned the bishop, 'seeing that we have learned not to inveigh against prophets, but to speak in their behalf and to feel proud of them; but we do not know that one who is revered among you.'[24]

According to a late-eleventh-century Pisan author, Muslims invoked Mohammed, 'the enemy of the Trinity and the Holy Faith.'[25] Around 1100, in Calabria, Luke of Bova reproached his flock for behaving like the 'followers of Mohammed' during funerals.[26] Readers of the Latin translation of the chronicle by the Byzantine author Theophanes, made by one of Italy's greatest intellectuals, Anasthasius the Librarian (ca. 815–ca. 878), could discover that 'Mohammed taught that he who kills an enemy, as he who is killed by an enemy, will enter Paradise.' This passage, copied by a southern Italian writer towards the end of the tenth century, was further spread to western Europe. Anasthasius also translated into Latin the proceedings of the ecumenical council of Constantinople (787), which contain some vague information about Islam, and a letter dating to 725. In this letter, Christians are suggested to respond to the Muslims' accusations of idolatry by accusing the Saracens themselves of worshiping a desert stone known as Chobar, thus referring to the Kaaba of Mecca that contains a piece of a meteorite.[27]

Hints at the beliefs and customs of the faithful of Islam are not absent either. At the beginning of the tenth century, a Neapolitan author notes that a Muslim leader incited his warriors to attack Italy, reminding them that such an undertaking would please God and that by doing so they could enter 'the Paradise of milk and honey,' clear references to jihad and to the rewards associated with it.[28] The Neapolitans had numerous encounters with the Saracens and therefore it should be expected that they learned something about them. The few Christians who had been imprisoned and then freed by the Muslims probably learned something about their captors as well. Elias the Younger, claims his biographer, preached Christianity successfully in Islamic territories and was therefore denounced to the authorities; he was also accused of criticizing the 'Prophet' and his prophesies (obvious allusions to Mohammed and Islam).[29] To convert some Saracens, the saint explained the fallacies and errors of their religion, resorting to typical arguments from anti-Islamic Byzantine treatises. Though presenting the Muslim religion as a sum of heresies and distorting some of their beliefs and practices, these passages nevertheless display a certain knowledge of Islam.

> Having yourselves circumcised, you follow the rules of the Jews, and having sexual intercourse with multiple women, you oppose God, because God gave man only one woman as a help, not many... in fact, your prophet, whom you divinize, by gathering the thorns of every heresy, passed down to you, and deceived you with the worst beliefs that are most widely held by sensual men. And you, observing them, think you are living a good life. And while, for every fact, which should be documented, you do not accept one testimonial, but two or three, and sometimes even

more, instead in matters of your superstition, you are not ashamed to have only one testimony.[30]

There is further confirmation of the awareness of the Saracens' religious otherness in accounts of conflicts with them, where the various ethnic and political allegiances of the inhabitants of the Peninsula are often replaced with the term Christians[31] and sometimes with similar definitions such as faithful, 'followers of Christ' and 'people of God';[32] in one case it was emphasized that the Saracens must be fought for 'love of the Christian faith' and to 'save the Christian people.'[33]

The 'contaminating' Muslims and the attacks against the Christian religion

The danger represented by the Muslims' otherness and especially the fear that their deeds could contaminate the holy spaces and objects of the Christians, thus making them ineffective, can be seen in the terminology sometimes utilized by writers in their descriptions of Saracen attacks. The most explicit account can be found in an anonymous Salernitan text about Saint Fortunatus, Saint Caius, and Saint Anthes. According to this work, during the siege of Salerno in 872, a Muslim tried to insult those saints by dirtying the altar of the church dedicated to them with his excrement.[34] Recounting how the followers of Islam devastated Calabria, the biographer of Saint Vitalis (tenth century) used disparaging adjectives for them such as 'filthy' and 'very dirty'.[35] A reference to this theme can be seen in the term 'impure' utilized for the Saracens in the biographies of Saint Sabas (ca. 910–ca. 991) and of Saint Neilos (ca. 910–ca. 1004).[36] In order to emphasize the entirety of the destruction some Muslims caused in a few churches of the Amalfitan coast, the word 'contamination' and the verb 'to contaminate' are used,[37] thus hinting at the fact that those churches had to be purified before being used again.

The biographer of Saint Vitalis utilizes this same terminology in the account of the transfer of that saint's relics into a town, thus suggesting that the Saracens may have sullied those precious remains. There is no doubt that the author of the *Life of Saint Luke* wished to express this idea as well. In the territory where that saint lived, the Muslims entered the 'holy place' devoted to the mother of God with their 'filthy feet' and dirtied it with 'nefarious crimes'.[38] These ideas appear in the *Life of Saint Neilos* too. Foretelling the Muslims' destructive actions, a companion of that saint was sorrowful at the loss of the churches that the Saracens would turn into stables. After the Muslims ransacked Neilos's cave, they were called 'filthy pagans'.[39] Having conquered Palermo in 1072, narrates Amatus of Montecassino, Roger of Hauteville and his brother Robert Guiscard had the church of Saint Mary, which the Muslims had turned into a mosque, cleaned of all 'dirt.' According to the same author, Robert Guiscard incited his men to attack Castrogiovanni by saying that they were going to assault a place made by the 'dirt of heresy'.[40] This type of terminology can be found in northern Italy as well, and it is not an accident that it is present in the chronicle of Novalesa, as the Muslims destroyed this monastery at the beginning of the tenth century. The historian of the abbey explains that, if the abbot of Novalesa had not fled, the Muslims would not have contaminated the entire monastery and the surrounding territory. According to the same author, the 'cruel rabies' of Fraxinetum's Muslims dirtied the entire world.[41] Around 1100, Donizo underlined his dislike for Pisa by remarking that he 'who goes to Pisa can see the monsters that come from the sea; that city is dirtied by pagans, Turks, Libyans, and Parthians as well'.[42]

These ideas concerning contamination also touched the sexual sphere. Even though he was an infidel, notes the tenth-century anonymous chronicler of Salerno, the Emir of Bari, Sawdān, did not 'contaminate' a Christian woman given to him as a hostage.[43] Noteworthy are the different words a late-eleventh-century chronicler employed to emphasize the violent deeds the Muslim warriors of Robert Guiscard's army committed against the women of Rome in 1084. He uses the terminology 'to corrupt' for the nuns, while he utilizes 'incest' (a term often employed to indicate any sexual activities between unmarried persons) for the other women.[44]

There are also descriptions of Muslims committing clear acts of disrespect for the Christian religion, which only enemies of God could carry out. A ninth-century Cassinese chronicler writes that 'the most nefarious' Emir of Bari, Sawdān, drank from the sacred chalices and used the incense burners of St. Vincent at Volturno.[45] Having entered the holy places of Rome in 846, recounts the tenth-century chronicler Benedict of St. Andreas, the Saracens danced around the altar of St. Peter's and one of them struck the face of Christ, painted on a wall, with his lance. To show how much this profanity wounded Christianity, the author adds that the image started to bleed as if it were a real man. The Muslims later stated that they had been defeated because 'they had seen the blood of the Christians' God,' thus acknowledging the great impiety they had committed.[46] According to Elias Spelaeota's biographer, the Muslims opened the tomb of Arsenius, the mentor of that saint, looking for precious objects. Frustrated because they found none, they decided to burn the saint's remains. They justified their actions by claiming that Arsenius was one of those who deceived foolish Christians, telling them that the Son is the same as the Father.[47] The tenth-century anonymous Salernitan chronicler relates that a Saracen general not only raped some Christian girls but blasphemously carried out the acts on a church altar.[48] According to Geoffrey Malaterra, in a raid against Calabria the Muslim leader Benarvet, the fiercest adversary of Roger of Hauteville, devastated several churches, defiled sacred images, and stole sacred vessels and vestments. Moreover, he also commanded his men to rape the nuns.[49]

In an anonymous text in Greek, there are a few concise reports about explicit attacks against the Christian religion in Sicily.

> In the year 6011 (903), having come from Africa in the middle of the Holy Fasting (i.e., Lent), the Cadi started to devastate the churches of Palermo and of that region, to destroy books, and to imprison churchmen.

> In the year 6014 (906), the monk Argentius was martyred in Palermo.[50]

According to archeological data that are difficult to interpret, the frescoes in a religious building in southern Apulia appear to have been pulled from the walls intentionally during a Saracen incursion into that area.[51] During the conquest of Sicily, some churches were destroyed, but it seems that these were the result of events that may have happened during war campaigns, rather than premeditated acts. In general, Muslims preferred to turn the most important churches into mosques, which the Normans subsequently changed back into churches. A Muslim Sicilian exile, Ibn Ḥamdîs (ca. 1056–ca. 1133), complains about this and about the fact the monks there rang the bells from morning until night.[52]

Holy war against the Muslims

A few Christian authors portray the clashes with the Saracens as holy war, thus further pointing out the religious otherness of the Muslims. On this subject, it is necessary to clarify what I mean by this definition. First, for this period, it is completely anachronistic to use terms like crusade or pre-crusade. By holy war, I mean episodes of war where the writers clearly state that God supported the Christians against their adversaries who were considered God's enemies.

One of the first and best examples of these descriptions can be found in the chronicle by Andreas of Bergamo (second half of the ninth century), who recorded some episodes of Emperor Louis II's campaign against the Saracens in southern Italy (866–871). According to this author, the Muslims decided to attack the emperor's troops on Christmas, believing that the followers of Christ, preoccupied with their prayers, would be unarmed and therefore easy to defeat. Before the battle, the Christians attended mass, taking Holy Communion and receiving the blessing of priests. Then, before beginning the fighting, Louis II's soldiers –

called the 'faithful of Christ' – addressed Jesus with a prayer in which the message 'God is with us and against our enemies' is quite evident.

> It was reported to the Saracens that the Christians would celebrate a great day, as it was a feast day, that is, the nativity of our Lord Jesus Christ. Therefore they said: 'They are worshiping their god on that day. They will neither fight nor take up arms. Let us go upon them and take them all in their guilelessness!'... The emperor then ordered that, at dawn, at the cockcrow, the bishops and the priests would celebrate solemn masses, and that the people would receive communion and the benediction, and they did so... the faithful of Christ prayed, saying: 'O Lord Jesus Christ, you said: 'He who eats my flesh and drinks my blood will remain in me and I in him.' So, if you are with us, what is against us?'[53]

The fact that there were no other reports of this kind in that period further emphasizes that Louis II's campaign represented one of the few times between the ninth and tenth centuries in which the Christians were successful against the Muslims. Almost as if he wanted to indicate the exceptionality of the elimination of the Muslim base on the Garigliano in 915, Liudprand of Cremona (ca. 920–972) did not limit himself to saying that the victory was obtained thanks to God's help, but also thanks to the prayers of Saint Peter and Saint Paul, who both appeared on the battlefield.

> In that battle the most holy Peter and Paul were seen by the pious faithful, and we believe that it was by their prayers that the Christians deserved that the Phoenicians (i.e., the Muslims) should flee and that they should deserve victory.[54]

A progressive strengthening of western Christians and a simultaneous weakening of the Muslims took place in the new millennium. The description of the Venetian Duke Peter II Orseolo's expedition to free Bari from the Muslims' siege in 1002 symbolizes this change very well. The contemporary Venetian chronicler, John the Deacon, did not limit himself to reporting that the Muslims were put to flight thanks to God's help. According to this writer, on Assumption Day, a star was seen passing through the sky from the West and falling in the port of Bari; this event was understood as a sign that military aid was arriving. In addition, the Venetian fleet reached Bari on the birthday of the mother of God. The 'spirit' of holy war is certainly not very strong in this account. It, however, assumes particular significance if we take into consideration the context in which it was written and the place where that clash occurred. The Byzantines nurtured a special veneration for

Mary and maintained that the Mother of God had protected Constantinople from enemies many times. Although Venice had been independent from the Byzantines for a long time, it still had strong ties to that world, and it should not be overlooked that Bari was, at that time, the capital of the Byzantine territories in Italy.

According to a German chronicler of that period, Pope Benedict VIII (1012–1024) reacted to the Muslim conquest of a Ligurian town by ordering all the 'supporters and defenders of the Holy Church' to join him in fighting against those 'enemies of Christ' and by reminding them that God would help them. After three days of ferocious fighting, explains the writer, God put 'those who hate him' to flight.[55] Describing the victory of the Byzantine general, Maniakes, against the Muslims in Sicily (ca. 1042), the biographer of Saint Philaretos, on the other hand, employs explicit references to the Old Testament, comparing this campaign to the Jews' wars to liberate their land. Beside the able and brave Christian commander, in fact, stood the 'God of Israel' who had saved the Jews by dividing the Red Sea. The 'barbarians,' therefore, confronted two adversaries at the same time, the imperial troops and the divine spirit, and their great army fell 'like dust beneath the feet' of the Byzantines.[56]

After enduring the catastrophic Muslim raids between the tenth century and the beginning of the eleventh, the Pisans and the Genoese began to fight the Saracens on the Tyrrhenian Sea successfully and even attacked them in Tunisia in 1087. A Pisan writer celebrated that event by composing a text dedicated exclusively to the episode. The author states clearly that God helped the Christians to reach the African coast and to defeat that 'pagan people and enemy of God,' and that his countrymen relied on the Lord without concern for their own lives or those of their children. He also makes numerous comparisons to Old Testament heroes: Gideon, who distinguished himself in his fight against the enemies of Israel and for never worrying about their numbers; David, the boy who killed the giant, Goliath; and Judah Maccabee, the valiant defender of Israel against pagan invaders. A saint with strong military connotations like the archangel Michael even played his trumpet to defend Christians in the same way that he did when he had faced the dragon. Saint Peter encouraged the Genoese and the Pisans with the sword and the cross. Moreover, the writer does not neglect to provide a strictly Pisan perspective to the battle, pointing out that it took place on the Feast of Saint Sixtus, the day on which Pisans had always obtained victory 'from heaven'.[57]

As has already been noted, the Norman chroniclers present their expeditions in Sicily as fought against the enemies of God. In the description of the only great field battle of that period, the spirit of holy war emerges quite forcefully. Before the fight, recounts Geoffrey Malaterra, the Normans purified themselves of their sins and commended themselves to God. The first victory was described as a success clearly obtained thanks to the Lord, and it was compared with the wars of the ancient Jews against the pagans. Subsequently, the Normans, fearing the great number of Muslims, were reminded that they were 'the soldiers of the Christian militia' and that they were carrying the symbol of Christ, who would not abandon them if they did not offend that symbol. Moreover, it was emphasized that their adversaries were a people rebellious against God and that forces not supported by God would soon be exhausted. Fear turned into courage when a knight on a white horse, with a white banner bearing a luminous cross, appeared among the Christian ranks. By charging the enemies, he encouraged the Normans to follow his example. That knight, explains the author, was Saint George, who was often portrayed as a knight killing a dragon (a symbol of evil) and was venerated by the Normans for his military virtues. On that occasion, many Christian soldiers also saw a cross hanging from the tip of their commander's spear, which only God could have placed there.

> Seeing that their men, normally so brave, were frightened by the great multitude of enemy forces, [they] tried to shake the fear from them with exhortations like the following: 'Arouse your hearts, O most valiant young soldiers of the Christian army. We are all inscribed with the name of Christ, who would not desert his sign unless offended. Our God, the God of gods, is omnipotent: and it is his hand that places flesh on everyone, even those who, not trusting in God, place their confidence in men. All the kingdoms of the world belong to God, and he bestows them upon whomsoever he wishes. This people [of the Saracens] has rebelled against God, and power which is not directed by God is quickly exhausted. They glory in their own power; we, on the other hand, are secure in the protection of God. There is no room for any doubt: it is certain that, with God leading us, the enemy will not be able to stand before us. Gideon wiped out many thousands of the enemy with only a few men because he never had any doubts about God's assistance.'
>
> After these things had been said and the Norman forces were rushing toward the battle, there appeared a certain knight, magnificent in his armor, mounted on a white horse and carrying a white standard with a splendid cross on it tied to the tip of his lance. It was as if this knight were advancing with our battle line and rushing at the enemy where they were the thickest with a most valiant attack, so as to make our men more confident and ready to fight. Seeing this, our men were elated, and they called out again and again, 'God and St. George.' Struck with the joy of such a

vision to the point where they were shedding tears, they eagerly followed the horseman who preceded them. Many also saw a banner containing a cross hanging from the top of the count's lance, a banner which only God could have placed there.[58]

To crown the resounding success reported on that occasion, Malaterra recounts how the pope then sent his blessing to all the Normans, absolution for their sins (present and future), and the banner of Saint Peter so that the Normans would be able to confront the Saracens with more confidence. The Normans had thus obtained a confirmation of the sacredness of their conquest from God's highest representative on Earth.[59]

Not only warriors fought against the Muslims. In a case of great danger, even an abbot and his monks clashed with the Saracens. According to his biographer, Luke of Demenna (tenth century), complaining that God was allowing the Muslims to humiliate, kill, and enslave Christians, begged the Lord for divine intervention, to which God answered with the same words that he had pronounced to Moses in the Old Testament. Luke was instructed to gather his brothers, take his staff, and crush those 'dogs.' The abbot subsequently chose his strongest monks and, having taken a cross, imitated the Biblical hero, Gideon, by assaulting and vanquishing many Saracens, who were portrayed as the Devil's emissaries. In addition to exhorting Saint Luke to confront the enemy, the Lord also helped him in battle. A burst of fire surrounded the white horse on which the abbot rode, and then this fire struck down the Saracens. The author of this text further emphasizes the similarities with the Old Testament by narrating how, after defeating his adversaries, Luke sang one of David's psalms: 'May God appear and disperse all His enemies and may all who hate Him flee before Him.'[60] The author of the deeds of Saint Martin of Monte Massico recounts how, invoked by the monks of his monastery during a Muslim incursion in the early tenth century, the saint had them take weapons and himself led their charge against the raiders. 'With the help of Christ, who gives victory to his saints', the biographer emphasizes, 'they inflicted a heavy defeat on the Saracens'.[61]

To end this overview, I wish to mention a different type of source that shows that the spirit of holy war was not only present 'at the writing desk' but was also used during the clashes with the Muslims. In the prayer for the blessing of the banner of Saint Eusebius of Vercelli (ca. 964), with allusions to the Old Testament, God was asked to protect his people from Saracen incursions and to force them to flee before the standard.[62]

The popes did not produce any theoretical works about how fighting against the Muslims should be perceived. Some details in their letters, however, show that such clashes were given special significance. Hadrian II (867–872) praised Emperor Louis II for conducting 'the wars for the Lord' against the Saracens. This pontiff also wrote a letter to the Frankish King, Charles the Bald, asking him not to attack the kingdom of Louis II, since the latter was engaged in 'the wars for the Lord, fighting the Saracens', i.e., the Christians' enemies.[63]

Despite not referring specifically to the Muslims, two ninth-century popes provide detailed information about the celestial benefits for all those fighting against non-Christians to protect the Church. Addressing the Frankish warriors, Leo IV (847–855), elected shortly after the Muslim sacking of Saint Peter's in 846, stressed that those who had died defending the Church against pagans would be accepted into the Kingdom of Heaven.[64] Because many regions of western Europe were under attack by the Vikings in that period, the pope used the term 'pagans' to refer to all non-Christian enemies. The fight against this kind of enemy was recalled in the correspondence between several Frankish bishops and John VIII (872–882), another pope who was very concerned by the Muslim presence in Italy. To the request for explanations regarding how to treat those who had died defending the Church, the pope responded that their sins would be forgiven and that they consequently deserved eternal life.[65]

The pontiffs also sponsored the alliances to destroy the Muslim base on the Garigliano River in 915 and to repel a Saracen attack on the Tyrrhenian coast at the beginning of the eleventh century. The lack of papal sources does not, however, allow us to know if they promised something to those who participated in these campaigns.[66] On the other hand, the popes of the second half of the eleventh century strongly underlined their role as leaders of the Church and used the instructions left by their ninth-century predecessors to promote wars against the Muslims. Once Roger of Hauteville had demonstrated the strength of his commitment against the Muslims in Sicily by vanquishing them on the battlefield, Pope Alexander II (1061–1073), as has been already mentioned, absolved the Norman leader and his men of all their sins. In addition, the pontiff showed his support for this action by sending them the banner of Saint Peter.[67] Pope Victor III performed the same actions for the members of the expedition to al-Mahdīya in 1087.[68] In this regard, it should be noted that the popes of this period behaved in this way with all those who fought the enemies of the Papacy and the Church, even in cases where the adversaries were not Muslims.[69] Gregory VII (1073–1085) had broader horizons than those of his predecessors. In the wake of the disastrous defeat of the Byzantines by the Turks in 1071 and the successive expansion of the latter into Anatolia (Turkey), the pope tried in vain to involve numerous European rulers in the organization of an expedition against the Turks by promising the remission of all their sins.[70]

Roger of Hauteville's biography is not the only text to emphasize the special features of some of the clashes that Norman leader had with the Muslims in Sicily. After the island's conquest, Roger did not neglect to mention his victories in his donations to ecclesiastical institutions when he addressed an audience composed of churchmen, and not his Muslim subjects, to whom he promised a policy of peaceful coexistence. He describes his gesture with great religiosity, presenting it as the fulfillment of a vow. The faithful of Islam are depicted as enemies of God who had devastated Sicilian churches with their tyranny, while Roger and his warriors are shown fighting those perfidious enemies to defend the Christian faith and to bring it back to the island. The new churches were obviously intended for all Christian people. Roger, however, also attempted to grant himself and his men a sort of remission of sins, stressing that the clergy receiving his generosity should pray for the salvation of his soul and for those of his soldiers, including those who had died fighting the Muslims, so that God would pardon their sins and give them eternal life.

> I, Count Roger, since I committed in my person, once I vanquished the enemies of the divine name, to restore the holy churches of God, devastated by the tyranny of those who used to dominate Sicily, to their ancient state so that the name of God is exalted and the followers of Christ can perform their divine offices in those churches, and can pray to God more efficiently and comfortably, to the advantage of all Christian people; for this reason, I had a church built in the castle of Troina, and I adorned it with pious objects and necessary decorations. I endowed it with properties for its financial support and appointed priests to administer the divine and most holy sacraments to the faithful and to me, and to instruct everyone in divine doctrine and dogma of the sacrosanct Catholic faith, so that the Christian believers would grow through their preaching. I therefore entrust you this church so that you administer it along with the priests ordained to it, and you pray to God for the salvation of my soul and all my warriors who came with me to acquire the island of Sicily, and also of those who died fighting the perfidious Saracens for the defense of the Christian faith, so that the merciful God will forgive us all the sins that we and they had committed and will lead us to eternal glory.[71]

Christians in Muslim texts

In Muslim Sicily, no text about Christians has survived and comments about Christianity are absent in all Muslim works. In them, however, the term 'polytheist' is often employed to describe the followers of Christ in order to emphasize the idea that their belief in the Trinity meant that Christians did not have only one God.[72] The epithet 'worshipers of the Cross,' used by a Muslim Spaniard in an account of his stay in Sicily in 1185, has a similarly derogatory meaning. The same author further emphasizes his disdain for the Christians by calling the churches of Palermo 'dens.'[73]

In the twelfth century, the Saracens of the Maghreb had to defend themselves from Christian attacks, and Muslim authors consequently used harsher terminology to describe their adversaries. The Christians are called 'enemies of God',[74] and their religion is classified as 'misbelief.'[75] The theme 'we are right, while they persist in their error because they are ignorant' is present as well. Referring to a victory against the Normans, Ibn Ḥamdîs (ca. 1056–ca. 1133) wonders ironically: 'Why did ignorance keep these barbarians in error for so long? Was there not one wise man among them?'[76]

According to Iraqi geographer and traveler Ibn Ḥawqal (tenth century), who visited southern Italy, in the main mosque of Palermo, there was a wooden chest, hanging in the air and containing the remains of the Greek philosopher Aristotle. He adds that the building was previously a church of the Christians, who highly venerated that tomb and used to ask Aristotle for relief during droughts and for protection from other calamities.[77] This writer does not criticize these beliefs, but he probably mentions them as a sort of strange custom in a foreign land. Nevertheless, such an anecdote also seems to hint at the superstitious nature of the Christians and, therefore, their inferiority. On the other hand, a derogatory intent can certainly be perceived in Hārūn b. Yaḥya's description of what the pope would do with the hair and nails of Saint Peter's body.

> In the church there is the golden tomb of two apostles: one called Peter and the other called Paul. Every year, at Easter, the King (i.e., the pope), comes and opens the door of the sepulcher; he descends into the tomb with a razor in his hand. There he shaves the head of the dead Peter, and also cuts his nails; when he returns, he gives a hair to every person present. This rite has been celebrated every year for nine centuries.[78]

The same goal can be seen when this author attributes the practice of head shaving, which he had probably observed among some ecclesiastics, to all of Rome's inhabitants.[79]

The reference in an anonymous text to the fact that some of the Lombards did not have any religion during their rule in Italy was probably the result of the echoes of papal criticism for that people and of rituals the Lombards performed when they were still pagans.

Currently the Lombards are mostly Christian, but among them, there are some with no religion at all. Their practices are the same as the Rūm, and some of them incinerate the bodies of the dead.[80]

There is no doubt about how the Muslims perceived the campaigns against the Christians in Italy. They were jihad, which, in those centuries, was considered a fight against the infidels in the *dār al-ḥarb* (The House of War), i.e., the territories governed by non-Muslims. For example, describing the campaigns of a Muslim leader, a chronicler points out that 'he carried out many expeditions in the House of War, so that the countries overseas, belonging to the Franks, Genoa and Sardinia, would fear him and pay tribute'.[81] An epitaph in verse, on the other hand, praises the deceased as 'fallen martyr, happy thou, on the field of jihad, surrounded by wretched barbarians'.[82] This feature can be found in the descriptions of the conquest of Sicily and the rest of southern Italy. The chronicler Alī ibn al-Athīr (ca. 1160–ca. 1230) presents the campaign of Emir Ibrāhīm II (d. 902) as a sort of religious duty, claiming that the ruler would make a pilgrimage to Mecca after conducting jihad in southern Italy.[83] According to this author, before attacking Taormina, Ibrāhīm II had ordered two verses of the Quran to be recited and said: 'Oh great God…today I confront the infidels for you'.[84] More detailed accounts are present in the descriptions of the fights against the Normans in the Maghreb during the twelfth century. When the Muslims were successful, they explicitly thanked Allah for conceding the victory to Islam.[85]

Ibn Ḥamdîs praised the victory of the governor of al-Mahdīya against the army of Roger II in 1124 in this way:

> God would not allow the victory not to be yours, or our faith not to destroy the edifice of misbelief, or the barbarians to return without being humiliated after such treatment, vilified by the defeat, which was the fruit of their guilt. Praise be to you for a victory in which the sword's thirst is quenched by their blood, the memory of which quiets the face of religion… it was the duty of God's armies to fight them…Groups of warriors from every tribe obeyed the call to jihad, no one could excuse himself from not taking a part in this. The Lord of the Throne exalted them through Mohammed's religion and welcomed them in the womb of his protection.[86]

Some authors specify that the Muslims attacked the enemy shouting 'Akbar Allah' (God is great).

> He moved with all of them against the Rūm who were already sacking and capturing women. Raising the cry 'Allah Akbar' against the Rūm who had

prepared for battle. . . . He attacked them, and God defeated them with his own hand.[87]

At night the Muslims emitted a dreadful cry so that the earth was shaking and attacked saying 'Akbar Allah'. Scared by this, the Franks (i.e., the Normans) thought that all of the Muslims were about to fall upon them and they quickly ran towards their ships to board them.[88]

At the same time, those who did not demonstrate enough fervor in their fight against the Christian invaders, or who had lost against them, were accused of showing a weak faith: 'It happened that a certain tyrant and chief of Arab bandits, motivated by his corrupt religious conscience and feeble faith, treacherously gave the enemy a castle'.[89]

Many Sicilian Muslims, explains Ibn Ḥawqal, became teachers in order to be excused from their duty to participate in jihad, an observation that suggests the existence of a great difference between theories, aspirations, praising tones, and reality.[90]

Notes

1 Amatus of Montecassino, *Ystoire de li Normant*, V, 23; *Vita di s. Nilo*, chapter 14; *Capitularia regum Francorum*, eds. A. Boretius, V. Krause, MHG, *Leges sectio* 3, 2 vols. (Hanover, 1883–1897), vol. 2, number 203, chapters 2, 9.
2 Geoffrey Malaterra, *De rebus gestis*, IV, 7.
3 *Chronicon Salernitanum*, chapter 112; *Vita Antonini abbatis Surrentini*, in *Acta Sanctorum, Februarii*, II (Venice, 1785), chapters 21, 22; William of Apulia, *La Geste de Robert Guiscard*, III, line 330.
4 *Liber pontificalis*, vol. 2, p. 81; Geoffrey Malaterra, *De rebus gestis Rogerii*, II, 45; *Vita di Sant'Elia il Giovane*, chapter 8, p. 12; *Vita Walfredi*, p. 62; *Vita S. Venerii*, in *Acta Sanctorum, Septembris*, IV (Antwerp, 1763), chapter 17; *Vita s. Lucae abbatis*, chapter 5; *Vita et Miracula Sancti Fantini*, in *Acta Sanctorum, Iulii*, V (Antwerp, 1727), chapters 52–53; *Miracula sancti Felicis Nolani*, in Peter the Subdeacon, *L'opera agiografica*, ed. E. D'Angelo (Florence, 2002), p. 212, paragraph 24.
5 *Vita S. Eliae Spelaeotae*, chapters 35, 69; *Vita e fatti del nostro padre Bartolomeo*, chapter 24 (twice).
6 *Vita di Sant'Elia il Giovane*, chapter 44, p. 66; *Historia et laudes SS. Sabae et Macarii iuniorum e Sicilia auctore Oreste Patriarcha Hierosolymitano*, ed. G. Cozza-Luzi (Rome, 1893), chapter 8, p. 81.
7 Geoffrey Malaterra, *De rebus gestis Rogerii*, II, 33, p. 44, II, 35.
8 Landulf the Elder, *Historia Mediolanensis*, eds. L. C. Bethmann – W. Wattenbach, in MGH, *Scriptores*, vol. 8 (Hanover, 1848), p. 100. Enemies of Christ in *Capitularia regum Francorum*, vol. 2, number 203, chapter 9.
9 *Carmen in victoriam Pisanorum*, stanza 26.
10 *Vita di Sant'Elia il Giovane*, chapters 16, 24.
11 *Chronica Monasterii Casinensis*, III, 71.
12 Nicholas, *Epistolae*, ed. E. Perels, in MGH, *Epistolae*, vol. 6 (Berlin, 1925), number 99, p. 579, chapter 103.
13 *Translatio sancti Severini*, p. 453.

14   *Translatio sancti Severini*, chapters 1, 3.
15   *La Vita di san Leone Luca di Corleone*, ed. M. Stelladoro (Badia Greca di Grottaferrata, 1995), p. 74.
16   *Vita di s. Luca vescovo di Isola Capo Rizzuto*, ed. G. Schirò (Palermo, 1954), p. 90.
17   *Liber pontificalis*, vol. 2, p. 109.
18   *Chronicon Salernitanum*, chapter 107.
19   William of Apulia, *La Geste de Robert Guiscard*, III, lines 199, 286–87; Geoffrey Malaterra, *De rebus gestis Rogerii*, II, 1.
20   William of Apulia, *La Geste de Robert Guiscard*, III, lines 332–36.
21   Geoffrey Malaterra, *De rebus gestis Rogerii*, II, 13.
22   Amatus of Montecassino, *Ystoire de li Normant*, I, 5.
23   Italian translation in *Regesti dei documenti dell'Italia meridionale (570–899)*, eds. J.-M. Martin, E. Cuozzo, S. Gasparri, M. Villani (Rome, 2002), p. 479, chapter 9.
24   *The Epistle of the monk Theodosius*, p. 95.
25   *Carmen in victoriam*, stanza 32. Mohammed is mentioned in stanza 52.
26   P. Joannou, 'La personalità storica di Luca di Bova attraverso i suoi scritti inediti', *Archivio Storico per la Calabria e la Lucania*, 29 (1960), pp. 214–16.
27   Kedar, *Crusade and Mission*, pp. 33–34.
28   *Translatio Sancti Severini*, chapter 1, p. 453.
29   *Vita di Sant'Elia il Giovane*, chapters 16–17, pp. 24–27.
30   *Vita di Sant'Elia il Giovane*, chapter 24, pp. 34–37.
31   For example, see *Liber pontificalis*, vol. 2, p. 113; Andreas of Bergamo, *Historia*, chapters 17, 18; William of Apulia, *La Geste de Robert Guiscard*, III, lines 242, 254; *Historia et laudes SS. Sabae et Macarii*, chapter 6, p. 13; *Vita Vitalis*, chapter 14; *Vita e fatti del nostro padre Bartolomeo*, chapter 24; *La vita di san Leone Luca di Corleone*, p. 74; *Vita Antonini abbatis Surrentini*, chapters 20, 22; Neilos, *Vita di san Filareto di Seminara*, pp. 48–49.
32   William of Apulia, *La Geste de Robert Guiscard*, III, line 218; Neilos, *Vita di san Filareto di Seminara*, pp. 44–45.
33   O. Vehse, 'Das Bündnis gegen die Sarazenen vom Jahre 915', *Quellen und Forschungen aus italienischen Archiven und Bibliotechen*, 19 (1927), p. 203.
34   The composition date of this text is unfortunately unknown. *Acta Fortunati, Caii, et Anthae*, in *Acta Sanctorum, Augusti*, XXVIII (Antwerp, 1743), p. 168, chapter 7.
35   *Vita Vitalis*, chapter 23, p. 33.
36   *Historia et laudes SS. Sabae et Macarii*, chapter 9, p. 17; *Vita di san Nilo*, chapter 30.
37   *Sermo de virtute Sancti Constantii*, chapter 10, pp. 1017–18.
38   *Vita s. Lucae abbatis*, chapter 10.
39   *Vita di san Nilo*, chapters 24, 30.
40   Amatus of Montecassino, *Ystoire de li Normant*, VI, 19, V, 23.
41   *Cronaca di Novalesa*, IV, fragmentum XXII, pp. 239–40, V, 1.
42   Donizo, *Vita di Matilde di Canossa*, ed. P. Golinelli (Milan, 2008), I, lines 1370–72, pp. 120–21.
43   *Chronicon Salernitanum*, chapter 108.
44   Landulf the Elder, *Historia Mediolanensis*, eds. L. C. Bethmann – W. Wattenbach, in MGH, *Scriptores*, vol. 8 (Hanover, 1848), p. 100.
45   *Cronicae Sancti Benedicti Casinensis*, II, 28.
46   Benedict of St. Andreas, *Chronicon*, pp. 148–51.
47   *Vita S. Eliae Spelaeotae*, chapter 35.
48   *Chronicon Salernitanum*, chapter 112.
49   Geoffrey Malaterra, *De rebus gestis Rogerii*, IV, 1.
50   *Cronaca Cassanese del X secolo*, ed. V. Saletta (Rome, 1966), p. 61.
51   P. Arthur, 'Saraceni, schiavi e il Salento', in *III Congresso Nazionale di Archeologia Medievale* (Florence, 2004), p. 444.

52 A. Borruso, 'Some Arab-Muslim perceptions of religion and medieval culture in Sicily', in *Muslim Perceptions of Other Religions: A Historical Survey Overview* (New York, 1999), p. 141.
53 Andreas of Bergamo, *Historia*, chapter 18.
54 Liudprand of Cremona, *Retribution*, in *The Complete Works of Liudprand of Cremona*, trans. P. Squatriti (Washington, D. C., 2007), II, 54.
55 Thietmar of Merseburg, *Chronicon*, VII, 45.
56 Neilos, *Vita di san Filareto di Seminara*, pp. 44–47.
57 *Carmen in victoriam Pisanorum*, stanzas 23–28, 33–34.
58 Geoffrey Malaterra, *The Deeds of Count Roger of Calabria and Sicily and of his Brother Duke Robert Guiscard*, trans. K. B. Wolf (Ann Arbor, 2005), II, 33, pp. 109–10.
59 Geoffrey Malaterra, *De rebus gestis Rogerii*, II, 33.
60 *Vita S. Lucae abbatis*, chapters 10–11.
61 H. Moretus, 'Un opuscule du diacre Adalbert sur S. Martin de MonteMassico', *Analecta Bollandiana* 25 (1906), chapter 8, pp. 254–55. The author claims to have witnessed that clash. The monastery of Saint Martin of Monte Massico was located in northwestern Campania, about ten kilometers from the Tyrrhenian coast.
62 *Benedizione del vessillo di Sant'Eusebio a Vercelli (964)*, in *Le carte dello Archivio capitolare di Vercelli*, eds. D. Arnoldi, G. C. Faccio, F. Gabotto, G. Rocchi (Pinerolo, 1912), p. 353.
63 Hadrian II, *Epistolae*, ed. E. Perels, in MGH, *Epistolae*, vol. 6 (Berlin, 1925), number 21, p. 725.
64 Leo IV, *Epistolae Selecta*, ed. A. de Hirsch-Gereuth, in MGH, *Epistolae*, vol. 5 (Berlin, 1899), p. 601, number 28.
65 John VIII, *Registrum*, p. 126, number 150.
66 The fact that in 1010 Pope Sergius IV wanted to organize an expedition to Jerusalem is based on a document which most scholars believe to be a forgery. For further information on this, see J. Flori, *La guerre sainte: la formation de l'idée de croisade dans l'Occident chrétien* (Paris, 2001), p. 302–4.
67 Geoffrey Malaterra, *De rebus gestis Rogerii*, II, 33.
68 This information is mentioned in a Cassinese chronicle where it is said that the pope gave the indulgence to the participants of an expedition against the Saracens in Africa. The chronicler likely refers to the raid of the Pisans and Genoese against that Tunisian city. *Chronica Monasterii Casinensis*, III, 71.
69 For example, Leo IX pointed out that those who had died fighting his enemies (i.e., the Normans of southern Italy) in 1053 had to be considered martyrs. Alexander II, in a similar gesture, sent the banner of Saint Peter to the Milanese faction that supported the reform of the Church. For further information about this topic, see Flori, *La guerre sainte*, pp. 178–205.
70 It seems that Gregory VII also wanted to reconquer Jerusalem. For further information about Gregory VII's project, see Flori, *La guerre sainte*, pp. 305–9.
71 *Documenti latini e greci del conte Ruggero I di Calabria e Sicilia*, ed. J. Becker (Rome, 2013), number 2, p. 41.
72 BAS, vol. 1, pp. 308, 372; vol. 2, pp. 7, 10, 15, 16, 18, 72, 74, 86, 147, 177, 301, 302.
73 *The Travels of Ibn Jubayr*, trans. R. Broadhurst (London, 1952; Reprint, Noida, 2001), p. 350.
74 BAS, vol. 2, p. 72.
75 Ibn Ḥamdîs, *Il Canzoniere*, Italian translation by C. Schiaparelli (Palermo, 1998), number 143, stanza 2.
76 Ibn Ḥamdîs, *Il Canzoniere*, number 143, stanza 40.
77 BAS, vol. 1, p. 11.
78 Borruso, 'Some Arab-Muslim perceptions of religion and medieval culture in Sicily,' p. 137. This author visited Rome around 900.

79 Borruso, 'Some Arab-Muslim perceptions of religion and medieval culture in Sicily,' p. 137.
80 Italian translation in Mandalà, 'La Longobardia, i Longobardi e Pavia', p. 347.
81 Italian translation in M. G. Stasolla, 'Arabi e Sardegna nella storiografia araba del medioevo', *Studi Maghrebini* 14 (1982), p. 197.
82 BAS, vol. 2, p. 409.
83 BAS, vol. 1, p. 403.
84 BAS, vol. 1, p. 394.
85 BAS, vol. 2, p. 74.
86 Ibn Ḥamdīs, *Il Canzoniere*, number 143, stanzas 1–3, 16, 64, 65.
87 BAS, vol. 1, p. 311.
88 BAS, vol. 1, p. 475. For other examples, see BAS, vol. 1, pp. 202, 372, 457, 458.
89 BAS, vol. 2, p. 73.
90 BAS, vol. 1, p. 24.

3   Perceptions

Muslims in Christian texts

Derogatory definitions for Muslims frequently appear in all the narrative works of this period. The most commonly utilized term, 'barbarian', immediately evokes the image of ferocious and destructive invaders.[1] The main reference work for the writers of this epoch, who one should always keep in mind were all churchmen, was the Bible. In the Holy Scriptures, the worst persecutors of the chosen people were the Pharaoh and the Egyptians. It is not surprising, therefore, that some authors compare the faithful of Islam to them. According to the biographer of Vitalis of Castronovo, this saint once addressed some Muslims and told them that their 'prince' was the Pharaoh who had drowned in the Red Sea with his army, thus emphasizing that he considered the Saracens as direct descendants of the biblical Egyptians.[2]

The Muslims are also described in more obviously disparaging terms. The most common are: 'iniquitous', 'ferocious' (a Neapolitan writer claims that their ferocity is insatiable),[3] 'nefarious', 'bastards', 'delinquents', 'crazed', 'very evil', 'abominable', and 'cruel'.[4] They are even called 'dogs'.[5] The Salernitan anonymous chronicler compares them to locusts,[6] insects well known for their voracity and destructivity. Similarly, in his description of Sicily's invasion, Erchempert equates them to a swarm of bees, insects extremely dangerous when they attack in large groups. The Saracens, explains that chronicler, indeed brought death and destruction to the island.[7] According to a Neapolitan author, the Muslims devastated Reggio Calabria with their 'usual rapacity'.[8] The author of the *Life of Saint Venerius* defines them as a 'tumultuous and unstable people', thus attributing their incursions to their very nature.[9]

Besides being terrible destroyers, the Muslims could also be sly and perfidious. In the account of Bari's conquest by the Saracen troops hired by the prince of Benevento and charged with the defense of that city, it is narrated that these mercenaries were placed outside Bari's walls but that they subsequently entered the city at night while its inhabitants were sleeping. This treachery, adds an anonymous Cassinese author, occurred in the usual manner, a clear reference to the fact that deceit and treason were considered standard Muslim tactics.

> At that time, through the Gastald of Bari, Pando, Prince Radelchis invited the Saracens from beyond the sea to come to his help. They stayed for a long time near Bari, afterwards they took possession of the city at night in the usual manner.[10]

In recounting the same episode, Erchempert points out that the Saracens were by nature shrewder and more skilled than others in committing evil.[11] On this topic and on the necessity not to trust them, Erchempert insists with a malignant observation – 'Who will cure the wizard once he is bitten by the serpent?' – when he mentions the havoc the Saracens had wrought in the lands of their former allies, the Neapolitans.[12]

Liudprand of Cremona emphasizes the slyness and perfidiousness of the Muslims in his description of the creation of their stronghold at Fraxinetum.

> Meanwhile the Provençals, the nation that was closest to them, began to squabble among themselves through envy, to throttle one another, snatch property, and to do whatever evil they could think up. But since one faction could not quite do for itself what envy and pain demanded, it called to its aid the aforementioned Saracens, who were no less clever than perfidious, and with them crushed a faction of neighbors. Nor was it enough to murder neighbors, but truly they reduced to desolation the fruitful earth. … The Saracens, since they could do little with their own men, defeating one faction with the help of another, ceaselessly increasing their troops from Spain, began to hunt down by all means those they at first seemed to defend. Therefore they ravaged, they exterminated, they made it so that no one was left.[13]

Placing too much faith in a certain Muslim cost Serlo of Hauteville, Roger's nephew, his life. To get rid of him, this Saracen pretended to ally with him and even made him his adopted brother. Luring Serlo out of a city by telling him that a small group of Muslims would attack, he ambushed him, confronting him with many Saracens, against whom the Norman inevitably lost his life.[14] The same fate awaited the Muslim ruler who allied himself with Roger of Hauteville; while he was looking for allies among his coreligionists in Sicily, he fell into a trap set for him by one of his warriors.[15]

The anonymous Salernitan chronicler refers to other qualities of the Muslims. During the siege of Salerno in 872, a Saracen, a sort of super-man endowed with three testicles, swaggeringly challenged a Salernitan to a duel. Moreover, he invited him to experience the 'virtue' of the Muslims, probably a word-play used by the chronicler to show the meager value of those virtues. Having accepted the invitation, the Christian, with the help of God, easily killed the arrogant Muslim.[16]

The first contact Saint Neilos (ca. 910–1004) had with the faithful of Islam provides the most detailed account of the degree of terror they inspired. First, the encounter is compared to that of Saint Paul's with a viper. Referring to the theory connecting physical features to moral characteristics, the biographer stresses how the swarthy complexion, the dark eyes, and murderous looks made the Saracens look like demons. Thanks to God, adds the writer, nothing happened. In order to emphasize the exceptional nature of that event, however, his biographer notes that Neilos began to tremble because of the danger that he had just escaped and that he expected to be treacherously hit in the back by a Muslim, as was the habit of those 'barbarians'. Inspired by the Lord, the Saracen, however, gave Neilos some bread.[17]

In the *Life of Saint Elias the Younger*, Muslims are accused of being as lecherous as animals, differing from them only because they perform homosexual acts.

> Being libertines, you are incontinent in your pleasure, and you are different from animals, that have no reason which rules passions, only because they know the limits of their natural impulse, while you look for femininity in the male and for virility in the female.[18]

Authors' points of view obviously influenced their perceptions. In the small town of Larino (Molise), the target of attacks by both Muslims and Hungarians, the destruction caused by the latter was described as much worse than that of the Saracens. Even the terminology utilized to characterize them seems to reflect such a difference. The Saracens, narrates an author of that region, were pagans, while the Hungarians were barbarians. At Larino, the result of the Muslim incursion was, however, catastrophic; the consequences of the Hungarian raid were minimized thanks to the intervention of Saint Pardus, whose remains were preserved in Larino. In the recounting of such events, it becomes apparent that the different results of the two attacks were influenced by the fact that, in the case of the Saracen assault, the inhabitants of that town had not acquired the relics of that saint yet. Consequently, the Hungarians were portrayed more ferociously than the Muslims to exalt the salvific intervention of Saint Pardus.[19]

The *Life of Saint Elias Spelaeota* reminds us that saints' biographies must not be read as a straightforward description of events but as a reflection of the views of the monastic communities in which they were written. The young companion of Elias, narrates the biographer, could not endure the harshness of the saint's ascetic life and, returning to his former life, was killed by Saracens. No comment is made about his tragic fate, but it is pointed out that the young man had thus 'died twice'. The author emphasizes how serious his abandonment of the ascetic life was by saying not only that he had 'acted like a dog that eats its own vomit', but by adding that Elias had grieved more for his young disciple's decision than for his death.[20]

In papal letters, Muslims appear most often in the rich correspondence of John VIII (872–882). He tried, without great success, to gain support for his fight against them, and to put an end to the 'impious accords' struck between the Saracens and the Christian rulers of southern Italy. Besides the already mentioned terminology about their religious otherness, the pope compares the destruction the Muslims caused to that of locusts, calling them 'odious to God', 'children of fornication', 'iniquitous', 'nefarious', and 'malicious people'.[21] In two letters, John VIII specifies that their incursions occurred surreptitiously; thus they were shrewd and cowardly.[22] On the other hand, Gregory VII (1073–1075) implicitly compares Muslims to ferocious animals, stating that it was necessary to help the Eastern Christians who were cruelly afflicted 'by the Saracens' bites'. To incite the European rulers to follow him in this enterprise, the pope stressed that the pagans arrived at the walls of Constantinople, devastating everything in their path and slaughtering Christians by the thousands as if they were cattle.[23]

Most of the early medieval archival sources are sales of land, donations to churches and monasteries, and wills. In these documents the goal of those involved was to register a transaction, not to provide their own opinions about Muslims or detailed information about their incursions. A few brief and generic comments about the Saracens do appear, but they are only mentioned in these sources when it was necessary to give an explanation of the conditions under which the charter was written. Regarding such sources in southern Italy, we should note that the extant documents are not equally distributed over all the geographic areas and historic periods examined in this study. Very little, and sometimes nothing, from the 'hottest' areas and periods has come down to us.

In Salerno, in July 872, a woman states that, since her brother was captured by 'evil Saracens' who were besieging the city, she will dictate her last wishes in the presence of two of her other relatives.[24] In the stipulation of a will, written in the same place and under the same conditions in February 882, the characterization of the Muslims is similarly brief, but more caustic, probably because this record preserves the pain of a mother. Indeed, the woman's two sons could not be with her because one had fallen into the hands of the Muslims, while the other one lived in another town and was unable to reach Salerno due to the siege set by the 'barbaric people of the Saracens'.[25]

In 893, in a lease of land belonging to the monastery of St. Vincent at Volturno, Muslims are called pagans. On that occasion it was specified that the decision to rent the property had been made necessary by the economic harshness the monks were experiencing after the Saracens had pillaged their abbey.[26] Describing similar destructions in the second half of the tenth century, some northwestern Italian churchmen define those dreaded enemies as 'nefarious and infidel'.[27] In the rental contract for the use of a mill in Tuscany in 875, it is specified that payment would not be due if pagans should destroy the mill.[28] In other archival documents, comments are conspicuously absent. For example, this is the case in a charter redacted in December 882, during the siege of Nocera by the Muslims, despite the fact that it also records the dramatic choice of a widow of that town who was forced to sell everything left by her husband in order to prevent starvation.[29] Other types of sources for this period are equally laconic, including the list of twenty-seven monks from St. Modestus of Benevento killed by Muslims and therefore honored during mass and the descriptions of how to deal with Saracens in the peace treaties between the principalities of Benevento and Salerno (849) and the Lombards and the Neapolitans (936–940).[30]

The tone is, on the contrary, notably harsh in the measures Emperor Lothar issued in 847 to organize an expedition against the Muslims in southern Italy. His campaign was a response to the sack of Rome by the Muslims in the previous year. Besides describing the logistical features of the campaign, the goal of this document was to underline Lothar's commitment to avenge the serious offense inflicted upon the heart of western Christendom and to galvanize his warriors. Muslims are called pagans, infidels, and 'enemies of Christ', and it is emphasized that they had looted St. Peter's. The emperor acknowledges that the terrible event happened because of the many sins of Christians and promises to stop all the crimes and immoral acts, including those concerning sexual activities. Moreover, he proclaims a general fast of three days to invoke God's help and he orders his troops not to pillage Christian territories in order to avoid divine wrath.

> No one doubts that, because of our sins, worthy of infamy, a terrible evil came to the Church of Christ, that the Church of Rome itself, which is the head of Christendom, was delivered into the hands of the infidels, and the ranks of the pagans prevailed in all the territories of our kingdom and of our brothers. We therefore believe it is absolutely necessary to reform all the things that we know offend God, with the help of his mercy, and to

commit to placate divine justice, by giving it adequate satisfaction until we are able to appease He whom we are feeling is angry.[31]

Christians in Muslim texts

When it happened that the Christians attacked and the Saracens defended themselves, the roles were reversed, and some derogatory definitions for the faithful of Christ appear in Islamic narrative works. Most Muslim authors are quite synthetic about these episodes and do not linger on details. In the descriptions of Norman campaigns in Tunisia during the twelfth century, however, it is the Christians who are called barbarians. In the narration of the Pisan and Genoese raid against al-Mahdīya in 1087, an inhabitant of that city defines the aggressors as snakes and states that there were so many of them that they looked like clouds of locusts and knots of worms.

> The enemies attacked our homeland in such number that [they looked like clouds of] locusts or [knots of] worms. / Twenty thousand of them gathered together from everywhere; alas, what an evil gathering! / They suddenly plummeted on a handful of men, inexperienced in war, rookies,/ used to a mellow and care-free life: but Destiny does not have languid eyes!/ Waking up from their morning sleep, they saw threatening stares and sharp swords before them./ They came on galleys that looked like mountains, but their summits were bristled with spears and swords. / ... They came upon us like snakes.[32]

In the account of the battle at Cape Dimas with the Normans in 1124, it is emphasized that 'ships came like a cloud of locusts that darkened the sky'. In addition to being called barbarians, the aggressors are also called swine, notoriously impure animals for Muslims: 'In their jihad the Bedouins fought the barbarians, pigs to be crushed by furious lions'.[33]

The ferocity of the enemies and the consequences of their attacks

Christians suffered Muslim attacks between the ninth and the tenth centuries, and therefore it is not surprising that several Italian writers provide detailed descriptions about the extremely violent behavior and ferocious nature of the Saracens. After sowing death and destruction in Rome in 846, recounts a Cassinese chronicler, the Muslims tried to take Montecassino. A violent storm, however, flooded a river, thereby preventing the Muslims from reaching the abbey. Describing their anger at being unable to reach their objective, the Cassinese author portrays them as madmen and remarks that, as was typical of their barbarity, the Muslims chewed their fingers, ground their teeth, and ran up and down in search of a place where they could cross the river. Moreover, they burned some religious buildings so that their attempted raid might not be fruitless.[34]

Explicit references to the fury of the Muslims are recorded in other texts as well. According to a Sorrentine writer, the inhabitants of the Campanian cities formed a league to free themselves from the 'rage' of the Saracens; the raiders, adds the same author, assaulted with 'blind fury' Saint Antoninus, who had appeared on one of their ships.[35] Furious because they did not find any satisfactory prey at the monastery of Vitalis of Castronovo (tenth century), some Saracens decided to behead the abbot.[36] Similarly, the presence of a modest amount of money in the monastery of Gregory of Cassano (ca. 930–ca. 1002) provoked the rage of other Muslims. Claiming that Gregory had lied, they tortured him by hitting his genitals.[37]

In his requests for military assistance, Pope John VIII emphasizes that the Muslims slaughtered a great number of Christians and enslaved those who had survived their raids. The Saracens devastated the entire region around Rome to the point that food was scarce. The pontiff adds that sterile women were lucky, since they would not have to cry for their children who would have been killed by those raiders.[38] To describe the extent of their cruelty, the pope explains that he would have had to pour out rivers of tears; moreover, he would have lacked both words and parchment.[39]

Describing the effects of their expeditions, Erchempert emphasizes that they destroyed everything down to the roots, so that not a germ of life remained after their passage, while, on another occasion, nothing survived but brambles; Calabria was as depopulated as it had been after the Noachian flood.[40] Having occupied the island of Ischia, recounts a Sorrentine author, the Saracens plundered the nearby mainland, burning fields, killing many peasants mercilessly, and capturing many of that region's inhabitants. Their destruction is even compared to that caused by a violent hailstorm.[41] At Lipari, they looted the whole island, either killing or capturing all the inhabitants, including the churchmen; they left unharmed just three or four old monks, who, because of their age, were not thought worthy of any consideration.[42] In addition to mentioning the devastation and the slaughter of monks and lay people by Muslims in Sicily, the biographer of Saint Sabas (ca. 910–ca. 991) also lingers on the catastrophic effects of their presence, providing macabre details that underlined the Christians' extreme despair. In that period the shortage of food became so critical that it led many Christians to eat human flesh; parents ate their children, children their parents, brothers ate brothers, and wives their husbands.[43]

Somewhat confusing his geography and occasionally exaggerating, Liudprand of Cremona (ca. 920–972) turns his attention to southern Italy as well. According to this bishop-writer, the Saracens occupied almost the entire southern part of the Peninsula and many cities of central Italy to the point that half of those urban centers were completely under their dominion. They also captured all the pilgrims going to Rome and freed them only after they paid a ransom.[44] Liudprand also makes the unusual comparison between what had occurred in the north and south of the Peninsula, observing that, despite the fact that Fraxinetum's Saracens and Hungarians ravaged the North, nothing was comparable to the tribulations the Muslims caused in the South.

> Although wretched Italy was oppressed by many misfortunes of the Hungarians and of the Saracens from Fraxinetum, still it was shaken by no devastations or epidemics like those brought by the Africans.[45]

According to this writer, the Saracens of Fraxinetum proved to be a true and persistent thorn in the side of northwestern Italy. They were not content with devastating the Italian towns close to the Alps. Indeed, one of their raids reached Acqui. In order to highlight the extent of their incursions, Liudprand notes that it was only forty miles from Pavia. This city was the capital of the Italian kingdom, and this detail shows that the Saracens could even raid the Po Valley easily. Liudprand also mentions that, on this occasion, the Muslims provoked such terror that no one dared to wait for 'their arrival unless in very heavily defended places'.[46] They were not the only ones who hit northern Italy either. North African Muslims, in fact, attacked Genoa, killing all the men, kidnapping women and children, and pillaging the churches.[47]

At the beginning of the tenth century, recounts the chronicler of Novalesa, the abbot of his monastery, afraid of Fraxinetum's Muslims, moved to the safety of Turin with his monks taking valuables and a great number of manuscripts with him. The 'most ferocious' invaders immediately occupied the monastery, stealing everything they found and burning all the structures. Following this destruction, the abbey remained deserted for many years. In order to survive, the abbot had to pawn a great deal of the treasure and codices of the monastery. Because of the turmoil provoked by the Muslims all these treasures were lost anyway. In Turin the unfortunate members of that monastic community also suffered losses at the hands of the Muslims. Two Saracens, kept prisoners in that city, burned the church of the Novalesa monks in Turin.[48] Muslims therefore played an extremely negative role in the history of that abbey. It is not surprising that, despite recounting these events many years later, the anonymous monk who wrote the history of his monastery shows his anger towards them, using particularly harsh language. He, in fact, compares one Saracen incursion to a flood that submerged everything in blood and fire.[49]

The serious situation created by Saracen raids in several regions of Piedmont in the tenth century is also documented in a papal letter.

> We have actually heard that the Bishopric of Alba has been so ruined by the Saracens that Bishop Fulcard, currently in charge of that Church, is without clerks and population, and he is furnishing his daily expenses not as a bishop from the resources of the Church, but as a peasant from his agricultural work.[50]

Authors sometimes linger on specific victims of the Muslims. These episodes, however, are not commented upon, almost as if to suggest that the stories alone are enough to demonstrate the Saracens' fierceness. During a raid in the hills around Montecassino in the 860s, the faithful of Islam killed an old man who had shown them the wrong path.[51] When Saracens reached the Abbey of Novalesa, they battered two old monks to death.[52] According to a Milanese chronicler, in Rome, in 1084, Muslim soldiers of Robert Guiscard's army raped nuns and Roman women and cut their fingers off to take their rings.[53]

One of the most detailed accounts of Saracen ferocity is that by the monk Theodosius who, unlike the aforementioned chroniclers, made some comments about what the Muslims did after the fall of Syracuse in 878.

> The barbarians took those whom they had made prisoners with the patrician, all born in Syracuse, and of high station, and some other captives also, and led them out of the city, and made them stand together within a circle; and they fell upon them with a rush like wild dogs, and slew them, some with stones, some with clubs, some with the spears they had in their hands... they consumed their bodies with fire.

A special treatment was reserved for a Byzantine soldier who, during the siege, daily cursed Mohamed in front of the Saracens.

> They separated him from the number of those who were to be slain, and they stretched him upon the ground on his back, and they flayed him alive from his breast downward, and they tore to pieces his protruding vitals with spears; and, moreover, with their hands they tore the heart out of the man while he yet breathed, and lacerated it with their teeth, most monstrously, and dashed it upon the earth and stoned it, and then at last were satiated, and left it.[54]

Muslim texts on the Norman conquest of Sicily are very concise and do not mention massacres of civilians or the killing of prisoners by Christians, but this detail may be due to a dearth of coeval chroniclers. The poet Ibn Ḥamdîs (ca. 1056–ca. 1133), who left the island in those years, complains because Christians humiliated his beloved homeland. He does not recall, however, any violent acts against Muslims, thus confirming the version of events presented by the Christian chroniclers.[55]

The recording of such atrocities is also absent from the Muslim accounts of the Pisan and Genoese expedition against al-Mahdīya in 1087. Moreover, the Islamic texts describe that campaign as a blockade of the Tunisian city which the governor of al-Mahdīya ended by paying tributes to the Pisans and Genoese and by liberating the Christian prisoners.[56] It is impossible to determine if the Muslim authors limited themselves to recounting just what they knew or if they preferred to minimize the extent of the enemies' success and therefore under-represented their brutality. These details suggest that one must not interpret the account of the civilians' massacre at al-Mahdīya by a Pisan writer as an accurate description of events; rather, his narrative seems to represent the author's desire to convey to his readers that an enemy, who had created serious problems for Pisa and Genoa, had been completely eliminated.

The tone of the Muslim writers, however, changes in their accounts of the Norman leaders' campaigns in Tunisia during the twelfth century. They do not record horrible massacres, but they do mention the execution of civilians after a siege, the presence of many refugees, and famines caused by the Norman attacks.[57] Instances of cannibalism are not mentioned in their works, but they do explain that the besieged populations reached such desperation that they were driven to eat animal carcasses.[58]

The leaders of the 'other'

Although they are quite rare, there are also accounts of extremely brutal Muslim leaders. In the biography of Saint Gregory of Cassano, a Saracen commander is portrayed as 'merciless' and a 'persecutor of the Holy religion'. His name, Scandalis, represents a play on words probably intended to stress his cruel nature. Moreover, his order to sack Cassano and its surroundings and to destroy everything in the towns and churches around is called tyranny.[59]

In the *Life of Saint Philaretos*, the governor of Sicily is called an impious tyrant, distinguishing himself by his greed and arrogance. When a Byzantine army reached Sicily, he deceitfully tried to get rid of his adversary's army by having iron nails thrown on the ground (the trick failed because the hooves of the Byzantines' horses were protected with horseshoes). The immense Muslim army was easily defeated, and their despicable and arrogant commander shamefully escaped to Africa.[60] The most detailed account of a Saracen ruler is found in a text about the transfer of Saint Severinus's relics to Naples. This text presents an extremely negative image of Emir Ibrāhīm II (d. 902), who was planning to conquer the southern part of the Italian Peninsula at the beginning of the tenth century. Often called tyrant, this Muslim leader is depicted as a cruel beast with an unquenchable thirst for Christian blood. He accused his son, who returned from a victorious campaign against Reggio Calabria, of not being his offspring because he had not exterminated every Christian in Italy. The ferocious emir decided to fight the faithful of Christ in person to eradicate them from the Earth. Even his followers held him in such great fear that everyone responded immediately to his call to arms.[61] Once he conquered Taormina, he carried out a massive slaughter, killing everyone, regardless of their age or sex.

The atrocities committed on that occasion were so numerous that the Neapolitan writer states that he could not narrate them all. He adds, however, that he wants to tell of the execution of the city's bishop, so that his brave behavior might serve as an example for others. The prelate responded in laughter to Ibrāhīm II's proposal that he convert and serve under him. The blood-thirsty emir, described as a rabid dog, grinding his teeth in anger, then ordered the extraction of the valiant clergyman's heart, which he promptly ate. Not satisfied with this, he ordered the still palpitating body of the bishop decapitated, as well as the other prisoners, and their corpses burned. The cruel Muslim ruler is also portrayed as a boastful megalomaniac. Refusing disdainfully the tributes offered to him by Italian cities, he declared that he would become the ruler of all of Italy and that he would treat all its inhabitants as he wished. He even adds that they should hold out no hope for help from the Byzantines and the Franks, because he would easily defeat them too; moreover, he intended to destroy Rome and reduce Constantinople to rubble.[62]

The invective of the Lombard chroniclers is, in large part, directed against Sawdān (857–871), the last emir of Bari. Such rancor was probably motivated by his excessively violent behavior in comparison to his predecessors and the danger he accordingly represented. It was for good reason that he was dubbed 'the enemy of all'.[63] In fact, he was guilty of attacking both the abbey of St. Vincent at Volturno and that of Montecassino. Among the most significant insults addressed to him, we find 'most iniquitous', 'impious and cruel thief', and 'pestiferous tyrant'.[64] As has already been emphasized, he drank from sacred chalices and used liturgical incense burners in obvious disdain for the Christian religion.[65] The entire range of cruel acts that could be committed in war was also ascribed to him. He conducted the expedition that put Benevento to fire and sword, leaving none alive. The emir of Bari, moreover, had his prisoners cruelly killed.[66] Sawdān is also depicted as a bloodthirsty monster.

On one of his expeditions, not a single day passed in which he did not kill at least five hundred men; he was even accustomed to sit on a pile of bodies, eating 'like a putrid dog'.[67] In this spine-chilling description, impurity, that is chaos, is an important element – the ingestion of nutrients necessary for life is occurring in the very face of death. This episode may, therefore, be understood as symbolic for the excessively violent behavior of this Muslim ruler, who refused to honor previous treaties with Christians – especially with the abbeys of the South. In breaking these treaties, he represented a powerfully disturbing element in that region.

The portrayal of an extremely fierce Muslim can also be found in one of the chronicles about the Normans in southern Italy. His name was Benarvet, and he was the Saracen leader who offered the most strenuous resistance to the campaigns of Roger of Hauteville. According to Geoffrey Malaterra, this Saracen was a fierce butcher who razed everything he encountered to the ground. As has been already underlined, in one raid in Calabria, his fury was unleashed particularly against the symbols of the Christian religion.[68] Furthermore, he was very deceitful. His words, explains the chronicler, never reflected his thoughts.[69]

The violent assaults against Sardinia by the Emir of the Spanish city of Denia, Mujāhid, shortly after the year 1000 were recorded in a twelfth-century Pisan chronicle. It is emphasized that the Muslim ruler had ordered some Sardinians to be bricked into walls while still alive.[70] Another Pisan writer depicts the governor of al-Mahdīya, Timun, even more negatively. Comparing him to the Anti-Christ and to a cruel dragon, he narrates how 'this impious Saracen' rained death and destruction on the entire Mediterranean so that 'there was neither country nor island in all the world that was not brutalized by Timun's perfidiousness'.[71]

In Muslim texts, the only negative descriptions of Christian rulers are in the accounts describing the Norman sovereigns' attacks against Tunisia in the twelfth century. The only one portrayed without any nuances is William (d. 1166), son of Roger II. Depicted as a man of evil behavior and sinister appearance, he is often called a tyrant. To obtain fealty from the Muslim governor of Sfax, William took the latter's father hostage. When the Tunisian ruler later disobeyed him, the Norman king had his father executed.[72]

Violent like, and more than, the Muslims

For some authors, Muslim devastation and ferocity were such that they became a point of reference against which to measure any violent act or evil behavior.

According to Pope Benedict III's (855–858) biographer, an ex-communicated priest organized an uprising during which he committed acts that even the

Saracens would have been unable to comprehend. Having entered Saint Peter's Basilica, he destroyed various paintings, among which was one of Christ and the Virgin Mary.[73] In 876, in a letter to Emperor Charles the Bald, Pope John VIII complains that the margrave of Spoleto and that of Tuscany behaved no better than Muslims.[74] Towards the end of his chronicle, Erchempert stresses his aversion to the Byzantines very harshly, observing that God allowed the Muslims to defeat them in order to punish them for their behavior. Not only does he claim that the 'Greeks' were Christians in name but not in deeds – he even redoubles his criticism, adding that the Byzantines were worse than the Saracens. The 'Greeks', explains the Lombard chronicler, were accustomed to committing the heinous crime of capturing Lombards, either to enslave them or to sell them to Muslims.[75] According to Saint Vitalis's biographer, the people of Turris reacted sorrowfully to the order of the governor of that region to transfer that saint's relics from Turris to Armento (Basilicata). They emphasized the iniquitousness of that action by stating that they were deprived of those precious remains neither by the Muslims nor another people but by their own lord.[76]

Referring to the Norman conquest of Apulia in the eleventh century, the Milanese chronicler Arnulf remarks that the rulers of the South had turned out to be worse than the previous ones, even fiercer than the Saracens.[77] This author was a supporter of the archbishop of Milan, and as such, averse to any reform of Church customs. His caustic observation about the Normans was probably aimed at those who, in the second half of the eleventh century, had become the defenders of the reformist popes. Similarly, another Milanese chronicler of this period, Landulf the Elder, mentions the Muslims as a point of comparison for criticizing adversaries of the Milanese and of his own party. The first case dates to the siege of his city at the end of the ninth century by the King of Italy, Lambert, who, on that occasion, proved himself worse than a Saracen.[78] The other episode was coeval with Landulf the Elder and concerned a very heated issue. According to this chronicler, also a supporter of the archbishop of Milan's party, the leaders of the opposing faction, proponents of a drastic reform of the Milanese Church, behaved like Muslims, instigating the population to violence against their enemies.[79]

Probably alluding to the presence of Saracens in the army of Robert Guiscard, who went to Rome in 1084 to defend Pope Gregory VII, the Bishop of Alba, Benzo (ca. 1010–ca. 1090), archenemy of that pontiff and supporter of the German ruler Henry IV (1050–1106), explains how 'the Agaren', that is, Gregory VII, prevented Henry IV from being crowned in Rome.[80] Therefore, Benzo does not state either that the pope's allies used Saracens to protect him or that his supporters behaved worse than the fierce Muslims; rather, he accuses the pontiff himself of being a Muslim. Such an accusation is underlined at a later point. Thanking God for not conferring victory on the enemy of Henry IV and exalting this sovereign, the author observes that the 'Ishmaelite', that is, Gregory VII, fled before the German king.[81] Such a person could certainly not be considered a legitimate pope; in fact, Gregory VII's opponents never acknowledged his election. Benzo alludes to this topic in the introduction to his work, commenting that his adversaries behaved like Ishmael, the founder of the Arab people.[82] This author, too, criticizes the Normans by associating them with the Saracens. Indeed, the Byzantine Emperor, claims Benzo, invited Henry IV to join him in freeing Christendom from Norman and Muslim 'filth'.[83]

These comparisons, however, were not only rhetorical figures used by authors in narrative texts. Maybe the memory of Muslim raids in the Tyrrhenian Sea or of the recent exploits of Pisa against the Saracens made it possible for a certain Pisan charter to state that some neighbors performed violent acts as if they were pagans and Saracens.[84]

The pleasure of narrating violence inflicted on the other

In the previous pages it has been shown that both Christian and Muslim writers describe the violence and destruction committed by their adversaries in vivid detail to emphasize their evil. Authors also recall their coreligionists' attacks against their enemies, but, in these cases, they tend to provide fewer details, probably because they do not wish to portray their compatriots as bloodthirsty monsters. In addition, for the Christian writers, because they were all church-men, they perhaps perceived lingering on the enemies' suffering inappropriate. Moreover, many writers, especially Muslim chroniclers, lived many years after the events they narrated, and their emotional involvement with those episodes was therefore less intense. In one of his most detailed descriptions of fighting between his coreligionists and Christians, 'Alī ibn al-Athīr (ca. 1160–c 1230) reports the following account.

> Muslims suffered their worst defeat. The enemy pushed them back to their tents, already certain of their victory. In such a situation, the Muslims, after deliberating that death was their only means of salvation, started to recite the saying of the poet: 'I pulled back to save my life, but my soul does not live if it does not march on. / Our heels are not bloodied with wounds; our blood seethes at the tips of our feet'... then the Rūm fled, shamefully vanquished, and the Muslims massacred them. Reaching the verge of a cliff, as deep as a pit, the fugitives fell into it fearing their enemies' swords. In so doing, they killed each other, as they fell one on top of the other, and the pit filled up with corpses. The battle lasted from dawn to dusk; Muslims killed their enemies for the entire night.[85]

A greater narrative involvement can, instead, be found in some authors contemporary to the events narrated in their works. The satisfaction and, at times, the pleasure of exalting what had been inflicted on their adversaries offer some insights into the mentality, the tastes, and, sometimes, the frustrations of those authors and their audience. Geoffrey Malaterra wrote his chronicle on the conquest of Sicily at the request of Roger of Hauteville. Influenced by his patron and his informants, he includes reports of 'fine soldiery' and episodes in which Roger and his men perform heroic acts against the Muslims. This chronicler, however, only once lingers on descriptions of violence, when he explains that the number of adversaries killed in a battle had been so high that the stink of their corpses made the air unbreathable.[86]

Such a detail also appears in the description of the campaign against al-Mahdīya in 1087. Yet the author of that text adds many more horrendous details. That work is pervaded by the spirit of holy war, and the writer was probably influenced by the biblical episodes in which the Hebrews massacred all those who had occupied Israel. His account about the indiscriminate killing committed on that occasion attempts to show that the Christians had completely eliminated the enemies of God (the absence of such details in the Muslim versions of this episode suggests that he could have exaggerated what had happened). In the case of the Pisan writer, it is incorrect to use the words pleasure and joy to describe his feelings, but the presence of some details reflects his satisfaction with the amount of harm his fellow citizens and their allies had inflicted on all the Muslims. Saracens who remained outside the walls of the city had been 'killed and chopped to pieces, almost like cattle'. Having entered the city next to al-Mahdīya, the Christians did not stop, and they killed 'married women, virgins, and widows, and newborns were crushed so that they could no longer live. In the whole city of Sibilia there was not a house nor a street that was not reddened with blood'. In the mosque of al-Mahdīya 'they maimed a thousand of the priests of Muhammad'.[87]

Pleasure and joy, on the contrary, clearly emerge in the brief poems by Ibn Ḥamdîs for his Maghreb patrons. In them, it is possible to perceive the deep satisfaction of the exile – obliged to leave his native Sicily because of the Normans – in recounting the massacres Muslims carried out against their enemy when the Christians attacked North Africa. Since he made a living writing verses, a very popular genre at the Muslim courts, it is very likely that his audience appreciated those descriptions as well.

> And so many tried to escape death by paying in gold, but gold was not accepted! / Here Islam quenched its burning thirst for their blood, breaking and chopping with spear and sword.[88]

On the island of Pantelleria you see the skulls of their ancestors; still
today the dust is filled with the shards of their skulls.[89]

Managing to capture the women of the enemy was a way of underlining that
victory had been completely achieved, and the poet stresses this with humiliating words.

Has not our invading army enslaved their sweet girls? So many women
were taken away from their husbands, in whose footsteps the little virgins
were dragged away![90]

A twelfth-century writer, on the other hand, mentions an anecdote where,
besides recording the killing of Normans who had surrendered in exchange
for their lives, he also makes fun of the enemy.

At Roger's court I saw a Frank with a long beard, who, touching the tip of
his beard, swore on the gospels not to cut a single hair of it before taking
revenge against the people of al-Mahdīya. Having asked news of him, I
was told that during his flight he tore his beard so much that his chin was
bleeding.[91]

Macabre trophies of victory

In describing the killing of Serlo of Hauteville (ca. 1065), Geoffrey Malaterra
also explains the end of the Norman's corpse and those of his men. The
Saracens quartered Roger's nephew, extracted his heart, and ate it in order to
gain his courage. Then they decapitated him and, putting his head on a pole,
exhibited it to show that all the Muslims' enemies had been defeated; the
heads of the other Normans were sent to Africa as a trophy.[92] This story was
told as evidence of Muslim cruelty; in addition to treacherously killing Serlo,
they also savaged his corpse. Furthermore, this episode implicitly emphasizes
how brave and feared that Norman warrior was.

This passage is, however, based on a fairly common practice. Several
Muslim authors mention the exhibition of the heads of Christians killed in battle
as well. Celebrating a victory over the Normans in Africa, one Muslim author
narrates how, if they had hung all the heads of their enemies around the walls
of a fortress, they would have encircled it like a necklace around a neck.[93] This,
moreover, was the same punishment reserved for other adversaries, including
other Muslims.[94] The use of such rituals for rebels in Byzantine Italy and the
Lombard Kingdom during the seventh century and in Venice around 830, indicates that this practice was not unknown among Christians.[95] Even Roger of

Hauteville was not completely immune to such types of exhibition. According to his biographer, 'striking him in the middle with one blow, he cut him in half. He then gave his opponent's horse and spoils to one of his men'.[96]

Are you what you look like?

Some episodes mentioned in the biographies of saints are significant both to describe the atmosphere of suspicion and fear existing in that period and to underline that because many Muslims were descendants of Christians who had converted to Islam, in southern Italy and the Mediterranean it was sometimes difficult to recognize an individual's identity immediately.

In Butrinto, near Corfu, a Byzantine official accused Elias the Younger and his companion of being Saracen spies and ordered them to be imprisoned. Gregory the Decapolite was similarly charged during his travel through Apulia in the 830s.[97] After being liberated from Egypt in the 980s, the bishop of Vercelli and many other Christians went to Constantinople where they were taken for enemies and incarcerated.[98] In the biography of John Terista (tenth/eleventh century), too, it is said that the saint was mistaken for a Muslim. In this case, however, the accusation was understandable. According to this text, to which we will return later, John was the child of Christian parents from the Calabrian town of Stilo. Conceived in Calabria, he was born in Palermo after the faithful of Islam had killed his father and taken his mother to that Sicilian city. Because she was married to a Saracen, this woman hid from John his Italian-Christian origin, although she did teach him the Christian faith. His stepfather, however, simultaneously tried to raise him according to the Islamic religion. When John was fourteen, his mother revealed his origins to him and told him to leave Sicily in order to be baptized, and John followed her suggestion. Once in Calabria, Christians believed he was a Muslim because of his 'barbaric clothes', but, after passing a test successfully, they understood that he was not a Saracen.[99]

In order to save their houses from a Muslim incursion, the inhabitants of a small Calabrian town dressed as Saracen warriors, and Saint Neilos (ca. 910–ca. 1004) recognized them only after they removed their turbans. On another occasion, Neilos was the one to disguise himself. In order not to be recognized by his fellow citizens, the saint put a fox pelt on his head. The strategy succeeded, but some boys started throwing stones at him, calling him Bulgarian, Frank, and Armenian.[100] In Calabria, which was located at the southwestern frontier of the Byzantine Empire, an individual dressed in such a strange fashion was not therefore identified with the Muslim neighbors, whose appearance was known, but with other peoples from areas bordering the Byzantine Empire.

The fact that people dressed in the same clothes, independently of their faith, and the contemporary desire of the Muslim authorities in Sicily to distinguish who was Christian is suggested by a brief text in Greek. It is explained that in 886/887, the Saracens mandated that all Christians in Palermo wear a symbol on their clothes, thus rendering them identifiable immediately.[101]

Such habits provoked completely different reactions in the Muslim traveler Ibn Jubayr, who visited Sicily in 1184–1185. Probably wishing to underline that, despite more than a century of Christian rule, the inhabitants of Palermo were still strongly influenced by Muslim culture (a clear indication of the superiority of Muslim civilization), he reports the following observation.

> The Christian women of this city follow the fashion of Muslim women, are fluent of speech, wrap their cloaks about them, and are veiled. They go forth on this Feast Day dressed in robes of gold-embroidered silk, wrapped in elegant cloaks, concealed by colored veils, and shod with gilt slippers. Thus they parade to their churches, or (rather) their dens, bearing all the adornments of Muslim women, including jewelry, henna on the fingers, and perfumes.[102]

Notes

1 For example, see *Epistola Theodosii monachi*, pp. 274–75; *Vita di Sant'Elia il Giovane*, chapters 22, 24, 57; *Vita S. Eliae Spelaeotae*, chapter 69; *Chronicon Salernitanum*, chapter 60; *Vita Vitalis*, chapter 14; Benedict of St. Andreas, *Chronicon*, pp. 149–50; John the Deacon, *Istoria Veneticorum*, IV, 23; *Vita et miracula sancti Bononii abbatis Locediensis*, eds. G. Schwartz - A. Hofmeister, in MGH, *Scriptores*, vol. 30, 2 (Leipzig, 1934), chapter 4; *Cronaca di Novalesa*, V, 2, 9; Neilos, *Vita di san Filareto di Seminara*, p. 42.
2 *Vita Vitalis*, chapter 14.
3 *Vita s. Athanasii*, in *Vita et Translatio s. Athanasii Neapolitani episcopi (BHL 735 e 737) sec. IX*, ed. A. Vuolo (Rome, 2001), chapter 4, p. 129.
4 For example, see *Miracula S. Euphebii episcopi Neapolitani*, in *Acta Sanctorum, Mai*, V (Antwerp, 1685), chapter 2, p. 237; *Epistola Theodosii monachi*, p. 276; *Liber pontificalis*, vol. 2, p. 99; *Vita di s. Nicodemo di Kellàrana*, chapter 18; *Cronicae Sancti Benedicti Casinensis*, II, 2; *Vita di Sant'Elia il Giovane*, chapter 57.
5 *Vita s. Lucae abbatis*, chapter 5.
6 *Chronicon Salernitanum*, chapter 93.
7 Erchempert, *Piccola Storia dei Longobardi di Benevento / Ystoriola Longobardorum Beneventum*, chapter 11.
8 *Translatio Sancti Severini*, chapter 1, p. 453.
9 *Vita S. Venerii*, chapter 16.
10 *Cronicae Sancti Benedicti Casinensis*, II, 2.
11 Erchempert, *Piccola Storia dei Longobardi di Benevento / Ystoriola Longobardorum Beneventum*, chapter 16.
12 Erchempert, *Piccola Storia dei Longobardi di Benevento / Ystoriola Longobardorum Beneventum*, chapter 77.
13 Liudprand of Cremona, *Retribution*, I, 4.

14 Geoffrey Malaterra, *De rebus gestis Rogerii*, II, 46.
15 Geoffrey Malaterra, *De rebus gestis Rogerii*, II, 22.
16 *Chronicon Salernitanum*, chapter 113.
17 *Vita di san Nilo*, chapter 6.
18 *Vita di Sant'Elia il Giovane*, chapter 24, pp. 34–35.
19 Radoynus, *Vita S. Pardi episcopi*, in *Acta Sanctorum*, *Mai*, VI (Antwerp, 1688), chapters 9, 11.
20 *Vita S. Eliae Spelaeotae*, chapter 8.
21 John VIII, *Registrum*, numbers 8, 31, 36, 230, 245, 246, 250, 279, pp. 7, 29, 35, 205, 214, 215, 218, 246. The definitions 'hateful to God', 'nefarious', and 'iniquitous' are also used in Leo III, *Epistolae*, ed. K. Hampe, in MGH, *Epistolae*, vol. 5 (Berlin, 1899), number 6, p. 96.
22 John VIII, *Registrum*, numbers 32, 47, pp. 31, 45.
23 Gregory VII, *Registrum*, ed. E. Caspar, MGH, *Epistolae selectae in usum scholarum*, 2 vols. (Berlin, 1920–1923), pp. 70–71, 75, 166.
24 *Codex Diplomaticus Cavensis*, vol. 1, eds. M. Morcaldi - M. Schiani - S. De Stefano (Naples, 1873), number 75, p. 98.
25 *Codex Diplomaticus Cavensis*, vol. 1, number 86, p. 110.
26 *Chronicon Vulturnense del Monaco Giovanni*, ed. V. Federici, 4 vols. (Rome, 1925–1940), vol. 2, p. 76.
27 A. A. Settia, 'I Saraceni sulle Alpi: una storia da riscrivere', *Studi storici* 28 (1987), pp. 136–37, notes 43 and 45.
28 A. A. Settia, *Castelli e villaggi nell'Italia padana: Popolamento, potere e sicurezza fra IX e XIII secolo* (Naples, 1984), p. 67, note 90.
29 *Codex Diplomaticus Cavensis*, vol. 1, number 97, p. 123.
30 H. Houben, 'Il saccheggio del monastero di S. Modesto in Benevento: un ignoto episodio delle incursioni arabe nel Mediterraneo', in Id. *Medioevo monastico meridionale* (Naples, 1987), p. 61; J.-M. Martin, *Guerre, accords et frontières en Italie méridionale pendant le Haut Moyen Âge. 'Pacta de Liburia, Divisio Principatus Beneventani' et autres actes* (Rome, 2005), pp. 202, 212, chapters 3, 24, p. 218, chapter 2.
31 *Capitularia regum Francorum*, vol. 2, pp. 65–66. Similar measures can be found in the document about the organization of Louis II's campaign in southern Italy in 866. *Cronicae Sancti Benedicti Casinensis*, p.10.
32 BAS, vol. 2, pp. 62–63.
33 Ibn Ḥamdîs, *Il Canzoniere*, number 143, stanza 61.
34 *Cronicae Sancti Benedicti Casinensis*, II, 5.
35 *Vita Antonini abbatis Surrentini*, chapter 20.
36 *Vita Vitalis*, chapter 14.
37 *Vita S. Gregorii abbatis Porcetensis prior*, chapter 9.
38 John VIII, *Registrum*, number 22, p. 20; number 31, pp. 29–30.
39 John VIII, *Registrum*, number 273, p. 241.
40 Erchempert, *Piccola Storia dei Longobardi di Benevento / Ystoriola Longobardorum Beneventum*, chapters 29, 35, 51.
41 *Vita Sancti Antonini abbatis Surrentini*, chapter 20.
42 *Translatio corporis sancti Bartholomei in Gallias*, in Anastasius Bibliothecarius, *Sermo Theodori Studitae de sancto Bartholomeo*, ed. U. Westerbergh (Stockholm, 1963), p. 5.
43 *Historia et laudes SS. Sabae et Macarii*, chapter 6, p. 13.
44 Liudprand of Cremona, *Antapodosis*, II, 44.
45 Liudprand of Cremona, *Retribution*, II, 44.
46 Liudprand of Cremona, *Retribution*, II, 43.
47 Liudprand of Cremona, *Antapodosis*, IV, 5.
48 *Cronaca di Novalesa*, II, 19, IV, fragment XXV, p. 242, V, 1.

49 *Cronaca di Novalesa*, IV, fragment XX, p. 236.
50 Letter by Pope John XII probably written in 969. Italian translation in A. A. Settia, 'L'alto medioevo ad Alba. Problemi e ipotesi', in *Studi per una storia d'Alba*, V. *Alba medievale. Dall'alto medioevo alla fine della dominazione angioina: VI–XIV secolo*, ed. R. Comba (Alba, 2010), p. 20 (digital version available in www.retimedievali.it).
51 *Cronicae Sancti Benedicti Casinensis*, II, 32.
52 *Cronaca di Novalesa*, IV, fragment XXIV, p. 240.
53 Landulf the Elder, *Historia Mediolanensis*, p. 100.
54 *The Epistle of the monk Theodosius to the Archdeacon Leo concerning the capture of Syracuse*, in F. M. Crawford, *The Rulers of the South*, 2 vols. (London, 1901), pp. 89–90.
55 In a letter dating to 1061/1062 a Jewish merchant, however, mentioned the killing of many Muslims by the Normans. A. Feniello, *Sotto il segno del leone. Storia dell'Italia musulmana* (Rome-Bari, 2011), pp. 197–98.
56 BAS, vol. 1, pp. 441–42.
57 BAS, vol. 1, p. 449.
58 BAS, vol. 1, p. 449.
59 *Vita S. Gregorii abbatis Porcetensis prior*, chapter 9.
60 Neilos, *Vita di san Filareto di Seminara*, pp. 42–47.
61 *Translatio Sancti Severini*, chapter 1, p. 453.
62 *Translatio Sancti Severini*, chapter 4, p. 455.
63 *Cronicae Sancti Benedicti Casinensis*, II, 32.
64 *Cronicae Sancti Benedicti Casinensis*, II, 25.
65 *Cronicae Sancti Benedicti Casinensis*, II, 28.
66 Erchempert, *Piccola Storia dei Longobardi di Benevento / Ystoriola Longobardorum Beneventum*, chapter 29.
67 *Cronicae Sancti Benedicti Casinensis*, II, 25.
68 Geoffrey Malaterra, *De rebus gestis Rogerii*, IV, 1.
69 Geoffrey Malaterra, *De rebus gestis Rogerii*, III, 30.
70 *Gli Annales Pisani di Bernardo Marangone*, ed. M. L. Gentile, *Rerum Italicarum Scriptores*, vol. 6/2 (Bologna, 1937), p. 4, year 1017.
71 *Carmen in victoriam Pisanorum*, stanzas 5–8.
72 BAS, vol. 1, p. 480; vol. 2, p. 50.
73 *Liber pontificalis*, vol. 2, p. 142.
74 John VIII, *Registrum*, number 22, p. 20.
75 Erchempert, *Piccola Storia dei Longobardi di Benevento / Ystoriola Longobardorum Beneventum*, chapter 81.
76 *Vita Vitalis*, chapter 24.
77 Arnulf of Milan, *Liber gestorum recentium*, I, 17.
78 Landulf the Elder, *Historia Mediolanensis*, p. 46.
79 Landulf the Elder, *Historia Mediolanensis*, p. 87.
80 Benzo of Alba, *Ad Heinricum IV. imperatorem libri VII*, ed. H. Seyffert, MGH, *Scriptores rerum Germanicarum in usum scholarum separati editi*, vol. 65 (Hanover, 1996), p. 542.
81 Benzo of Alba, *Ad Heinricum IV*, p. 552.
82 Because Ishmael was Abraham's illegitimate son, it is also possible that the author wished to utilize this charge to emphasize that Gregory VII was an illegitimate pope. Benzo of Alba, *Ad Heinricum IV*, p. 354.
83 Benzo of Alba, *Ad Heinricum IV*, p. 226.
84 Settia, *Castelli e villaggi*, p. 120.
85 BAS, vol. 1, pp. 426–27.
86 Geoffrey Malaterra, *De rebus gestis Rogerii*, II, 33.
87 *Carmen in victoriam Pisanorum*, stanzas 36–39, 52.

88 Ibn Ḥamdîs, *Il Canzoniere*, number 143, stanzas 36–37.
89 Ibn Ḥamdîs, *Il Canzoniere*, number 143, stanza 47.
90 Ibn Ḥamdîs, *Il Canzoniere*, number 143, stanza 46.
91 BAS, vol. 2, p. 36.
92 Geoffrey Malaterra, *De rebus gestis Rogerii*, II, 46, p. 54.
93 BAS, vol. 2, pp. 400–1. For another episode, which took place in the tenth century, see BAS, vol. 1, p. 423.
94 BAS, vol. 2, p. 45.
95 Paul the Deacon, *Historia Langobardorum*, eds. L. Bethmann – G. Waitz, in MGH, *Scriptores rerum Langobardicarum et Italicarum saec. VI-IX* (Hanover, 1878), V, 41; John the Deacon, *Istoria Veneticorum*, II, 41.
96 Geoffrey Malaterra, *The Deeds of Count Roger*, II, 4.
97 *Vita di Sant'Elia il Giovane*, chapter 28; C. Mango, 'On re-reading the Life of St. Gregory the Decapolite', *Byzantina* 13 (1985), p. 637.
98 *Vita et miracula sancti Bononii abbatis Locediensis*, chapter 9.
99 A bishop asked him to enter a cauldron containing hot oil. Yet, when he saw that John was going to do so, he understood that John was telling the truth and, consequently, stopped him. *Vita di San Giovanni Terista*, ed. S. Borsari, *Archivio Storico per la Calabria e la Lucania* 22 (1953), chapters 1–3.
100 *Vita di san Nilo*, chapters 30, 41.
101 Schreiner, *Die byzantinischen Kleinchroniken*, p. 334, number 28. In territories under Muslim rule Christians had to wear similar identification badges. It is not possible, however, to determine if this order was always enforced.
102 *The Travels of Ibn Jubayr*, pp. 349–50.

4 Some light in the darkness

Reading between the lines of the zealots' criticism

In the previous pages, it has been noted that some authors were extremely critical of those who established friendly relationships with Muslims instead of rejecting or annihilating them. We have no record of these peoples' points of view, but these criticisms are themselves proof of the presence among Christians of different opinions about dealing with the faithful of Islam. According to Erchempert, the fact that the Emir of Bari, Sawdān, was not executed brought the wrath of God on Emperor Louis II, who was thus guilty of having forgotten the Bible's lesson concerning the infidels. Indeed, the prophet Samuel ordered King Saul to kill all the Amalekites in order to cleanse Israel of all idolaters. Tired of massacres, the Jewish king had spared the life of his enemies' king, and, for this reason, he was cursed by Samuel, who then slit the Amalekite's throat.

> Having captured Bari and Sawdān, the most despicable of all men, Louis II did not have him killed without mercy, as the Lord wanted, because he deserved it. Instead, Louis forgot Samuel's treatment of Saul over the affair of the fat king of the Amalekites, Agath, and that Samuel tore him to pieces.[1]

This comment is probably only an interpretation of events filtered through Scripture; nevertheless, the real existence of a group among Christians, especially among the clergy, in favor of giving no quarter to the Saracens should not be ignored. It should also be remembered that the emperor's decision to spare the emir of Bari was almost certainly determined more by practical considerations than by a spirit of clemency. In this period, Muslims had not yet been expelled from the Italian peninsula, and, in subsequent diplomatic bargaining, or as a simple deterrent against reprisals, Sawdān would prove more useful alive than dead. Indeed, he was later released to end the attacks of the Muslims of Taranto.[2]

The warning of Neilos to Bishop Blatton not to have any relationships with the Saracens and the saint's refusal of the invitation from the emir of Sicily to come to his lands and of his gifts underline the Calabrian monk's intransigent position on this topic.

> Listen to my advice, lord. Do not return to that brood of vipers; for after they excessively flatter and honor you, they will kill you with a sword and drink your blood. Also, you should not toil for the peace of Calabria, nor insist on it, for the Lord of all things is not in favor of this.

> Upon hearing this, the godly Neilos was amazed at God's dispensation toward him, and recited the riddle of Samson, 'Truly now meat came forth from the eater', and kindness from the misanthrope'. He added also this to the emir's promises, that 'All these things I will give to you, if you will fall down and worship me'.[3]

His biography, therefore, seems to express the viewpoint of the Christians opposing any form of peaceful contact with Allah's followers. At the same time, these passages also emphasize the existence, among both Christians and Muslims, of people who were in favor of friendly interactions. Even if it was clearly willed by God, in Neilos's first contact with Islam's believers, they not only left him unharmed, but gave him bread,[4] an act showing the possibility of a peaceful encounter between Christians and Saracens. Such charitable qualities, as well as the desire to respect religious buildings and a famous monk, like Neilos, are also evident in the episode concerning the Sicilian emir. Besides inviting the saint to his land and sending him gifts, the Saracen leader ordered three of Neilos's fellow monks, who had been captured during a raid against the saint's monastery, to be freed without ransom. Moreover, he told Neilos that had he known that the abbey was his, he would have ordered it to be protected.[5]

Christian nuances

Up to this point, the image of the Muslims that has emerged from this analysis has been extremely negative. In some of the texts examined, however, there are relevant nuances that render the general picture more varied and that suggest the existence of relationships between Christians and Muslims that were not based purely on conflict.

The anonymous ninth-century Cassinese author, who began his chronicle by stating that he wanted to explain why the Saracens were dominating Campania and Apulia, mentions two episodes that have such features. Both concern Massar, the Muslim leader who took possession of Benevento around 848.

According to the chronicler, during a bloody and destructive raid under Massar's leadership, the Muslim chieftain reached the gates of Montecassino and not only ordered them to be locked so that his men could not enter but also forced one of his dogs to free a goose belonging to the monastery. Shortly after, he refused to take advantage of a recent earthquake and sack Isernia, whose walls were severely damaged, stating that the 'Lord of all' already expressed his anger in that place and that he saw no reason for further violence.[6] Massar's behavior towards Montecassino is attributed to divine intervention rather than to the Saracen leader's own desire to respect a holy place like that abbey. In the second episode, however, the chronicler ascribes deep religiosity and other humane qualities to Massar, qualities which are difficult to find in any epoch (including our own). Therefore, it is doubly significant that he chose to mention them, especially since Massar was not only an enemy but a Muslim. In connection with this, the expression 'Lord of all' is particularly relevant because it implies the existence of a single divine entity common to both Christians and Muslims. Nonetheless, one should bear in mind that this account still represents a strictly Cassinese viewpoint. The difference between Massar and Sawdān is that the former did not do any damage to the monks of Montecassino. If the stories of any of his victims (among whom were many clerics, according to the same chronicler) had been taken into account, his characterization would probably have been worse. That Louis II had Massar executed after his capture indicates how dangerous he was considered to be.[7]

That anonymous Cassinese author was not, however, the only one to express this kind of idea. In 1076, in a letter to the Emir of Bougie (Algeria), am-Nāṣir, Pope Gregory VII underlines that the emir's gesture of freeing Christian prisoners was inspired by 'God, the Creator of All'. In addition, the pontiff states that among Christians and Muslims there was a special relationship, unknown to other peoples, because, though in different ways, they believed in one God and they venerated him every day as the creator of the whole world. Gregory VII finished his missive by blessing the Muslim ruler and wishing him happiness and prosperity in this life. Additionally, he prayed that, upon the emir's death, am-Nāṣir might be welcomed by God into the bosom of Abraham.[8] This letter reveals, beyond doubt, an excellent example of the nuances existing in the relationships between Christians and Muslims and, particularly, how Christians could see Muslims in a favorable light. We should remember, however, that such a source needs to be read as the product of very special circumstances and that it cannot be taken as the definitive thought of this pope about Islam. In fact, a few years later, Gregory VII claimed that those who professed the Muslim religion could not obtain salvation.[9]

There is also a range of views in the accounts about Sawdān. Despite the fact that he was an infidel, says the anonymous Salernitan chronicler, the emir of Bari did not harm the prince of Benevento's daughter who had previously been given to him as a hostage.[10] This author seems to imply that on this occasion Sawdān did not behave as one would have expected from a Muslim. According to this author, the emir was also very clever and the Beneventan ruler, uncertain whether to imprison Emperor Louis II, who had become a dangerous ally, asked for his advice.[11] A Byzantine source, similarly, portrays Sawdān as a wise man. It is told that during his captivity in Benevento, the emir of Bari stopped laughing and persisted in this dourness to the extent that Louis II offered a large sum of money to anyone who was able to change his behavior. The Muslim, however, started to laugh again without any help, explaining how the sight of a cart wheel revolving led him to understand the fleeting nature of human happiness and the vanity of his pride. At the same time, he understood that from so low he would be able to rise again to the top. Struck by these reflections, the emperor invited him to his table. According to the same writer, this crafty Muslim managed to convince the Beneventans to put Louis II in jail by telling them that the emperor had given orders to prepare the chains for their imprisonment.[12]

The anonymous Salernitan chronicler lived in a tragic period for the history of Salerno. The family that had ruled the city for over a century was deposed because of the betrayals of some of the prince of Salerno's relatives. Moreover, the neighbors of the Salernitans profited from this moment of weakness to take possession of the principality. The influence of these events can be seen clearly in several of this chronicler's accounts, as he sometimes uses the past as a sort of parable to indicate what could happen if promises were broken or if someone's honor was offended. Such concerns, however, were valid on any occasion, even when the 'dangerous' Muslims were involved. In these episodes, Allah's followers therefore lose the features of ferocious raiders against whom anything was licit and assume those of persons to be respected.

This author recounts that the Prince of Salerno, Siconolf (839-849), had a very cordial relationship with Apolaffar, the commander of the Muslim troops at his service. Siconolf, however, did not account for the fact that one of his gestures could be interpreted as an insult. He put the Muslim, who was rather short, on a staircase three steps higher than the prince, then hugged him and kissed him. Apolaffar perceived this as an offense and, despite the prince's apologies, left Salerno with his men. Siconolf's rival, the Prince of Benevento, Radelchis (839–851), then allied himself with that Saracen and from that moment Allah's followers ravaged the Salernitan territory.[13] During the subsequent siege of Benevento by the Salernitans and their allies, Apolaffar humiliated Guy of Spoleto, the prince of Salerno's brother-in-law, in combat and the Spoletan promised to raze the city to the ground if the Beneventans did not hand over all the Muslims in their service to him. Radelchis agreed to the request and had Apolaffar captured while he was sleeping, after which the prince's men escorted the Muslim to the city gates just as they had found him, i.e., barefoot. To the prince of Benevento asking why they were carrying him without shoes, Apolaffar answered, spitting: 'You do not care about my head and you ask about my feet?' making the prince blush with shame.[14] The insult to the warrior honor of a Christian was thus cleaned up ignobly. Yet the Salernitan author did not stop his narrative here. Indeed, unlike the Christians, Apolaffar lost his life but not his honor; he had the moral satisfaction of shaming his betrayers.

The chronicler was so sensitive to treachery and the necessity to keep faith with any agreements that he recounts the following episode. After establishing a non-aggression pact with the Muslims, the Salernitans secretly took up arms to attack them. Allah's followers, however, turned to Jesus, stating that they would recognize him as king of heaven and of earth and the lord of all creation if he would destroy the perjurers. God welcomed their request because the Christians had broken their oath, and, although the Saracens had fewer troops than the Salernitans, they inflicted a heavy defeat on them.[15] For this author, keeping one's word was even more important than eliminating dangerous infidels.

The chronicler also presents positive examples, that is, he insists that one should act uprightly not only in wartime but also in daily life. In the period following the elimination of Bari's emirate, a follower of Allah, by name Arrane, while he was in a street of Salerno where he had resided for some time, asked the Prince of Salerno, Guaifer (861–880), to give him his headgear, which the Christian ruler did immediately. Having gone back to his home in Africa, the Muslim found out that his coreligionists were preparing a fleet to attack Salerno. Having seen some Amalfitans and ascertained that one of them knew Guaifer well, Arrane exhorted him to inform the prince of the forthcoming assault and to give him detailed information about how to strengthen the city's fortifications.[16]

The setting of this story well highlights the absence of rigid 'physical barriers' between Christians and Muslims. Arrane was probably living in Salerno as a merchant and the Amalfitans were certainly in northern Africa for the same reason. Similarly, the behavior of Guaifer and of Arrane indicates that even 'mental barriers' between those two groups could be sometimes overcome. This is emphasized especially by the gesture of Arrane, who reciprocated the prince's courtesy to an extreme degree, thus showing a well-defined scale of values. According to these values, before an ethnic or religious solidarity, there was a respect for friendship and one's word.

Such nuances are absent in the chronicles of the Norman campaigns in southern Italy. This absence does not mean, however, that the image of the Muslim in these sources is completely monochromatic. In the account of the Normans' assault on the walls of Palermo, William of Apulia observes that 'both peoples made the same effort, but for different reasons—one to take the city, the other to defend it. One side fought for themselves, their children and their wives; the other wished to please the duke by conquering the city'.[17] The author does not therefore conform to the view that one had to fight against the Saracens because they were enemies of God; rather he attempts to show the true motives for the conflict. The chronicler's explanation is all the more important because he puts aside the glorious martial aspects of the campaign.

Geoffrey Malaterra often praised the military talents of Roger and the other Hautevilles. Underlining the martial skills of certain Muslims was probably a way to embellish further the qualities of the Norman heroes, who had succeeded in defeating their worthy adversaries. Such descriptions, however, also seem to suggest a certain respect for Allah's followers by the author and probably by the Normans as well. For example, the people of Messina doggedly resisted Roger's attacks. Despite their small numbers and prior defeats, they manned the walls of their city along with their wives and prepared to defend themselves. In this way, they convinced the Normans to retreat for fear that other Saracens, inspired by their fight, would come from all over Sicily to aid Messina.[18]

Respect for the honorable behavior of the enemy clearly appears in the case of a Messinese Muslim who preferred to kill his sister rather than let her be raped and forced to renounce Islam.[19] The chronicler does not express any judgment in response to this action, but it is extremely revealing that he devotes an entire chapter to this person, who was after all still an enemy, and that the chronicler also mentions the inglorious behavior of his own compatriots. Such a presentation of events seems to reveal a desire to give ample room to the defense of one's family honor, even if this went against his great affection for his sister, a fundamental principle for the audience Geoffrey Malaterra addressed.

A variegated image of the Muslims is also present in Theodosius's account about his captivity. According to the Sicilian monk, a few of Allah's followers convinced a fanatical group of their coreligionists to abandon their plan to sacrifice the archbishop of Syracuse, explaining that such an action was actually against Islam.

> In the celebration of this day, strange madness, they took council to burn
> the archbishop and to offer the most holy pontiff of Christ to their evil

demons... but certain old men with wise grey beards, and elders honorably clad in mantles, turned to the people and condemned the thing.[20]

Saints' biographies obviously aim to exalt those 'champions' of Christianity who were able to interact successfully with, and to gain the respect of, dangerous enemies such as the Muslims (sometimes this respect was reciprocal). These works are particularly relevant, however, because they also present a diversified image of Allah's followers and of the relationships between Christians and Muslims. Noteworthy is the fact that the nuances are recorded in the lives of the Calabrian and Sicilian saints, who lived in areas characterized by frequent and close contacts with Islam's believers. In the course of his stay in Africa, Elias the Younger earned the admiration and respect of an emir for healing a Muslim who had been seriously wounded by a Christian. The saint's intervention also saved the aggressor from the death penalty, thus avoiding tensions between the faithful of the two religions.

> Two men, a Christian and an Ishmaelite, were quarreling with each other. The Christian took a club and broke the head of the Ishmaelite. The relatives of the victim grabbed and tied the Christian, and laid the other one, in agony, on a stretcher. Then they brought both of them before the emir. The latter, surprised by the unusual affair, ordered the Saracen, already at death's door, to be taken home, and the Christian to be beheaded. The admirable man (Elias) heard about the episode, went swiftly to the wounded and, by holding his head with his two hands and secretly marking him with the sign of the cross, restored him to health, so that the latter could immediately get up, go to the emir and announce the miracle to the people. Having seen this and having his indignation turned into admiration... the emir absolved the culprit and allowed the saint to carry out his work freely.[21]

Having returned to Calabria, Elias predicted that a peasant would go to Africa and for this reason he asked him to extend his warmest greetings to the head of Allah's followers. The prophesy came true because a group of Muslims caught that man and took him to their country. Remembering what the saint had told him, the Christian managed to meet their ruler and did as Elias had instructed. Although he is called 'barbarian', the Saracen leader was inspired by God to recognize Elias as a 'true servant of God' and thanks 'to his love' he freed the peasant. In Egypt, the Muslims, so says the biographer of Saint Bononius, put aside their 'barbarian ferocity' and showed such great respect for the Bolognese saint's exemplary way of life that they allowed him to restore the churches in their land and to practice his mission freely. Bononius also succeeded in convincing the sovereign of Egypt to free many of his fellow Christians who had been captured by that lord.[22]

On the other hand, an anonymous Christian subject contrasts the maliciousness of a Muslim officer who falsely accused the court physician John of having insulted Mohammed and the barbarity of the Muslim crowd who, in addition to lynching him, burned and ate his body, with the integrity of Palermo's ruler. In fact, the latter did not believe the false accusation and encouraged his doctor to flee when his officer incited the people against John.[23]

Believing that Allah's followers too could be forgiven and shown the right way, Vitalis (tenth century) cured the Muslim who had been struck by lightning for trying to kill him, and convinced him and his companions not to attack Christians anymore. Returning good for evil, Saint Gregory of Cassano healed his Saracen torturers' arms that had been paralyzed by God and cured one of them of a painful toothache.[24] Additionally, a charitable gesture was accomplished by Saint Martin of Monte Massico, who healed the wife of a Saracen when she asked for help at the saint's tomb.[25] So even these terrible adversaries were sometimes perceived as fellow people who could be helped by the Christian saints.

Muslim nuances

Muslim authors showed greater interest towards Christians when the latter either occupied some parts of the 'House of Islam' or launched attacks against it. In general, their tone is fairly harsh and their accounts aim to emphasize the destruction caused by their enemies. Even these accounts, however, possess remarkable nuances. After subjugating Sicily, 'Ibn 'al 'Atir remarks that Roger 'had the Rūms and the Franks settled with the Muslims, not leaving either a bath, shop, windmill, or oven to the inhabitants'.[26] According to the same author, Roger II (d. 1154), however, followed a radically different policy, adopting the customs and administrative system of the Saracen rulers and behaving as a just king at all times.

> Roger followed the customs of the Muslim kings, instituting in his court aide-de-camps, chamberlains, squires, bodyguards and other offices of this type. He therefore distanced himself from the customs of the Franks, among whom none of these positions were known. Under Roger, a court of injustices was established, to which any plaintive could bring his case, and the king granted them justice, even if he had to go against his son. Roger respected Muslims greatly, had great familiarity with them, and defended them from the Franks.[27]

Particularly noteworthy is the description of Roger's irreverent answer to the proposal of participating in a crusaders' campaign against the Muslims of northwestern Africa.

> Roger called together his companions and consulted them about these proposals. 'This will be a fine thing both for them and for us!' they declared, 'for by this means these lands will be converted to the Faith!' At this Roger raised one leg and farted loudly, and swore that it was of more use than their advice. 'Why?' 'Because if this army comes here it will need quantities of provisions and fleets of ships to transport it to Africa, as well as reinforcements from my own troops. Then, if the Franks succeed in conquering this territory they will take it over and will need provisioning from Sicily. This will cost me my annual profit from the harvest. If they fail they will return here and be an embarrassment to me here in my own domain. As well as all this Tamim will say that I have broken faith with him and violated our treaty, and friendly relations and communications between us will be disrupted. As far as we are concerned, Africa is always there. When we are strong enough we will take it'.[28]

This text represents a clear example of the *realpolitik* adopted by the Norman leader towards his Muslim neighbors, according to which peaceful co-existence, trade, and economic interests could not be compromised by a military campaign, even if motivated by religious ideals. That this type of account is present in a Muslim text shows that its author wanted to describe Roger as a ruler ignorant of good manners, yet it indicates above all how Allah's followers were aware that the 'Franks' of Sicily had a different mentality from those who had conquered Jerusalem in 1099.

To confirm the fact that Norman rulers did not turn Sicily into a hostile land for Saracens, in 536 (1142/1143), narrates a Muslim author, many Tunisians went to the island when a very serious famine devastated their region.[29] In the passages regarding Roger II's campaigns against Tunisia, the king is called 'enemy of God' and 'the accursed',[30] yet the Muslim chroniclers also recognize that, once the 'enemy of God' had conquered some cities, he reestablished order, favored commerce, bestowed help on the poor, and entrusted the administration of justice to a follower of Allah who was liked by the local population.[31] A Muslim historian also recounts how one of Roger II's commanders proved to be so benevolent to the people after the fall of al-Mahdīya that those who fled on that occasion met a far worse fate; they all died of thirst. That commander later gave food and even lent money to the population.[32]

The desire to highlight both the arrogance of the Normans and the wisdom of one of their kings and his admiration for Muslim scholars emerges from the following account.

> The King of Sicily sent a naval expedition that ravaged Tripoli in North Africa. Now there was in Sicily a learned, God-fearing Muslim whom the King held in great respect, relying on his advice rather than that of his own priests and monks; so much that the people used to say that the King was really a Muslim. One day, as the King was standing at a window overlooking the sea, he saw a small boat come into the harbour. The crew told him that his army had invaded Muslim territory, laid it waste and returned victorious. The Muslim sage was dozing at the King's side. The King said to him: 'Did you hear what they said?' 'No'. 'They told me that we have defeated the Muslims in Tripoli. What use it Muhammad now to his land and his people?' 'He was not there', replied the old man, 'he was at Edessa, which the Muslims have just taken'. The Franks who were present laughed, but the King said: 'Do not laugh, for by God this man is incapable of speaking anything but the truth'. And a few days later news came from the Franks in Syria that Edessa had been taken.[33]

Although Ibn Jubayr's wish to praise the superiority of the Islamic religion and civilization probably conditioned his writing, his description of his stay in Sicily is noteworthy. His work is structured as a diary, and the author clearly communicates the change from his first, extremely negative, impressions to those of surprise at the unexpected atmosphere of tolerance he found at the court of King William II (d. 1189) in Palermo. Having disembarked in Messina in December 1184, he highlights the total absence of Muslims in that city, full of 'smell and filth' and of 'worshipers of the Cross', where the foreigner can know no form of courtesy.[34] Even as he notes with displeasure that his fellow coreligionists were obliged to pay a special tax in Sicily (a humiliating duty because the Christians had to pay it in the 'House of Islam'), he is forced to admit, however, that in general Muslims were treated well in Sicily. The situation in Palermo was completely different from that in Messina. There were many of Islam's faithful in that city and they lacked neither mosques nor markets. To Ibn Jubayr's great surprise, King William II even knew how to read and write in Arabic. In addition, his court and lifestyle were very similar to those of Muslim rulers. In the royal palace, practically everyone, from the councilor to the cook, servants, and slaves, was Muslim, and their true faith did not concern the king at all. According to this author, when an earthquake occurred, invocations to Allah and Mohammed were heard all over the royal residence, and the servants felt very embarrassed when they saw the king.

Yet William II reassured them, asserting that everyone should call on his own God and that those who had faith would be comforted. The royal palace is described as having such a strong Muslim atmosphere that all Christian women who were living there converted to Islam thanks to the influence of the Muslim domestic staff.[35]

A further example of tolerance is recorded in Trapani, where, yet again, Ibn Jubayr was surprised because he saw that Allah's followers could celebrate the end of their annual fast openly and joyously.[36] Another surprise was caused by the existence of hospitals similar to those in the 'House of Islam'.[37] The author himself experienced the different atmosphere characterizing Palermo. He and his companions were welcomed and treated politely by the local Christians. To tell the truth, the suspicious traveler describes this friendly manner as a subtle form of behavior used by Christ's followers to allure simpletons. It is no coincidence that he added an invocation to Allah, asking him to prevent Muslims from falling prey to such seductions. The following episode, which astonished him greatly, was also considered a form of entrapment. At the gate to a city, a Christian guard stopped him, claiming that he had some goods with him for which he had not paid customs duty. Another Christian quickly rebuked the accuser, telling him that those travelers were under the king's protection and had nothing to fear.[38]

Notes

1 Erchempert, *Piccola Storia dei Longobardi di Benevento / Ystoriola Longobardorum Beneventum*, chapter 37.
2 Erchempert, *Piccola Storia dei Longobardi di Benevento / Ystoriola Longobardorum Beneventum*, chapter 38.
3 *The Life of Saint Neilos of Rossano*, edited and translated by R. L. Capra, I. A. Murzaku, D. J. Milewski (Harvard, MA, 2018), pp. 211, 217.
4 *Vita di san Nilo*, chapter 6.
5 *Vita di san Nilo*, chapter 71.
6 *Cronicae Sancti Benedicti Casinensis*, II, 8, 10.
7 *Cronicae Sancti Benedicti Casinensis*, II, 14.
8 Gregory VII, *Registrum*, pp. 287–88.
9 The *'Epistolae vagantes' of Gregory VII*, ed. H. E. J. Cowdrey (Oxford, 1972), number 54, pp. 130–33.
10 *Chronicon Salernitanum*, chapter 108.
11 *Chronicon Salernitanum*, chapter 109.
12 Constantinus Porphyrogenitus, *De administrando imperio*, eds. G. Moravcsik - J. H. Jenkins (Washington, DC, 1967), vol. 1, chapter 29.
13 *Chronicon Salernitanum*, chapter 81.
14 *Chronicon Salernitanum*, chapter 83.
15 *Chronicon Salernitanum*, chapter 126.
16 *Chronicon Salernitanum*, chapter 110.
17 William of Apulia, *La Geste de Robert Guiscard*, III, lines 311–14.
18 Geoffrey Malaterra, *De rebus gestis Rogerii*, II, 6.

19 Geoffrey Malaterra, *De rebus gestis Rogerii*, II, 11.

20 *The Epistle of the monk Theodosius*, p. 97.

21 *Vita di Sant'Elia il Giovane*, chapter 15, pp. 22–25.

22 *Vita di Sant'Elia il Giovane*, chapter 57, pp. 88–90; *Vita et miracula sancti Bononii abbatis Locediensis*, chapters 3–7.

23 G. Mandalà, 'The Martyrdom of Yūḥannā, Physician of Ibn Abī 'l-Ḥusayn Ruler of the Island of Sicily: Editio Princeps and Historical Commentary', *Journal of Transcultural Medieval Studies* 3 (2016), pp. 93–94.

24 *Vita Vitalis*, chapter 14; *Vita S. Gregorii abbatis Porcetensis prior*, chapter 9.

25 Peter the Deacon, *Vita, translatio, et miracula S. Martini abbatis, in Acta Sanctorum, Octobris, X* (Bruxelles, 1861), chapter 14. About this episode, it is necessary to point out that the author wrote 'uxor Saraceni', that is 'the wife of a Saracen'. Another translation, however, could be 'the wife of Saracen', i.e., of a Christian called Saracen; as emphasized in another chapter, Christians used this name in southern Italy.

26 BAS, vol. 1, p. 449.

27 BAS, vol. 1, pp. 449–50.

28 *Arab Historians of the Crusades*, trans. F. Gabrieli (Berkeley, 1969), pp. 3–4.

29 BAS, vol. 2, p. 102. According to the same author, Roger II profited from the famine to assault al-Mahdīya. Probably willing to criticize those who had decided to go to Sicily, 'Alī ibn al-Athīr narrated how those persons had been cruelly treated in Sicily. BAS, vol. 1, p. 469.

30 BAS, vol. 2, pp. 291–92.

31 BAS, vol. 2, p. 295.

32 BAS, vol. 2, pp. 77–78. A similar account can be found in BAS, vol. 1, p. 475.

33 *Arab Historians of the Crusades*, pp. 52–53.

34 *The Travels of Ibn Jubayr*, pp. 338–39.

35 *The Travels of Ibn Jubayr*, pp. 340–42.

36 *The Travels of Ibn Jubayr*, p. 353.

37 *The Travels of Ibn Jubayr*, p. 346.

38 *The Travels of Ibn Jubayr*, pp. 345, 347.

5   Supernatural events

The interventions of God and of his saints

Influenced by the expectations of their audience and by the atmosphere of the period in which they lived, Christian authors do not fail to report the miracles of the saints and God's intervention; these miracles worked to reassure the Christian faithful of the divine presence, even during dramatic circumstances, and, sometimes, to protect them from Muslim assaults. Moreover, the saints, i.e., the champions of Christendom, provided models for imitation. These types of accounts are, therefore, quite useful for reconstructing the fears, frustrations, and hopes of the authors and their audience, thus revealing important aspects of their mentality.

In the ninth and tenth centuries, the scarcity of Christian troops rendered the defense of churches and monasteries, which were typically located outside fortified centers, very problematic. Their lack of defense and abundance of precious items made these places ideal targets for Muslim raiders. The accounts about God's and the saints' intervention under these circumstances clearly emphasize the incompetence of the secular rulers as well as the deep dissatisfaction of the churchmen, who thus highlight that only the Lord and his emissaries did not abandon the Christians.

For example, when the Muslims tried to pillage his monastery, Saint Elias Spelaeota put them to flight with a sudden darkness followed by an intense light. Saint Bartholomew also used darkness to prevent the Saracens from capturing the ship carrying his relics.[1] Saint Severinus and Saint Constantius provoked a violent storm with big hailstones that pushed back the Muslim ships heading to Capri. Moreover, these saints comforted a terrified old woman of that island, who could not flee because of her age, by telling her that the enemies would not come. To dispel any doubt about who had put the Muslims to flight, a man, who had remained on Capri, stated that he had heard the sound of a trumpet and the noise of a great number of people coming out from the church of St. Constantius, followed by a voice saying: 'The Saracens had been expelled from here'.[2]

One of the most detailed and original accounts about a violent storm caused to protect Christians is present in an anonymous ninth-century Cassinese chronicle. After having plundered the church of St. Peter in Rome and having defeated the Franks, the followers of Allah attempted to pillage Montecassino as well. Being without any protection, the monks were sure that the end was near. Abbot Bassacius, however, had a dream in which one of his predecessors appeared and comforted him by saying that, if the monks prayed to God, Saint Benedict would assure their salvation. When Bassacius awoke, he called upon his brothers to turn to God, reminding them that the Lord always saves those who confide in him. Then, although the sky was clear, a violent storm suddenly broke out, and the heavy rain caused a dry river to overflow its banks, effectively blocking the Saracens' route to Montecassino.[3]

On another occasion, narrates the anonymous tenth-century Salernitan chronicler, God used a storm to bring relief to some Christians. As a Muslim force was unable to conquer a castle due to the fierce resistance of its inhabitants, the attackers deprived the Christians of water in order to force their surrender. After the defenders had prayed to the Lord, however, a beautiful dove flew around the castle and alighted on the roof of its church. God then sent rain only to that specific location, thus quenching the thirst of its inhabitants and allowing them to collect a great amount of water. Having seen this, the Saracens decided to abandon the siege.[4]

God also protected the saints and the particularly devoted and brave churchmen. For example, he paralyzed the arms of the Muslims who were torturing Gregory of Cassano.[5] In order to save Saint Vitalis, who was going to be decapitated by a Saracen, the Lord first enveloped the executioner with a very thick fog, then struck him with lightning, thus terrifying his companions.[6] When a Muslim raid caught a priest outside Naples' walls, the ecclesiastic neither grew frightened nor ceased to celebrate mass in the church of St. Euphebius. Thanks to that same saint's intercession, God rewarded the courage of his faithful priest and rendered him invisible to Allah's followers. At the end of the mass, the churchman, following God's command, took a stick and sowed terror and death among the Saracens with it; those who managed to flee later died in their homeland. He was able to convince his incredulous fellow-citizens of the danger's end and of what had happened only by showing them the corpses of the Muslims.[7]

The Lord and the saints provided a fundamental help on the battlefield as well. A decisive role in the victory of an army of Sorrentines, Gaetans, and Neapolitans against the Saracens is attributed to Saint Antoninus and other saints whose bodies were preserved in Sorrento. Three days before the battle, Antoninus and his companions boarded the Muslims' flagship and terrorized them through a series of appearances and disappearances. Having deduced that they were 'gods of the Christians', called to defend and avenge them, and having interpreted their arrival as the prediction of their adversaries' victory, the Saracen commander ordered a retreat from that area.[8] At that moment, however, the Christians assaulted Allah's followers and inflicted a heavy defeat on them. Probably motivated by the rivalry between Sorrento and Naples, the Sorrentine author of that account adds that, the night before the battle, Antoninus appeared to a Neapolitan elder and that the saint reproached the Neapolitans for their laziness and for having failed to invoke the help of all the defenders God had given them. Furthermore, the saint maintained to have asked Saint Januarius to assist the Neapolitans, and he exhorted the old man to make an offering to obtain the protection of Naples' patron saint, which he did immediately. During the first clash with the Muslims, seven Neapolitans died because of that delay, while only a single Sorrentine was wounded.[9] On another occasion, the mere appearance of Saint Felix to the Saracens who wished to sack Nola sufficed to terrify them and to convince them to abandon their goal.[10]

In the mid-tenth century, Saint Januarius and Saint Agrippinus had the biggest ship of the Saracen fleet sunk while it was moving towards the walls of Naples. This event cheered up the Neapolitans, who found the strength to repel their enemies' assault. Concerning this episode, the author of this text, however, seems aware of the fact that he could not modify what had happened on that occasion. Indeed, he adds that the Muslims ended their attacks against Naples because of the news of the imminent arrival of a Byzantine fleet and because the Neapolitans had given them tribute.[11] In the course of the Muslim siege of Salerno in 872, a Salernitan accepted a challenge to duel with the strongest warrior in the Saracen army. The Christian, asking for the help of God and Saint Cosmas and Saint Damianus, whose church was nearby, managed to kill Allah's follower easily.[12]

The mother of Christ, for whom the Byzantines had a great veneration, intervened as well. Her preferred weapon against the Muslims seems to have been fire, a likely allusion to the Greek fire that the Byzantines often employed against their enemies. According to the text that describes the miracles of the Sicilian Saint Fantinus the Elder, on the day of that saint's feast a Muslim ship approached Saint Fantinus's shrine with hostile intentions. Because of a sudden tempest, however, the ship was sunk. The Saracen survivors recounted that they had seen a boy holding a torch and a woman clothed in purple; as she made a sign, he threw the torch at the ship, which sunk immediately.[13] Obviously these two persons were Mary and Saint Fantinus. The role of Christ's mother is even more active and bellicose in the *Life of Saint Neilos*. Indeed, she often appeared in Rossano (Calabria), throwing torches against the Muslims who were climbing its walls.[14] The saint's hometown was thus implicitly likened to Constantinople, for whose defense it was believed Mary had intervened several times.[15]

As already seen, in Sicily Saint George led the Normans' charge in a battle against Allah's followers, Saint Luke of Demenna and Saint Martin of Monte Massico did the same with their monks, and Saint Michael and Saint Peter encouraged the Pisans and their allies in the course of the expedition against al-Mahdīya. On another occasion, Saint Peter and Saint Paul appeared during the battle of Garigliano in 915. Elias the Younger (ca. 823–ca. 903) was never present on the battlefield, but, because God had told him that the Christians would defeat the Muslims, he commanded the Calabrians not to flee, telling them: 'Do not be afraid, O men! 'The Lord will fight for you and you will keep silent''.[16] Moreover, there is reference to the special protection given by some objects. According to the biographer of Pope Gregory II (715–731), the inhabitants of southern France were not hurt in the battles with the Saracens thanks to the ingestion of a piece of the blessed sponges the pontiff had sent them.[17] Nobody, however, provided such help for the Christians of the Italian peninsula.

On various occasions, God and his champions punished the Muslims who had committed heinous actions. The Saracens, who could not pillage Montecassino because of the flooding of a river, decided to return home. When they had almost reached their own shores, they met a boat carrying a monk and a cleric, to whom they spoke of their victories. The Muslims asked the pair who they were, and the churchmen replied that they would soon find out. Afterwards, the heavens opened to unleash a great tempest that sank the Saracen vessels and drowned all onboard. The author of the account emphasizes that not one of them was thus able to recount his deeds to his compatriots.[18] When all had seemed lost (the Muslims had taken over a major Christian holy place and defeated the Franks, the strongest warriors in the West), Montecassino proved its sacredness and its founder's power. The monk and the cleric on the boat were obviously Saint Benedict and Saint Peter,[19] and the destruction of the Muslim fleet clearly represented divine punishment for having dared to attack places dedicated to these saints.

As happened to the ancient Egyptians who died in the Red Sea pursuing the Jews, the Lord, remarks the biographer of Pope Leo IV (847–855), brought about the drowning of the Muslims guilty of pillaging St. Peter's and St. Paul's churches in Rome in 846.[20] According to Erchempert, before provoking a storm that destroyed a Saracen fleet returning from a raid in southern Italy, God threw an immense torch among the enemies' ships.[21]

In the course of the Saracen siege of Salerno in 872, the Muslim commander was accustomed to rape Christian girls on a bed placed on the altar of a church. When one of them put up a strong resistance to him, the angels made a roof beam fall, thus killing the rapist. The author of the account explains that this beam was at a great distance from the altar and so the faithful of Allah could not believe that this had happened by accident.[22] According to a Neapolitan writer, at the beginning of the tenth century Saint Peter, Christ's favorite disciple and, more importantly, the first bishop of Rome, saved Christendom from the cruel Emir Ibrāhīm II. During the siege of the Calabrian city of Cosenza, the Muslim leader entered a church to find relief from the heat. He subsequently fell asleep and, while dreaming about the way in which he would destroy Rome and the other Italian cities, an angry old man came out from an ancient fresco, hit the emir with his stick, and then disappeared. When he woke up, a great terror entered Ibrāhīm II's mind. Having discovered that the image of the fresco portrayed Saint Peter, he died a few days later.[23] According to the biographer of Elias the Younger, however, Elias, not Saint Peter, brought about the death of Ibrāhīm II by utilizing his 'spiritual weapons', i.e., his prayers.[24]

The fact that Allah's followers were often able to take prisoners during their raids constitutes further proof of the Christians' inability to defend themselves effectively. Moreover, only the rich could afford to be ransomed. It is therefore no accident that the liberation of captives, often of low social status, is also among the miracles attributed to God and the saints. Saint Agnellus and Saint Elias the Younger once appeared to two Christians, who were held prisoners by the Muslims of Bari and by those of northern Africa respectively, freed them, and allowed them to return home.[25] Having heard that Saracen pirates had captured one of his monastery's boats, Saint Bartholomew of Simeri (ca. 1050–ca. 1130) immediately obtained the release of the crew by praying to the Lord.[26] While being brought in chains to Sicily by some Saracens, nine inhabitants of Bisignano were able to return home thanks to the prayers addressed to Saint Nicodemus of Kellàrana (tenth/eleventh century).[27] This saint, too, had fallen into the hands of Allah's followers. Because God saw that Nicodemus kept praying despite the scorn of his captors who told him that he should have done that before being captured, the Lord saved the saint by causing the Saracens to kill each other.[28]

When Elias the Younger was on a Muslim ship that was heading to Africa to sell him along with two hundred twenty other Christians, Saint Anania appeared to him in a dream.[29] Besides heartening Elias and revealing to him that he would be going back to his parents soon, Anania told the faithful of Islam to liberate their prisoners, warning them that, if they did not, the Byzantines would capture them. As they mocked him, the saint's prediction was fulfilled.[30] In another case, Saint George intervened personally. A sacristan of a Roman church devoted to that saint was captured by the Muslims on the Latium coast and brought to Sicily, but Saint George appeared on a white horse and took him home.[31]

Supernatural events regarding a monk of Montecassino who died in captivity in Africa and was buried in a local church, act as a reminder, demonstrating that God had not forgotten those who died in Muslim lands. At the same time, this account emphasizes the concern for the Christians under Saracen rule. According to the Cassinese writer Peter the Deacon (twelfth century), the dead churchman produced great surprise by appearing to some faithful of Islam in front of the church in which he had been inhumed shortly before. Furthermore, the flame of the lamp placed on his grave kept glowing despite all the Muslims' attempts to extinguish it. The Saracens even prohibited all Christians from entering the building, as they were suspected of lighting it secretly, but to no avail. When the ruler of that region saw the beam of a star light the lamp, he let the faithful of Christ have free access to the church.[32]

Similar concerns are present in some episodes about the period Elias the Younger spent in the Muslim lands. By healing a follower of Allah who had been hit by a Christian during an argument and was at death's door, the saint kept the offending Christian from being decapitated. Also during this time, God saved Elias when he had been sentenced to death for having converted some Muslims.[33]

The theft of sacred objects by the Saracens or their use as tribute to Allah's followers undoubtedly represented material and spiritual harm to the Christians. Indeed, their loss underlined the Christians' inability to protect an essential component of their communities' identity. Consequently, it is no surprise to see some saints engaged in the recovery of those relics and treasures that had been lost. Saint Constantius appeared to the custodian of the church devoted to him in Capri and made him happy by telling him where he could find the church's door that the Saracens had stolen shortly before.[34] More directly involved, Saint Agrippinus and Saint Januarius helped some Neapolitans recover from Sicily the sacred objects that the inhabitants of the Campanian city had given to the Muslims to convince them to end their attack against Naples.[35]

Obtaining the spontaneous conversion of Saracens undoubtedly constituted an important achievement that emphasized the power of the Christian faith, and, consequently, gaining converts is another of the miracles attributed to the saints. Acknowledging the superiority of Christianity, the Muslims who survived the failed attack against Saint Fantinus the Elder's shrine, accepted baptism. While he was traveling on a Muslim merchants' ship, Bononius made converts by calming a storm with his prayers, and the miracles of Elias the Younger and Simon converted Saracens as well.[36]

Accounts about miracles and divine intervention like those described so far are lacking in the works of Muslim writers who, however, sometimes mention storms provoked by God to damage the enemy. For example, according to 'Alī ibn al-Athīr (ca. 1160–ca. 1230), a strong wind, sent by God, prevented a Norman fleet from reaching al-Mahdīya.[37] Storms that destroyed enemies' ships are recorded in these texts, but they are not attributed to divine intervention (such intervention seems to be understood). There is, however, an exception. In this case, those punished were not Christians but Allah's followers. Condemning the immoderate greed of some Muslims, 'Alī ibn al-Athīr remarks that the Lord thus chastised those who had hidden loot obtained in an incursion against Sardinia for not sharing it with their community.[38]

Predictions and prophesies

At the beginning of his religious experience in southern Italy, Elias the Younger gave moral support to the Byzantine soldiers and the inhabitants of Reggio Calabria by predicting the Christians' victory over the Muslims and by telling them that God would fight for them.[39] This is an exceptional case, however, because, in the Sicilian-Calabrian saints' biographies, the predictions about the Saracen attacks are always connected to the theme of the impiety of the Christians, unable, because they were sinners, to understand the warnings of God's messengers (several biblical prophets had the same experience). In this way it was also possible to justify the successes of Allah's followers in a period in which they were invincible. Elias the Younger distinguished himself in these activities since his childhood. Emphasizing the foolishness of some Christians and the great number of sinners among them, his biographer recounts how, as a young man, the exactitude of his vaticinations earned him a reputation as a soothsayer and prophet of misfortunes, while his words were mocked in his old age.[40] God let Saint Luke of Demenna (tenth century) know of a forthcoming Muslim attack upon Calabria, which the Lord was going to send to punish that region's sinners. Nevertheless, unlike Elias the Younger, Luke did not reveal it to the Calabrians, and, believing that his prayers were useless, he left his cave and moved into a fortified center. Saint Neilos's predictions were, on the other hand, addressed to specific individuals. Warning Bishop Blatton not to have any relationships with the Muslims, the saint foretold his death by the Saracens. To the Byzantine commander's offer to build a church with the loot obtained from fighting Allah's followers, Neilos replied that it was useless because the Muslims would destroy that building and devastate Calabria.[41]

In ca. 850, probably influenced by the crisis that the division of the Carolingian Empire and the ensuing civil war had provoked in western

Europe, the Muslim incursion against Rome in 846, and the widespread corruption of the Ravennate clergy, the chronicler Agnellus of Ravenna predicted that many calamities would strike his city and the rest of Europe. In the first part of his vaticinations he did not say anything about the enemies who would pillage 'the head of all' and the neighboring cities. Mentioning other invaders coming from the sea, he adds that they were 'ignorant of God', and therefore it is possible that he was referring to the Vikings, who were devastating several parts of northwestern Europe in these years. On the contrary, in a following passage he states that the raiders would be the Muslims.

> The people of the Agarens will rise from the east and will plunder the cities located in the seacoast, and there will not be anyone to get rid of them. For in all the regions of the earth there will be kings needy and desiring wealth, and they will oppress the peoples subject to them, and the empire of the Frankish Romans will perish, and kings will sit on the imperial throne.[42]

The work of Agnellus is, however, the only one in which the faithful of Islam are present in this type of prophecy. They are also mentioned in some prophetic texts recorded in Liudprand of Cremona's account about his diplomatic mission in Constantinople in 968. In this case the tone is not apocalyptic at all. Indeed, the bishop-writer is not interested in the Saracens and his interpretation of those predictions is just an expedient for finding another way to criticize the Byzantines and praise his lord, the German ruler Otto.[43]

The devil

Because the Muslims are often portrayed as a destructive element, it is not surprising to find out that they are often associated with the devil. The Italian authors, however, do not often utilize this narrative device, which is also used for 'evil' Christians (some writers never employ it).

The demon, remarks Pope John VIII (872–882) in one of his letters, instigated the Amalfitans to make an agreement with Allah's followers.[44] According to Pope Gregory VII (1073–1085), the devil was trying to eliminate Christianity in the Byzantine empire, and his followers (the Turks) were slaughtering many Christians every day.[45] In the *Life of Saint Elias the Younger*, a Muslim ruler is called 'servant of Satan'.[46] The 'enemy of the human kind', writes the biographer of Saint Luke of Demenna, incited the Saracens 'against us'.[47] According to the account about the transfer of Saint Bartholomew's relics to France, the devil instigated the faithful of Islam to throw away the remains of that saint after having pillaged the monastery dedicated to him.[48] In the *Life of Saint Vitalis*, it is emphasized that, being disappointed by the lack of loot in this saint's abbey, the Saracen raiders took on the semblance of demons.[49] Some Muslims, portrayed as tempting devils, are remembered in Saint Neilos's biography. The 'enemy of all' organized the meeting of the young Neilos with Allah's followers to hinder his plans to become a monk. One of the Saracens, all of whom looked like demons, tried to dissuade him from entering a monastery. An allusion to this theme is present in another part of the work when Saint Neilos refuses the friendly invitation of a Muslim ruler to go to his land by equating it with the temptation of the devil to Jesus in the desert.[50]

The connection between the faithful of Islam and Satan can be found in some chronicles as well. According to William of Apulia, Muslims were subjects of the 'demons',[51] and the mosque of Palermo was the seat of Mohammed and the 'demon'.[52] Having taken a Muslim city in Spain, thanks to God's help, the Normans and other Christians, recounts Amatus of Montecassino, were subsequently defeated because of their sins. Indeed, envious of the victories the Christian faith had obtained, the devil astutely ignited a passion for the Saracen women in those knights, thus making them lose what they had conquered.[53] Playing with the assonance between Satan and the name of the Muslim leader *Sagdan*, the anonymous Salernitan chronicler narrates how the bishop of Salerno had not wanted to live in his residence anymore because the Salernitans hosted an ambassador of *Satan* there.[54] After the elimination of Bari's emirate, narrates Erchempert, the devil complained because his followers, that is the Muslims, had lost. He therefore started to sow discord among the Christians by inspiring the Franks to harass the Lombards of Benevento.[55] Thanks to the conquest of al-Mahdīya, writes a Pisan author, 'Hell was plundered and Satan vanquished'.[56] To Emir Ibrāhīm II's proposal to convert, the bishop of Taormina replied, saying that the demon put those words in his mouth. Afterwards the cruel Muslim leader paid for his wrongdoings by ending up in hell.[57] Geoffrey Malaterra differs from the other authors by assigning Satan a positive role. Indeed, according to the chronicler, the devil wanted to give a miserable death to Benarvet, the worst enemy of Roger of Hauteville, and therefore he instigated the Muslim leader to attack the flagship of the Norman fleet.[58] In two other works the devil was, on the other hand, the tool used for punishing Saracens who had behaved in a very reproachable manner.[59]

Notes

1 *Vita S. Eliae Spelaeotae*, chapter 10, p. 876; *Translatio corporis sancti Bartholomei apostoli Beneventum et miracula*, in Anastasius Bibliothecarius, *Sermo Theodori Studitae de sancto Bartholomeo*, ed. U. Westerbergh (Stockholm, 1963), p. 12.

2 *Sermo de virtute Sancti Constantii*, chapters 11–12, pp. 1018–19; *Sermo de transito Sancti Constantii*, ed. A. Hofmeister, in MGH, *Scriptores*, vol. 30, 2 (Leipzig, 1934), chapter 9, p. 1022.

3 *Cronicae Sancti Benedicti Casinensis*, II, 3–5.

4 *Chronicon Salernitanum*, chapter 139.

5 *Vita S. Gregorii abbatis Porcetensis prior*, chapter 9.

6 *Vita Vitalis*, chapter 14.

7 *Miracula S. Euphebii episcopi Neapolitani*, chapters 2–4.

8 *Vita Antonini abbatis Surrentini*, chapters 21–22.

9 *Vita Antonini abbatis Surrentini*, chapters 22–24.

10 *Miracula sancti Felicis Nolani*, p. 213, paragraphs 30–32.

11 *Ex miraculis Sancti Agrippini*, in MGH, *Scriptores rerum Langobardicarum et Italicarum saec.* VI–IX (Hanover, 1876), chapter 11, pp. 464–65.

12 *Chronicon Salernitanum*, chapter 113.

13 *Vita et Miracula Sancti Fantini*, chapters 53–54, pp. 565–66.

14 *Vita di san Nilo*, chapter 2.

15 During the sieges an icon of Mary was carried in procession on Constantinople's walls.

16 *Vita di Sant'Elia il Giovane*, chapter 25. Cf. Exodus 14,14.

17 *Liber pontificalis*, vol. 1, p. 401.

18 *Cronicae Sancti Benedicti Casinensis*, II, 6.

19 Their identity is clearly indicated in a later work. *Dialogi de miraculis sancti Benedicti auctore Desiderio*, eds. G. Schwartz – A. Hofmeister, in MGH, *Scriptores*, vol. 30/2 (Hanover, 1934), I, 2.

20 *Liber Pontificalis*, vol. 2, p. 107. According to the Neapolitan John the Deacon, God did the same with the Muslims who had besieged Gaeta. John the Deacon, *Gesta episcoporum Neapolitanorum*, chapter 60.

21 Erchempert, *Piccola Storia dei Longobardi di Benevento / Ystoriola Longobardorum Beneventum*, chapter 35.

22 *Chronicon Salernitanum*, chapter 112.

23 *Translatio Sancti Severini*, chapter 8, p. 458. According to a brief anonymous text, Ibrāhīm II died because the sword of God struck him. *Translatio Sancti Severini*, p. 457, note 1.

24 *Vita di Sant'Elia il Giovane*, chapter 53, pp. 82–83.

25 A. Vuolo, *Una testimonianza agiografica napoletana: il 'Libellus miraculorum s. Agnelli' (sec. X)* (Naples-Rome, 1987), pp. 152–53; *Vita di Sant'Elia il Giovane*, chapter 55. Elias also comforted those telling him their sufferings during their captivity. *Vita di Sant'Elia il Giovane*, chapter 44.

26 *Vita e fatti del nostro padre Bartolomeo*, chapter 24.

27 Their chains disappeared immediately after invoking the saint. *Vita di s. Nicodemo di Kellarana*, chapter 19, pp. 126–28.

28 *Vita di s. Nicodemo di Kellarana*, chapter 18, pp. 124–26. According to his biographer, Nicodemus always asked if someone had been captured and if it was necessary, he supported their relatives. *Vita di s. Nicodemo di Kellarana*, chapter 8. Other saints who freed prisoners are Simon of Calabria, John Terista and Athanasius of Naples; the latter, however, did not perform any miracle for doing that. *Synaxaria Selecta* [50], in *Synaxarium Ecclesiae Constantinopolitanae*, in *Acta Sanctorum, Nov.* XIX (online edition), pp. 237–39; A. Acconcia Longo, 'S. Giovanni Terista nell'agiografia e nell'innografia', in *Calabria bizantina. Civiltà bizantina nei territori di Gerace e Stilo* (Soveria Mannelli, Catanzaro, 1998), p. 146; *Vita s. Athanasii*, chapter 4, p. 129.

29 Anania of Damascus (first century) is remembered especially for having baptized Saint Paul.

30 *Vita di Sant'Elia il Giovane*, chapters 7–8.

31 This account is recorded in a collection of miracles written in Rome between the eleventh and the twelfth century. C. Erdmann, *The origin of the idea of crusade*, trans. M. W. Baldwin and W. Goffart (Princeton, 1977), p. 280.

32 *Chronica Monasterii Casinensis*, IV, 51, p. 517.

33 *Vita di Sant'Elia il Giovane*, chapters 15, 17.

34 *Sermo de transito Sancti Constantii*, chapter 8, pp. 1020–21.

35 *Ex miraculis Sancti Agrippini*, chapter 11, pp. 464–65.

36 *Vita et Miracula Sancti Fantini*, chapter 54, pp. 565–66; *Vita et miracula sancti Bononii abbatis Locediensis*, chapter 5; *Vita di Sant'Elia il Giovane*, chapters 16–17, 23–24; *Synaxaria Selecta* [50], pp. 237–39.

37 BAS, vol. 1, p. 471.

38 Stasolla, 'Arabi e Sardegna nella storiografia araba del medioevo', p. 186.

39 *Vita di Sant'Elia il Giovane*, chapter 25.

40 *Vita di Sant'Elia il Giovane*, chapters 5, 50.

41 *Vita S. Lucae abbatis*, chapter 5; *Vita di san Nilo*, chapters 69, 72.

42 Agnellus of Ravenna, *The Book of Pontiffs of the Church of Ravenna*, trans. D. Mauskopf Deliyannis (Washington, D.C., 2004), chapter 166.

43 Liudprand of Cremona, *Relatio*, chapters 39–43.

44 John VIII, *Registrum*, number 250, p. 219.

45 Gregory VII, *Registrum*, pp. 173, 189.

46 *Vita di Sant'Elia il Giovane*, chapter 16.

47 *Vita S. Lucae abbatis*, chapter 5. A similar explanation can be found in *Historia et laudes SS. Sabae et Macarii*, chapter 5, p. 13.

48 *Translatio corporis sancti Bartholomei in Gallias*, p. 5.

49 *Vita Vitalis*, chapter 14.

50 *Vita di san Nilo*, chapters 5, 6, 71.

51 William of Apulia, *La Geste de Robert Guiscard*, III, line 287.

52 William of Apulia, *La Geste de Robert Guiscard*, III, lines 332–36.

53 Amatus of Montecassino, *Ystoire de li Normant*, I, 7.

54 *Chronicon Salernitanum*, chapter 99.

55 Erchempert, *Piccola Storia dei Longobardi di Benevento / Ystoriola Longobardorum Beneventum*, chapter 34.

56 *Carmen in victoriam Pisanorum*, stanza 46.

57 *Translatio Sancti Severini*, chapters 3, 8.

58 Geoffrey Malaterra, *De rebus gestis Rogerii*, IV, 2.

59 *Rythmus de captivitate Lhuduici imperatoris*, in *Italian Carolingian Historical and Poetic Texts*, edition and English translation by L. A. Berto (Pisa, 2016), lines 22–27; *Acta Fortunati, Caii, et Anthae*, chapter 7.

6   Why is the enemy attacking us and winning?

Divine punishment for the Christians' sins is the most common explanation in the Italian texts to justify the attacks and victories of the Muslims. According to his biographer, Elias the Younger warned the faithful of Christ about their behavior and offered the Christians positive examples. Indeed, to a Byzantine admiral asking if his fleet would defeat the Saracens, the saint recommended that he convince his men to follow God's precepts. Moreover, he reminded him that because of fornication and drunkenness, the strong Jewish hero Samson had become the toy of his enemies' children. The commander followed Elias's suggestions and won a great victory.[1] The uniqueness of such an episode and the ubiquity of the Muslims' successes implicitly emphasize that the Christians continued to behave dissolutely. Taormina's inhabitants, in fact, considered Elias's warnings about conducting a temperate life and imitating the virtuous behaviors of two non-Christian military leaders of Antiquity – the Greek Epaminondas and the Roman Scipio – to be nonsense. A large army of Allah's followers arrived shortly thereafter and the Taorminians paid for their wrongdoing with the destruction of their city and the loss of their own lives.[2]

On the other hand, the author of the biography of the Bishop of Naples, Athanasius (849–872), focuses on specific crimes that the Lord punished by inciting the Saracens to assail the Christians. The first was the treatment reserved for the churchman by the Duke of Naples, Sergius II (868–878). This ruler first had Athanasius imprisoned, then relegated him to a small island near Naples, and eventually ordered his men, among whom were some Muslims, to attack the bishop.[3] The second crime was Louis II's imprisonment by the prince of Benevento in 871 after the emperor had eliminated the emirate of Bari. To underline further the gravity of what happened, the writer compares that deed to the vengeance wrought for Christ's death by the Roman Emperor Vespasianus and his son Titus (the author refers to the destruction of Jerusalem by the Romans in 70 AD, which was believed to have occurred to punish the Jews guilty of having crucified the son of God).[4]

Specific sins are also recorded to explain the raid against Rome in 846. According to the biographer of Pope Sergius II (844–847), God sent the Muslims to punish the widespread practice of selling ecclesiastic offices.[5] In the introduction to his chronicle, Liudprand of Cremona (ca. 920–972) presents the creation and survival of the Saracen base of Fraxinetum as the perfect example of Christians' insanity, and he emphasizes that God utilized those Muslims to chastise the inhabitants of that area.[6]

Nor do these authors fail to accuse the Christian rulers of inefficiency and, above all, of factionalism. Although it is not always explicitly stated, the ninth-century Cassinese chroniclers emphasize that the problems Allah's followers caused in southern Italy should be imputed to the Christian rulers. Too occupied with defending their own petty interests, they often provoked fratricidal fights, thus preventing the formation of a common front against the Muslims and weakening their land. This was a burning issue for the great monasteries of that area because the riches stored in them and the lack of defenders made them very desirable targets for the Saracens. In the 860s, an anonymous monk of Montecassino highlighted the stark contrast between the exemplary past of the Lombards and the present in which they were behaving irrationally. The Lombards killed their rulers and divided the principality of Benevento, thus permitting the Muslims to sack the region. It is no coincidence that the chronicler links the two periods with biblical quotations: 'Every kingdom divided against itself is heading for ruin' and 'what one sows is what one reaps'. Moreover, he offers a comparison to the Jews – the Chosen People par excellence – who, after quarreling among themselves, had been dispersed all over the world. The Lombards, therefore, reaped what they had sown; the division of the principality of Benevento did indeed bring about their weakness and ruin.[7]

Another Cassinese chronicler of these years began his work in a manner that clearly emphasizes his goal: 'If by accident you want to know... for which reason the Saracens dominated the region of the Beneventans, there is this opportunity'.[8] This reason was the factionalism and the inefficiency of the Lombard aristocracy. The author does not make any open accusations, but he does narrate some episodes that clearly allude to these problems. His contempt for the secular lords is noticeable, especially in one of their defeats at the hands of the Muslims. After one of Sawdān's bloody expeditions, the Christians tried to counter-attack, but, in this case, the words of the chronicler are as sarcastic as previously they were harsh in describing the emir of Bari. The author emphasizes how the Lombards, at last, seemed to be waking from a long sleep, yet this awakening was beset with countless 'miseries'. Their intentions may have been praiseworthy, but they were useless due to their endless internal problems. The Lombards faced their enemy 'not in unified ranks' and 'not under a single leadership', thereby suffering a heavy defeat, upon the details of which the chronicler bitterly lingers. The author's insistence on the ordered mode of attack practiced by the followers of Allah compared to the Lombards' disorganization is probably a metaphor describing the overall picture of southern Italy at that time, when the Muslims were taking advantage of divisions between Christian factions and easily becoming the dominant power.[9] Also noteworthy is the chronicler's comment about a Lombard victory over the Neapolitans. He immediately extinguishes the enthusiasm for that success by reporting Sawdān's evaluation of that battle. Indeed, the emir of Bari observed with irony how tow and wadding had fought.[10] In this way the writer does not merely emphasize the Muslims' lack of respect for both the Lombards and the Neapolitans. Indeed, he also underlines that, although the odious Neapolitans had been beaten, the real enemies, i.e., the Muslims, were still at large taking advantage of the wars among the Christians and even making fun of those clashes.

These themes constitute some of the main ideas running through the chronicle of the Cassinese monk Erchempert. In this work, however, dramatic tones and anger replace the metaphors and irony of his Cassinese brother, probably because Erchempert had lived through the tragic destruction of Montecassino by Allah's followers in 883. He explains the presence of the Muslims in Bari as one of the consequences of the civil war between the Beneventans and the Salernitans. Pressed by the need for more troops, the prince of Benevento unwisely hired Muslim warriors to defend Bari; as already seen, they took possession of it with ease. Because of that conflict, everyone was predisposed to evil and came to resemble sheep without a shepherd, and the Saracens profited from it, occupying even Benevento. According to this author, the Muslims had no regard for the Lombard nobles, going as far as to whip them like 'incompetent servants'. For Erchempert the elites of his homeland were therefore on the same level as the worst of the 'last'.

In search of allies in the South, Pope John VIII (872–882), too, helped to complicate the situation in that area by agreeing to a request to split the Capuan bishopric in two parts. By ignoring the warnings of Montecassino's abbot, emphasizes Erchempert, the decision of the pontiff sparked 'such a fire that all the territory of Benevento and the same Rome were completely devastated'. The church, in which the consecration of the new bishop had recently been celebrated, was torched by the Muslims who were in the service of one of the Christian factions. It is in this chaotic period that Montecassino's destruction took place. The ruler of Spoleto did not set a good example either. Having heard that Emperor Charles the Fat had died, he immediately went beyond the Alps in the hope of obtaining the crown, thus leaving his lands without defense, and, consequently, the Saracens pillaged them.[11]

Although with less dramatic tones, references to the Christians' inefficiency and to their inability to create a common front against Allah's followers are present in other works as well. The Muslim raid against Rome in 846
was successful because the local inhabitants disregarded the news of a large
Saracen fleet's imminent arrival. In their opinion, the Muslims could not be so
powerful as to accomplish such a deed. At the solicitation of a few Romans,
messages were sent to the peoples of the neighboring towns asking them to
guard the coast, but this request was completely neglected. Moreover, when
the enemies' ships arrived on Latium's shoreline, the locals did not offer any
resistance; instead, they abandoned their houses immediately.[12]

The Muslim base of Fraxinetum in Provence, explains Liudprand of
Cremona, could only have been created and continue to prosper thanks to
the ineptitude and factionalism of the Christians in that area. According to
the same author, rivalries and hatreds among local rulers contributed to the
survival of that settlement. After having destroyed the Muslim ships with the
help of a Byzantine fleet and having forced Fraxinetum's Saracens to take
refuge on a mountain, the King of Italy, Hugh (926–946), did not eliminate
them but, on the contrary, made a pact with them. Moreover, the sovereign
let them block the Alps' passes in order to prevent one of his adversaries
from attacking him from Germany. Due to that decision, not only did the
nest of those raiders survive, but a great number of pilgrims heading to Rome
lost their lives in those mountains.[13] Central Italian rulers, remarks Pope John
VIII, were not only passive towards Allah's followers, but were behaving like
caterpillars, eating what survived the 'Saracen locusts'.[14]

When the Christians took the offensive and achieved victories against the
faithful of Islam, the themes of the litigiousness and inefficiency of their own
rulers appear in the Muslim texts as well. In the chronicle by 'Alī ibn al-Athīr
(ca. 1160–ca. 1230) the account of the Norman conquest of Sicily is preceded
by the description of a long series of internecine conflicts that put an end to
the unity of the Muslims in Sicily. That author's evaluation of this period is
very eloquent: 'Everything went upside down. The most wicked men came to
power; everybody declared himself independent in his own territory'.[15] Roger
of Hauteville's arrival on the island occurred because of the clash between
two of these leaders. The governor of Catania, recounts 'Alī ibn al-Athīr, had
a big fight with his wife and, under alcohol's effects, ordered her assassina-
tion. The woman managed to flee and take refuge with her brother, the head
of Castrogiovanni. The lord of Catania was then defeated by his brother-in-
law and therefore asked for Roger's military help in order to defeat his rival.
Profiting from internal division among Sicilian Muslims and of the conflicts
among those of northwestern Africa, the Normans were able to take possession of the island.[16]

On the other hand, the success of the Pisans and the Genoese at al-Mahdīya in 1087 was attributed to the carelessness of the local governor, who was guilty of not repairing the city walls and of not having believed the news of a large Christian fleet's arrival. It was not even possible to face the enemy, because most of the garrison was out of town to crush a revolt.[17] Similar factors facilitated Roger II's victories in the Maghreb in the 1140s. For example, the taking of Tripoli in 540 (1146/1147) was due to a clash between two factions of that city's inhabitants. Too busy fighting each other, they left the walls undefended, thus allowing the enemy to conquer Tripoli easily.[18]

Notes

1 *Vita di Sant'Elia il Giovane*, chapter 43, p. 64.
2 *Vita di Sant'Elia il Giovane*, chapters 49, 51, 53.
3 *Vita s. Athanasii*, chapters 6–7.
4 *Vita s. Athanasii*, chapter 8, pp. 139–40. The Cassinese chronicler Erchempert, too, reports the second explanation. Erchempert, *Piccola Storia dei Longobardi di Benevento / Ystoriola Longobardorum Beneventum*, chapter 34.
5 *Liber pontificalis*, vol. 2, pp. 98–99.
6 Liudprand of Cremona, *Antapodosis*, I, 1. A similar explanation can be found in Hugh of Farfa's work. *Destructio monasterii Farfensis edita a domno Hugone abbate*, in *Il Chronicon Farfense di Gregorio di Catino: precedono la 'Constructio Farfensis' e gli scritti di Ugo di Farfa*, ed. U. Balzani (Rome, 1903), vol. 1, p. 31.
7 *Cronicae Sancti Benedicti Casinensis*, I, 5.
8 *Cronicae Sancti Benedicti Casinensis*, II, 1.
9 *Cronicae Sancti Benedicti Casinensis*, II, 26.
10 *Cronicae Sancti Benedicti Casinensis*, II, 22.
11 Erchempert, *Piccola Storia dei Longobardi di Benevento / Ystoriola Longobardorum Beneventum*, chapters 16, 19, 47, 79.
12 *Liber Pontificalis*, vol. 2, pp. 99–100.
13 Liudprand of Cremona, *Antapodosis*, I, 3–4, V, 16–17.
14 John VIII, *Registrum*, number 22, p. 20.
15 BAS, vol. 1, p. 445.
16 BAS, vol. 1, pp. 446–49.
17 BAS, vol. 2, pp. 32, 63.
18 BAS, vol. 2, p. 100.

7   Rewriting history

The memory of the Muslim presence in Italy did not fade away in the centuries following the early Middle Ages. Moreover, it was sometimes believed necessary to fill the gaps left in works written by authors of that period and to change or delete details of their accounts that were not consonant with later concepts held about Christian and Muslim relationships.

After the 860s, no text about the abbey of Montecassino was written until the beginning of the twelfth century, when a Cassinese monk named Leo composed the history of his monastery from its foundation to the eleventh century. Having at his disposal the chronicle of his ninth-century brother, Leo almost verbatim copied what he had written about the providential rain that prevented the Muslims from sacking the monastery in ca. 846 and about the ensuing storm that caused the wreckage of the Muslim ships.[1] As for the Saracen leader Massar, Leo believed that the episodes the ninth-century chronicler mentioned about him did not correspond to the manner in which the Muslims had behaved. In the explanation of why Massar had forbidden his men from pillaging Montecassino and freed one of the monastery's geese that had been caught by his dog, unlike his source, Leo described this Muslim chieftain as a 'barbarian' and cited God as the reason behind his change of heart.[2] Even more revealing is that Leo omitted the detail that Massar had refused to take advantage of an earthquake that had destroyed the walls of Isernia in order to pillage that city, saying that 'the Lord of all was angry in that place'.[3] Leo noticed the reference to a divine entity common to both Christians and Muslims and probably judged the implied similarity as being inappropriate.

Leo, however, did not neglect to mention the destruction of Montecassino and the killing of Abbot Bertharius by the Muslims in 883. That terrible episode had never been written down before. The same chronicler, Erchempert, who was a member of the Cassinese community that had taken refuge in Capua after the sack of Montecassino, strangely did not find an opportunity in that tragedy to stigmatize the behavior of the southern Italian Christian lords, who were busy fighting each other and did not protect the abbey; instead, he briefly described that event without recording Bertharius's death. The episode was, perhaps, too shocking to be remembered; the name of Bertharius is not even reported in early medieval Cassinese calendars. Leo did not blame anyone for the destruction of the monastery. Before narrating it, however, he explains that the duke of Gaeta made a pact with the Saracens and let them settle near the Garigliano River. Leo wrote that those Muslims had caused significant destruction and shed the blood of many inhabitants of that region because of the sins of the Christians living there.[4] Nevertheless, he did not use disparaging language for the faithful of Islam and neutrally described the devastation they had wrought. Even though he referred to Bertharius as 'a saint martyr of Christ', he utilized the same neutral style in the narration of the killing of the abbot near a church altar.[5]

This information was mentioned in the same way a few years later in a work on the most important characters of the monastery of St. Benedict; it was, however, added that the abbot had been beheaded.[6] It was necessary to wait until the mid-fifteenth century to create a text on the life and dramatic end of Bertharius. The necessity to emphasize the relevance of Montecassino in a period of strong crisis for that monastery, as well as the tragic events that had greatly awakened a fear of the Muslims among Europeans (the disastrous defeat of the crusaders against the Turks in Bulgaria in 1444 and, above all, the Turkish conquest of Constantinople in 1453) probably induced a Cassinese writer to compose Bertharius's biography. Interpreting that work as the desire to create an explicit correspondence between events and characters of the fifteenth and those of the ninth century is a bit forced. What clearly emerges from this text is the wish to present Bertharius as the last bastion against the Saracens in southern Italy.[7] There is also a strong desire to underline the courage of the abbot, who, despite the Muslims barging into the building, did not interrupt the holy office of the mass, but was then symbolically killed in the act of taking the Eucharist. The biographer suggests that just as Christ died to save humanity, so Bertharius accepted martyrdom to save the monks of Montecassino.[8]

In 881, Muslims also pillaged and destroyed St. Vincent at Volturno, which was the other great Benedictine abbey of southern Italy. In this case, too, it was necessary to wait until the twelfth century to have a full account of that tragic episode. By performing a 'cut and paste' operation and rewriting of Cassinese texts,[9] in the 1130s, John, a monk of St. Vincent, provided the historical background of that period, making evident chronological mistakes in the process. For example, a raid against that monastery by the Emir of Bari, Sawdān, which had occurred in about 860, is used to describe the attack in 881.[10] The sources that the St. Vincent writer used to recount the battle over the abbey and the massacre of the monks are unknown. Yet it is noteworthy that Bertharius's death by decapitation was briefly recorded at Montecassino at the beginning of the twelfth century. John was, perhaps, influenced by that account and, in a sort of competition over who had suffered more in the past, he recounted how in 881, the Muslims had beheaded a good nine hundred of his brothers, among whom was Abbot Maio.[11] Moreover, in contrast to the monks of Montecassino, those of St. Vincent defended their abbey tenaciously and were only defeated because they were betrayed by their servants.[12]

An evident example of re-writing about certain events is found when comparing the two biographies of the Calabrese monk Gregory of Cassano (ca. 930–ca. 1002), who moved to Germany in 995, where these two works were written. The first text was composed shortly after his death and was based on the testimonies of some of the saint's followers, probably from southern Italy; the second one was likely written in the twelfth century. In the latter work, the saint is portrayed as a champion of Christendom who was tortured by Muslims for being a Christian and refusing to deny his faith.[13] According to the first biographer, however, the Saracens wanted to torture Gregory because they did not believe his statement about the poverty of his monastery, and they hoped that he would confess the location of his abbey's riches to them. The twelfth-century author described his torture with greater drama, lingering on the details. The most important difference between the two works, however, concerns the saint's behavior towards the Muslims. Unlike the eleventh-century writer, the second biographer omitted that Gregory had cured the arms of his torturers, which had been paralyzed by Divine Providence, and relieved the painful toothache of a Saracen.[14] For the twelfth-century author, who was obviously influenced by completely different values from those found in the first biography, the Muslims could not be worthy of the saint's charitable gestures.

In the case of John Terista, who lived in Sicily and Calabria in the tenth and eleventh centuries, the instances of re-writing concern the saint's parents. According to two brief texts in verse written in Greek, probably based on a lost biography and composed before 1101/1102, John's father was a Muslim, while his mother was Christian.[15] Thanks to this woman's teaching, John decided to become Christian, but the Saracen fiercely opposed his son's choice. Moreover, it is narrated how the 'children of darkness' beat John because they could not stand to see him going to church. Incited by his mother and a dream, the young Sicilian ultimately left his home and went to Calabria, where he was baptized.[16]

In contrast, the biography of the saint, which was written between the twelfth and thirteenth centuries, specifies that John was conceived in Calabria by Christian parents, but was born in Palermo, because Muslim raiders killed his father and took his mother to Sicily. A Muslim man later married John's mother and raised him as a Muslim.[17] This biography also mentions that John's mother taught her son the Christian religion.[18] In this text, however, it is added that she convinced him to go to Calabria to be baptized because Christianity had completely disappeared from Sicily.[19] The birth of the saint from two parents of different faiths and the union between a free Christian woman and a Muslim man were considered tolerable in the first work (composed when Sicily was under the control of the Saracens). Conversely, these situations were believed to be unacceptable in the later text, which was written when the Christians had reconquered the island more than a century earlier. Both versions are, therefore, the product of two periods during which such unions were perceived in a completely different light. Moreover, in contrast to the first, in the second biography, the author also wanted to describe Sicily under the Muslims as a land without any Christians because the writer could not accept the idea of Christians subjugated to Islamic rule.

The author of the fourteenth-century Neapolitan text known as the *Chronicle of Parthenope* mentioned episodes from the early Middle Ages as well,[20] and it reported various events in which Neapolitans of those centuries had battled against Muslims. Even though there are references to the fact that the Saracens were dangerous enemies, one notes the absence of any negative judgment or pejorative description of the faithful of Islam. Their presence in this work does, however, serve some particular purposes. In 787, the chronicler claimed, there had been a Saracen attack on Naples that is not otherwise mentioned in early medieval sources.[21] The author recounts how the Saracens killed many Christians with no regard for age or sex: 'they put all Christians whom they took to the sword, with no mercy for females, children or old women'. After long battles, the enemies were defeated, thanks to the help of the Lombards and Franks. The motivation for inventing this fanciful episode is not clear. It is possible, however, that the distant memory of Muslim raids against the Campanian region[22] during the early Middle Ages was distorted in the fourteenth century to underline that Naples, then under the dominion of the French dynasty of the Angevins, had not been inhabited by pure Neapolitans for very long. According to this work, a great number of Neapolitans perished in these fights, and, in order to re-populate the city, it was necessary to invite numerous people from southern Italy and various other parts of the Mediterranean to settle in Naples; at that time, many individuals from France moved to that city as well. These immigrants were so many that 'at that same time Neapolitan blood was contaminated'.[23] Attempts by 'pure' Neapolitans to delegitimize the Angevin government on the grounds that the French were foreign to Naples, therefore, found no historical justification.

The author of this Neapolitan chronicle did not appreciate the close adherence to facts in the early medieval text about the miracles of Saint Agrippinus. According to this source, towards the middle of the tenth century, Saint Agrippinus and Saint Januarius defended Naples against a Muslim attack, but news of the imminent arrival of the Byzantine fleet and a payment of tributes to the Saracens were fundamental in putting an end to the siege.[24] To underline how special his city was, the chronicler erased these details and attributed the Muslims' retreat exclusively to the intervention of the two saints: 'Thanks to these saintly martyrs, the biggest ship was sunk, all of the army was distressed to see this, and they fearfully retreated'.[25]

In order to exaggerate the divine favor his fellow citizens had enjoyed, the author of the *Chronicle of Parthenope* committed an even bolder case of 'delete, translate, and paste'. The chronicler explains[26] that in the age of Emperor Lothar (839–855) and Pope Gregory IV (827–844), the Neapolitans caused all Muslims to be drowned through just one prayer to the Lord.[27] The author, thus, modifies an event recounted in another text. That prayer, in fact, constitutes the first part of an oration written in the biography of Pope Leo IV (847–855), composed soon after his death.[28] In his prayer, the pontiff asked God to intercede, so that the Neapolitans would defeat the Muslims who were heading for Rome. According to the papal source, while the Neapolitans were fighting, a strong wind, willed by God, blew up, separated the two fleets, and pushed the Muslim ships towards the coast, thereby scattering them and preventing them from sailing forward. Many Saracens thus died, by drowning, starvation, or at the hands of Christians.[29]

Bishop Blatton, who freed some Christian prisoners in northern Africa, is only remembered in the biography of Saint Neilos (ca. 910–ca. 1004). The author of this text, however, probably re-elaborated some episodes that were similar to those concerning Blatton in order to demonstrate what could happen to those who had friendly relations with Muslims. This churchman's claim to be a relative to the sister of a Saracen ruler, the liberation of Christian prisoners, and the subsequent killing of the bishop at the hands of Muslims recall some details about the Patriarch of Jerusalem, Orestes, and the metropolitan Bishop of Cairo, Arsenius. First, these latter men were brothers of a Christian concubine of the Fatimid Caliph al-Aziz (d. 996), who ruled a large part of the Near East, Maghreb, and Sicily. Orestes has been identified as the monk sent to Sicily by that Muslim ruler to accomplish various tasks. On this occasion, the churchman tried to ransom some Christian prisoners, but his mission failed.

Orestes died a natural death, but Arsenius was killed by Muslims, around 1010, in attacks ordered by Caliph al- Ḥākim, son of al-'Azīz.[30]

A very evident distortion of events for propagandistic ends is present in the apologetic work by Benzo of Alba (ca. 1010–ca. 1090) about Emperor Henry IV, which was composed during the heated years of the clash between that ruler and the papacy. In this text, Benzo briefly describes the deeds of Henry IV's predecessors in order to underline the beneficial role that the German emperors always played for Christendom. About Otto II (d. 983), he recounts how that ruler eliminated the Muslims from the Adriatic coasts,[31] thus falsifying what happened in reality. In the only campaign of that emperor against the Saracens (982), Otto II suffered a terrible defeat that both early medieval Italian and German sources recorded.

In a collection of brief papal biographies, known as *Roman Annals* and probably composed in the twelfth century,[32] the period of great tension between Pope Leo IX (1049–1054) and the Normans of southern Italy, which culminated in the disastrous setback of the pontiff's troops and the capture of Leo IX at Civitate in 1053, was, on the other hand, deleted by changing the name of the enemy in that battle. The biographer narrates how on that occasion, the army of the pope fought against the Agarens, i.e., the Muslims. No mention was made of the Normans, who later became protectors of the popes. An embarrassing episode for both the papacy and the new rulers of southern Italy thus disappeared from the history of the pontiffs.[33]

Notes

1 *Cronicae Sancti Benedicti Casinensis*, II, 5, 6; *Chronica Monasterii Casinensis*, pp. 77–81.
2 *Cronicae Sancti Benedicti Casinensis*, II, 8; *Chronica Monasterii Casinensis*, p. 82.
3 *Cronicae Sancti Benedicti Casinensis*, II, 10; *Chronica Monasterii Casinensis*, I, 28, p. 82.
4 *Chronica Monasterii Casinensis*, I, 43.
5 He also recorded that Bertharius had been buried in the church of Saint Benedict near the brothers' chapter. *Chronica Monasterii Casinensis*, I, 43, 44, p. 114.
6 Peter the Deacon, *Ortus et vita iustorum cenobii Casinensis*, ed. R. H. Rodgers (Los Angeles, 1972), p. 51.
7 *Passio s. Bertharii abbatis Cassinensis*, in *Acta Sanctorum, Octobris*, IX (Paris – Rome, 1869), chapters 39–40. This work was written by the Cassinese prior and archivist Ignatius of Prague.
8 *Passio s. Bertharii*, pp. 670–82. In spite of the composition of this text, the cult of Saint Bertharius was approved much later (on August 26, 1727).
9 The author used Erchempert's chronicle and probably the work by Leo Marsicanus.

10 *Chronicon Vulturnense del Monaco Giovanni*, vol. 1, pp. 362–63. Cf. *Chronica Monasterii Casinensis*, pp. 95–96. Leo rephrased what had been recounted in *Cronicae Sancti Benedicti Casinensis*, II, 28.

11 *Chronicon Vulturnense del Monaco Giovanni*, vol. 1, p. 368.

12 *Chronicon Vulturnense del Monaco Giovanni*, vol. 1, pp. 363–62.

13 *Vita S. Gregorii abbatis Porcetensis posterior*, ed. O. Holder-Egger, in MGH, *Scriptores*, vol. 15, 2 (Hanover, 1888), chapter 7.

14 *Vita S. Gregorii abbatis Porcetensis prior*, chapter 9. In the second biography, it is narrated how the saint cured a person of a toothache, but nothing is said about the identity of the sick. *Vita S. Gregorii abbatis Porcetensis posterior*, chapter 8.

15 A. Peters, *Joannes Messor, seine Lebensbeschreibung und ihre Entstehung*, Diss. (Bonn, 1955), pp. 8, 11; Acconcia Longo, 'S. Giovanni Terista', pp. 144–45.

16 Peters, *Joannes Messor*, pp. 8–11; Acconcia Longo, 'S. Giovanni Terista', pp. 145–48.

17 *Vita di San Giovanni Terista*, pp. 136–37.

18 According to this text, when John was fourteen, his mother revealed his origin to him. *Vita di San Giovanni Terista*, pp. 137–38.

19 *Vita di San Giovanni Terista*, p. 138.

20 Written in Neapolitan vernacular in mid-fourteenth century, the *Chronicle of Parthenope* reports episodes from the foundation of Cuma by the ancient Greeks to the beginning of Queen Joan's rule (1343–1382).

21 A very similar account was also written in Latin. *Neapolitanorum victoria ficta*, ed. G. Waitz, in MGH, *Scriptores rerum Langobardicarum et Italicarum saec. VI–IX* (Hanover, 1878), pp. 465–66. It is only preserved in a fifteenth-century manuscript. On the basis of this detail, Samantha Kelly believes that the author of the Latin text copied this account from the *Chronicle of Parthenope*. The 'Cronaca di Partenope': An Introduction to and Critical Edition of the First Vernacular History of Naples (c. 1350), ed. S. Kelly (Leiden, 2011). p. 310. It is not, however, possible to establish its date of composition. That text could therefore be a copy of an earlier work.

22 Naples was and still is the main city of that region.

23 The '*Cronaca di Partenope*', chapter 50, pp. 233–38.

24 *Ex miraculis Sancti Agrippini*, chapter 11, pp. 464–65. The hagiographer added that the objects had been recovered thanks to the saints' help.

25 The '*Cronaca di Partenope*', chapter 53, p. 242.

26 Some manuscripts of this chronicle, however, mention Pope Leo IV (847–855). The '*Cronaca di Partenope*', p. 313.

27 The '*Cronaca di Partenope*', chapter 54, p. 242.

28 *Liber pontificalis*, vol. 2, p. 118.

29 *Liber pontificalis*, vol. 2, pp. 118–19.

30 For further details about these similarities, see V. Von Falkenhausen, 'La Vita di s. Nilo come fonte storica', in *Atti del Congresso internazionale su S. Nilo di Rossano* (Rossano-Grottaferrata, 1989), pp. 294–95; and A. Luzzi, 'La vita di san Nilo da Rossano tra genere letterario e biografia storica', in *Les vies des saints à Byzance. Genre littéraire ou biographie historique?*, eds. P. Odorico - P. A. Agapitos (Paris, 2004), pp. 187–88.

31 Benzo of Alba, *Ad Heinricum IV*, p. 136.

32 They are in the appendix in one of the versions of the *Liber pontificalis*.

33 *Liber pontificalis*, vol. 2, p. 333. The author of this text or his source knew that on that occasion, the adversaries of the pope had been the Normans. The writer states that the pontiff annulled the excommunication against those adversaries, which is confirmed by eleventh-century primary sources. Because the Muslims belong to another religion, they obviously could not be excommunicated.

8   The enemy is coming

Moving the saints

Saints' relics were very precious for the Christians. They represented a tangible access to God and his saints and constituted a relevant component of the identity of both ecclesiastical and secular communities in the areas where they were preserved. The fear that they could be either taken by the Muslims or lost because of their raids was widespread, and this fear induced secular and ecclesiastical authorities to move them to safe locations. This necessity was felt from the moment the Muslim presence in the western Mediterranean began to become permanent. Indeed, the first provision of that type was taken around 717/725 when, because of the Saracens' attacks against Sardinia, the King of the Lombards, Liudprand, had the relics of Saint Augustine moved from the island to the capital of his kingdom.

> Liudprand also, hearing that the Saracens had laid waste Sardinia and were even defiling those places where the bones of the holy bishop St. Augustine had been formerly carried on account of the devastation of the barbarians and had been honorably buried, sent his men and, by giving a great sum, obtained them and carried them over to the city of Ticinum and there buried them with the honor due to so great a father.[1]

At the beginning of the tenth century, having heard of the arrival of a large Saracen army in Calabria and of their plans to conquer the whole of Italy, the bishop of Naples transferred Saint Severinus's remains from the unsafe Castrum Lucullanum to Naples.[2] The Prince of Benevento, Sicard (832–839), ordered the relics of Saint Bartholomew to be taken from Lipari to Benevento. In this case, however, Allah's followers had already devastated that island, and the removal occurred in order to prevent the loss of the saint's bones, which had been scattered because of the Saracens' incursions.[3]

Relocations of relics are also recorded in other areas of the Peninsula that were hit by Muslim raids. On the Tuscan coast this happened for those of

Saint Venerius, which were moved twice for this reason. When Novalesa's monks abandoned their abbey for fear of Islam's followers, Saint Secundus's remains were transferred to Turin.[4] The body of Saint Mark, stolen from Alexandria by two Venetian merchants in 827/828, was in a territory occupied by the Muslims about 190 years earlier. The possibility that the Saracens removed columns and slabs from the Alexandrian church in which the evangelist's remains were preserved was, however, considered by the Venetians a satisfactory reason for their gesture.[5]

Except for the attempt to burn the body of Arsenius, Elias Spelaeota's mentor – the Saracens' frustration at not finding precious objects in his grave motivated this act[6] – the destruction of relics by Allah's followers is not recorded;[7] there were no cases of relic theft either. On the contrary, some Christians profited from Muslim raids. Around 874, an Alaman of Emperor Louis II's army stole some saints' remains from a Campanian church that had been abandoned for fear of the Saracens, and he donated them to a German monastery. The inhabitants of the Apulian town of Lesina, on the other hand, took away those of Saint Pardus from the nearby Larino (Molise), which had been deserted because of a Muslim raid.[8]

Running away

The Sicilian–Calabrian monks' biographies emphasize that, besides creating problems for their security, the Muslims' incursions rendered it impossible for the saints to lead their secluded lives. So, at the news of the Saracens' arrival, they often moved to areas more remote than those in which they usually lived. If the danger was too great and lasted for too long, they migrated to other regions. Being a lover of quiet, during the attacks of the Muslims, Elias Spelaeota (ca. 860–ca. 960) preferred to abandon his monastery and hide in the neighboring mountains.[9] When the Muslims began to pillage the surroundings of Cassano, Saint Gregory (ca. 930–ca. 1002) fled from his monastery located near that town.[10] One day when Stephen, hermitage companion of Saint Neilos (ca. 910–ca. 1004), was visiting some neighbors, the Saracens raided that area. Unable to go back to his cave, Stephen went to a castle, while Neilos left his grotto and took shelter in a more secluded location. His decision was wise because the Muslims discovered his dwelling place.[11] Since that area was no longer safe, he abandoned it and settled in an even more remote area.[12] The subsequent Calabrian saint's relocation to Latium was due to the continuous Saracen raids against the South of the Peninsula.[13] For the same reason Sabas (ca. 910–ca. 991) first left Sicily, then Calabria.[14]

Foretelling the Muslims' advent and the defeat of the Byzantine army, Elias the Younger (ca. 823–ca. 903) decided to leave Taormina, still under imperial control, and go to Greece with one of his disciples.[15] Pope John VIII (872–882) writes that the central Italian bishops, frightened by Allah's followers, had to abandon their churches and to take shelter in those of the apostles in Rome.[16] In northern Italy, the best example of monks fleeing their monastery concerns the monks of Novalesa. Fearing an assault by Fraxinetum's Saracens, they relocated to Turin at the beginning of the tenth century, and their monastery remained in ruins for many years.[17]

Churchmen and saints were not the only ones to flee for fear of invaders and raiders. Indeed, in the ninth and tenth centuries, the people living in areas indefensible from the Muslims' attacks abandoned their homes. 'Cities, castles and villages are without inhabitants and are in ruins', emphasizes the pope in 876.[18] On some occasions people wanted to avoid the danger, as did Elias the Younger's parents in Sicily who moved from Castrogiovanni to a fortified center because of the imminent coming of the Muslims from northwestern Africa.[19]

People sometimes fled at the mere news of the Muslims' onset, as, for example, those residing near Turris did; some of them took shelter in neighboring castles, while others went to areas defended by nature.[20] During the raid that came within forty miles of Pavia, the locals fled into cities and strongholds.[21] On the other hand, when Allah's followers began their campaigns to conquer Sicily, Joseph the Hymnographer's parents preferred to migrate to Greece.[22] For fear of the Saracens in the 840s, the people of a Sardinian town moved to Latium, while the inhabitants of Centocelle fled into the woods, as the poor condition of their city walls could not guarantee effective protection.[23] In such circumstances, the saints sometimes helped the civilians. When Sabas was still in Sicily, at his mother's request, he took her and other persons to a safe place in the mountains.[24] On that occasion there was also his father Christopher, who, 'almost like a new Moses', led the refugees through mountains and forests to a fortified town.[25] In the areas not conquered by Allah's followers, the populations went back to their homes after the raiders withdrew. This, for example, is what the inhabitants of Porto and Ostia did in 846.

When the Normans assaulted northwestern Africa in the twelfth century, it was the Saracens' turn to flee, and Muslim authors do not fail to recount how the peoples of that region abandoned their homes at the news of those enemies' imminent arrival.[26]

In support of the fact that migrating to another territory was not at all easy and of the good treatment the Normans reserved for Islam's faithful in Sicily, the Muslim chroniclers report that only the scholars abandoned the island.[27] Among them was the learned writer Ibn Ḥamdîs (ca. 1056–ca. 1133). He managed to utilize his literary gifts at the courts of several lords in Spain and northern Africa, but he always felt a longing for Sicily.

Remaining behind the walls

At the news of the Saracens' coming, the Christians generally preferred not to face their adversaries on the battlefield but decided to stay inside their cities and fortresses, hoping that the attackers would not want to besiege them for a long time. Often used in the early Middle Ages (also against other enemies), this strategy was adopted above all because of the scarcity of troops. The worry of losing everything in a few hours on the battlefield likely played a role in this choice as well. 'There was no one who would await their arrival unless in very heavily fortified places' explains Liudprand of Cremona in his account of a Muslim incursion into the Po Valley.[28] After being defeated by Allah's followers in 827, the Sicilians followed this approach, and the Muslim conquest of Sicily basically became a long series of sieges, as the Muslims slowly conquered the main cities of the island. The same thing happened in the South of the Peninsula. In some cases, especially when Islam's faithful did not have large armies and when military help arrived, like in Salerno in 872 and in Naples around 950, these tactics were successful. When the Christians attacked, the Muslims often behaved in the same way. After being defeated by Emperor Louis II's army, Emir Sawdān withdrew into Bari where he held out for a few years. This also occurred on several occasions during the Norman campaigns to conquer Sicily.[29]

The threat of Muslim attacks did not result in the construction of many new fortified centers. In general, it was preferred to reinforce existing defenses, works previously made for protection against Christian enemies. Pope Gregory IV (827–844) had Ostia fortified to shelter it from the Saracens' assaults.[30] Having been warned of a forthcoming Muslim fleet, in 872 the prince of Salerno ordered the erection of several towers.[31] Having heard the news of Emir Ibrāhīm II's campaign in Calabria, in 902 the citizens of Cosenza strengthened the defenses of their city. On the other hand, the duke of Naples commanded the destruction of Castrum Lucullanum, located outside the city walls, because it was difficult to defend; he also did not want to give the enemy a fortified base.[32] For protecting Rome and preventing another pillage of St. Peter's, Pope Leo IV (847–855) had the city walls repaired and walls built around the basilica, and Emperor Lothar made a drive to raise money to finance their construction.[33] Roughly thirty years later, in Rome, Pope John VIII fortified the area around St. Paul. Moreover, Pope Leo IV gave a town to those Sardinians who had fled from their island for fear of Allah's followers and had been wandering for some time. On his initiative, a new center was erected for the inhabitants of Centocelle who had abandoned their town, because it was without walls, and were living in the woods.[34] Montecassino's riches rendered it a desirable target for the Muslims, and, consequently, Abbot Bertharius ordered a castle to be built to defend the abbey.[35]

Notes

1 Paul the Deacon, *History of the Lombards*, trans. W. D. Foulke (Philadelphia, 1907), VI, 48. The historian of the Lombards copied this passage from the Anglo-Saxon author Bede.

2 The same thing happened with the remains of Saint Vitalis, which were moved into Turris by the bishop of that town. *Vita Vitalis*, chapter 23.

3 *Translatio corporis sancti Bartholomei apostoli Beneventum et miracula*, pp. 10–12. For the same reason the relics of Saint Herasmus were transferred to Gaeta from the ruins of Formia several years after the town's destruction by the Muslims. *Passio Sancti Herasmi*, in D. Lohrmann, 'Die Jugendwerke des Johannes von Gaeta', *Quellen und Forschungen aus italienischen Archiven und Bibliotheken* 47 (1967), p. 381.

4 *Vita S. Venerii*, chapters 17, 23; *Cronaca di Novalesa*, IV, fragment 25, p. 242. During the Muslim raids in eastern Latium the body of Saint Victoria was moved into a castle that the abbot of Farfa ordered to be built. *Destructio monasterii Farfensis*, p. 32.

5 *Translatio Marci Evangelistae Venetias*, chapters 9–12.

6 *Vita S. Eliae Spelaeotae*, chapter 35.

7 The relics of the saints were sometimes scattered because of the Saracen incursions. For example, see *Translatio corporis sancti Bartholomei apostoli Beneventum et miracula*, p. 10; *Sermo de virtute Sancti Constantii*, chapter 10.

8 *Translatio S. Fortunatae et sociorum*, ed. O. Holder Hegger, in MGH, *Scriptores*, vol. 15, 1 (Hanover, 1887), p. 473; Radoynus, *Vita S. Pardi episcopi*, in *Acta Sanctorum, Mai.* VI (Antwerp, 1688), chapter 9. It is also recounted how an Alaman carried off the relics of Saint Januarius and of other saints from Nola, but it is suspected that this account was invented. *Translatio S. Ianuarii et sociorum*, ed. O. Holder Hegger, in MGH, *Scriptores*, vol. 15, 1 (Hanover, 1887), p. 473; Houben, 'Il saccheggio del monastero di S. Modesto in Benevento', pp. 59–61.

9 *Vita S. Eliae Spelaeotae*, chapter 69. In the same situation Saint Nicodemus hid himself in a place located in woods and mountains that was 'inaccessible to most people'. *Vita di s. Nicodemo di Kellarana*, chapter 6.

10 *Vita S. Gregorii abbatis Porcetensis prior*, chapter 9. Saint Luke moved from his cave to a fortified center during a Muslim incursion. *Vita s. Lucae abbatis*, chapter 5.

11 *Vita di san Nilo*, chapter 29.

12 *Vita di san Nilo*, chapter 36.

13 *Vita di san Nilo*, chapter 73.

14 *Historia et laudes SS. Sabae et Macarii*, chapters 7, 9, pp. 14, 17.

15 Elias later abandoned his monastery in Calabria because of the Saracens' persistent incursions and went to Greece again. When he was in the mountains of Catanzaro's province looking for solitude, the saint foretold the arrival of the Muslims and therefore decided to return to his monastery in Calabria. *Vita di Sant'Elia il Giovane*, chapters 26, 38, 39.

16 John VIII, *Registrum*, number 22, p. 20. The monks of Farfa left their abbey for the same reason. *Destructio monasterii Farfensis*, p. 31.

17 *Cronaca di Novalesa*, II, 19.

18 John VIII, *Registrum*, number 22, p. 20.

19 *Vita di Sant'Elia il Giovane*, chapter 3.

20 *Vita Vitalis*, chapter 23. For another example, see *Vita S. Gregorii abbatis Porcetensis prior*, chapter 9.

21 Liudprand of Cremona, *Antapodosis*, II, 43.

22 McCormick, *Origins of the European Economy*, p. 899, number 314.

23 *Liber pontificalis*, vol. 2, pp. 126–27, 131–32.

24 *Historia et laudes SS. Sabae et Macarii*, chapter 6, p. 14.

25 *Historia et laudes SS. Sabae et Macarii*, chapter 9, p. 82.

26 BAS, vol. 2, pp. 38, 77.
27 BAS, vol. 1, p. 448; vol. 2, p. 98.
28 Liudprand of Cremona, *Antapodosis*, II, 43.
29 For example, see Geoffrey Malaterra, *De rebus gestis Rogerii*, II, 41, III, 11, 18.
30 *Liber pontificalis*, vol. 2, pp. 81–82.
31 *Chronicon Salernitanum*, chapter 111.
32 *Translatio Sancti Severini*, chapters 4–5.
33 *Capitularia regum Francorum*, vol. 2, p. 66, chapter 7.
34 *Liber pontificalis*, vol. 2, pp. 123–24, 126–27, 131–32; F. Marazzi, 'Le 'città nuove'
    pontificie e l'insediamento laziale nel IX secolo', in *La storia dell'alto Medioevo
    italiano (VI-X secolo) alla luce dell'archeologia*, eds. R. Francovich - G. Noyé
    (Florence, 1994), pp. 269–71.
35 *Cronicae Sancti Benedicti Casinensis*, II, 15. After abandoning his abbey for fear of the
    Muslims, the abbot of Farfa had a castle erected on a mountain where he moved with
    his monks. *Destructio monasterii Farfensis*, p. 32.

9   Prisoners

The fate of those who were not able to flee and who were not killed during battles or raids was capture. Death could be their destiny, especially if the inhabitants of a city had defended themselves tenaciously. Such a result was not unusual in the premodern period. In fact, the Old Testament recommends that, upon the capture of a city, all the men be killed and the women and children enslaved. Several Christian writers mention the execution of prisoners by the Muslims. For example, at Taormina in 902, recounts a Neapolitan author, Allah's followers massacred all the inhabitants regardless of age or sex.[1] Another writer reports that, on that occasion, many Taorminians, including the bishop and the churchmen of the city, were locked in a church, which then was set on fire because they had refused to convert to Islam.[2] According to Theodosius, the Muslims also wrought a terrible carnage after their conquest of Syracuse in 878. Moved by God, remarks the ecclesiastic, the Saracens only spared the archbishop of the city and those who were with him (two clerks and Theodosius).[3] The list of the twenty-seven monks of St. Modestus of Benevento who were killed by the Muslims during a raid on their monastery (it is explained that only one monk survived) indicates that these accounts were not always exaggerations.[4]

Descriptions of prisoners' executions after the taking of the city or a victory on the battlefield are not lacking in Muslim works either. This is what 'Alī ibn al-Athīr (ca. 1160–ca. 1230) narrates in his accounts about the conquests of Syracuse, Taormina, and Rometta.

> Eventually the Muslims took the city and killed many thousands of men... A few Christians of Syracuse survived here and there.

> 'Ibrāhīm ordered the fighters to be put to death.

> They took the city, killed all the men, and imprisoned women and children.[5]

The Rūms captured at Pantelleria in 833 were all beheaded.[6] In a raid against Sicily in 516 (1122/1123), specifies ibn Idhāri (thirteenth–fourteenth century), the Muslim raiders took away women and children and killed the elders.[7] No Christian survived 'the swords of the Bedouins' in a clash that occurred during a Norman campaign in Tunisia in the twelfth century.[8] On another occasion the Christians of a fortified center were promised their lives in return for their surrender, but were all slain as soon as they came out.[9] According to a Muslim chronicler, Norman rule in Tunisia was hated by his coreligionists so much that, on the occasion of a revolt in 1156/1157, every Christian residing in Sfax was slain.[10]

In the ninth and tenth centuries, the balance of power between the Muslims and the Christians was such that the former were usually those who did the capturing. Roles, however, occasionally changed. In 812, in Lampedusa, writes Pope Leo III in a letter, the Byzantines killed all the faithful of Islam to the last man. The same detail is mentioned in the description of the battle recounting the elimination of the Saracen base on the Garigliano in 915 (perhaps, in these clashes an order was given not to take prisoners).[11] On other occasions, Muslims fell into Christian hands and were treated in various ways. The biography of Pope Leo IV (847–855) presents the best example of such variety. Three years after St. Peter's was looted, the followers of Allah returned to Latium's coasts, but this time the Christians reacted to the new threat effectively. Some of the Saracens, who survived the clashes and a storm, were executed immediately, while the others were taken to Rome to show the victory that had been obtained. Several of them were later hanged because it was believed that they were too many. The remaining were put to work on the construction of the walls around the basilica of St. Peter.[12]

After capturing Massar in ca. 849, Emperor Louis II had him beheaded. He was probably the chief of the Saracen mercenaries at the prince of Benevento's service and proved to be very ambitious (and therefore dangerous to the Christians) by taking possession of his employer's capital.[13] A few years earlier the same treatment was reserved for Apolaffar, the leader of the Muslim troops in the service of the prince of Benevento, who gave him to his adversaries to avoid the destruction of Benevento.[14] In the tenth century, after being captured and taken to Turin, two Saracens were crucified, but they were executed because they had managed to set a church on fire.[15] In another case, the thirst for revenge was so strong that the Christians forgot the biblical precept about using the death penalty only for warriors. Indeed, the members of the expedition against the Muslim ruler, who occupied Luni in ca. 1016, decapitated his wife as punishment for her husband's deeds.[16]

In some cases, Christian writers mention the killing of prisoners by Allah's followers to underline the ferocity and barbarity of their enemies and, sometimes, the bravery of the Muslims' victims. The most detailed descriptions are those already mentioned about the conquest of Syracuse in 878 and of Taormina in 902. Among the various infamies attributed to the Emir of Bari, Sawdān, there is also the cruel death reserved for those who fell into his hands, but it is not explained how this happened.[17]

Most prisoners were, however, destined for the profitable slave trade in the Mediterranean and in western Europe, while some others enriched the raiders through their ransom. Many texts mention this and sometimes clearly indicate that prisoners were considered part of the war booty. Having settled on the island of Ischia, recounts a Campanian writer, the Saracens assailed the mainland every summer for many years, capturing whomever they found.[18] 'Who flees fire or sword', observes Pope John VIII in 876, 'is turned into a prey, led into captivity and destined to perpetual exile'.[19] According to Novalesa's chronicle, besides sowing destruction, the Muslims plundered gold, mares, cows, jewels, girls, and children.[20] After occupying Taormina, Allah's followers, adds 'Alī ibn al-Athīr, took possession of all the goods of the city, the women, and the children.[21] As evidence that raiding was a way to obtain beautiful and exotic women, in his account of his stay in Sicily, Ibn Jubayr, struck by the beauty of Trapani's Christian women, wishes that Allah would let his compatriots capture them.[22]

Muslim troops were utilized during the civil war in the 840s between the Beneventans and the Salernitans and the lands 'beyond the sea', highlights Erchempert, got rich with 'the prisoners of our people of both sexes and all ages'.[23] Such circumstance is confirmed by a Frankish monk, who embarked a few years later in Taranto, then in Muslim hands, to go to the Holy Land. In the port of that city he saw six ships loaded with Lombard captives and headed to the African coasts.[24] In ca. 904 the supporters of Pope Sergius III, on the other hand, threatened to send the pontiff's adversaries to Naples where they would be handed to the Saracens, thus presenting a further proof of the Neapolitans' familiarity with the Islamic world.[25] In 880, thanks to the renewed interest of Constantinople in southern Italy, the roles were reversed in Apulia. A Byzantine army ended Muslim rule in Taranto and the sale of the city's inhabitants greatly enriched both the imperial troops and the emperor.[26] The fact that around 870, in Calabria, Emperor Louis II's soldiers attacked the followers of Allah who were harvesting their fields along with their Christian prisoners indicates that the latter were also utilized in farming in the lands conquered by the Muslims.[27] Many Christians captured in the Peninsula were taken to Sicily, but prisoners captured in the eastern Mediterranean were taken to the island as well.[28] On the contrary, the bishop of Vercelli followed the opposite path. Having fallen into Muslim hands after the defeat of Emperor Otto II's army in Calabria in 982, he ended up in prison in Egypt.[29]

There are several references to specific individuals captured by the faithful of Islam. Among them are Saint Elias the Younger (ca. 823–ca. 903), Saint Vitalis of Castronovo (tenth century), Saint Nicodemus of Kellàrana (tenth/eleventh century), and some monks of Saint Neilos's monastery (ca. 910–ca. 1004).[30] In 835, near Castrogiovanni, the wife and son of a Byzantine commander suffered this fate.[31] This could also happen to Jews living in Christian territories. In a brief autobiographical note, the learned Apulian Jew Shabbetai Donnolo explains that, at the age of twelve, he was captured during the Muslim raid against Oria in 925 and that his parents ransomed him in Taranto shortly thereafter.[32]

This type of misadventure became part of the family memory of the author of Novalesa's chronicle. Indeed, after having fallen into Saracen hands, the brother of his grandfather and a servant of the latter were put on sale and ransomed by his grandfather.[33] This episode indicates that the faithful of Islam sometimes tried to sell their captives right away or to obtain a ransom from their relatives. If this did not happen and the Saracens could not take them to their lands, the prisoners ran the risk of being killed. The risk was lessened if the attackers had ships. For example, around 1075, a Muslim fleet coming from Africa raided a Calabrian town, and many of its inhabitants were captured. The day after their raid, the Saracens went back to that place and let the survivors ransom the young boys and all the persons believed to be useless. All the others were taken to Africa.[34]

Nevertheless, the ransoming of the captives also occurred after they had been carried to the 'House of Islam'. In the tenth century the bishop of Capua did so for a churchman,[35] while Bishop Blatton arrived in Calabria from Africa, bringing with him numerous Christians whom he had liberated.[36] Pope Benedict IV (900–903) asked all his faithful to help a bishop of the eastern Mediterranean, who had gone to the pontiff telling him that, after having fallen into Saracen hands and having been freed by some coreligionists, he started a journey to collect the necessary money to liberate his thirty companions who were still prisoners of the Muslims.[37] Roger of Hauteville's intervention, on the other hand, saved Montecassino from paying the sum collected to free some monks captured by Saracen pirates. Having been pushed by the winds, those who had to take the money to Africa arrived in Sicily and told the Norman leader their story. Roger then sent a message to the ruler of that land saying that he had to give him those monks if he wished to keep having a peaceful relationship with him.[38]

As already emphasized, when the power relationships between Muslims and Christians changed, the roles reversed more often. Thirteen mules with thirteen Saracens were among the gifts Robert Guiscard donated to the abbey of Montecassino.[39] In 1087, on the occasion of the expedition of Genoese and

Pisans against al-Mahdīya, the ruler of that city immediately ransomed those who had fallen into Christian hands.[40] During the Normans' campaigns in Tunisia in the twelfth century, such episodes became quite common. In several cases the Muslim authors highlight that the Christians killed all or most of the adult males and took away women and children.[41] Being unable to leave a garrison in a city, King Roger II's warriors brought the governor of that place and his family to Sicily where they kept them until he was ransomed.[42] In one case it is recounted that the captives were sold to the Sicilian Muslims.[43] But it is not clear whether the latter ransomed them to prevent their coreligionists from being enslaved by the Christians and later planned to release them. If the ransom was not paid or the prisoner was considered a dangerous enemy, he could die in captivity. This happened to an officer of Emir Ibrāhīm II, who had fallen into the hands of the Byzantines in the strait of Messina in ca. 900; he was brought to Constantinople where he passed away for unknown reasons. This learned Muslim wrote some verses about his experience, complaining about his adverse fortune and the hardships of his captivity and hoping that God would save him.[44]

References to Christians fallen into the hands of Allah's followers can be found in archival documents when it was necessary to provide legal clarifications. At Naples, in 883, a couple sold its property on behalf of their son, who was held captive by the Saracens.[45] According to a donation charter to a monastery in 895, if the donor's son, captured by the Muslims several years earlier, returned, he would receive half of the properties that were donated.[46] In 872 and in 882, two Salernitan women could not dictate their last wills in the presence of their relatives because the Saracens had taken them.[47]

A Beneventan document from 764 seems to suggest that Muslim slaves were present in Christian territories. In fact, two slaves with names deriving from countries under Islamic rule are mentioned in it: Egypt and Mauretanus (in Roman times Mauritania included most of northwestern Africa).[48] Because of the lack of further information about them, it is possible that they were Christians coming from those areas. Some free men named Saracen are recorded in a few Campanian charters dating to the eighth century and the first half of the following one; some of them were landowners, while others acted as witnesses for sales and donations. Perhaps, either they or their ancestors had been Muslim slaves who had been redeemed. Yet we cannot rule out the possibility that Saracen was a nickname assigned to people who had either an exotic appearance or a complexion darker than the average person. If so, this concerned very few individuals. Moreover, this name appears only when the Muslims did not create any problems for the inhabitants of those areas.[49]

The most accurate description of a period of captivity can be found in a letter by the monk Theodosius, who fell into Muslim hands along with the archbishop of Syracuse and two clerics after the conquest of that city in 878.[50] He complains of the harsh conditions of his transfer to Palermo and of his prison in that city, but they do not seem too severe. In fact, he only mentions the unfavorable climatic conditions during his journey from Syracuse to Palermo and the fact that they traveled night and day. His jail in Palermo was underground, dark, very hot, filled with annoying insects, and crowded with persons of different ethnic backgrounds; various Christians and the bishop of Malta were among them.

> We were thrown into the common prison; and this is a den having its pavement fourteen steps below ground, and it has only a little door instead of a window; here the darkness is complete, and can be felt, the only light being from a lamp, or some reflection by day, and it is impossible ever to see the light of dawn in this dungeon, nor the rays of the moon. Our bodies were distressed by the heat, for it was summer, and we were scorched by the breath of our fellow-prisoners; and besides, the vermin and the lice, and hosts of fleas and other little insects, make a man miserable by their bites; promiscuously with us there were confined in the same prison, to trade (as it were) with these miseries, Ethiopians, Tarsians, Jews, Lombards, and some of our Christians, from different parts, among whom was also the most holy bishop of Malta, chained with double shackles.[51]

Besides a generic observation about the treatment received during the trip and the fact that the Maltese churchman was 'chained with double shackles', the Syracusan monk does not mention any violence or mistreatment against him and his companions. Rather, he recounts how in Syracuse Allah's followers showed respect for the local archbishop. Moreover, in Palermo they did not punish the prelate for refusing to acknowledge the superiority of Islam.[52]

No narrative text reports the conversion of Christian prisoners to Islam, but an allusion recorded in the biography of Saint Sabas (ca. 910–ca. 991) indicates that this could happen in some circumstances.[53] On the other hand, the letter of Patriarch Photios, dating to 880/886, to the Calabrian Archbishop Leo constitutes clear evidence that conversions did occur. This source also proves how relevant was the problem that the Christian captives could practice their faith. If no respectable women were available, explains the patriarch, women of another faith – wishing to help the Christians – could give the Eucharist to the prisoners.[54] This detail emphasizes that the Muslims could be respectful of their prisoners' spiritual needs as well. An epistle by Pope Stephen V from 887/888 clearly highlights that being a captive of the Saracens had to be considered a special period during which the 'normal' rules did not apply. In fact, the pontiff forgave a bishop of Corsica who had killed some men when Allah's followers captured him.[55]

It was a special period for female prisoners too, but no exceptions were made for them. The suspicions about their sexual behavior in these circumstances are well portrayed in Photios's letter. According to the patriarch, the churchmen whose wives[56] had consensual sex with the Muslims during their captivity had either to leave their wives or to give up their office. The same verdict applied if the women did not oppose their rape either for fear or for other reasons, but they were forgiven. On the other hand, there was no penalty if it happened by the use of force – for example, their legs and hands were tied. Yet, Photios recommends divorce and that the women become nuns, because it was difficult to prove that women had resisted their rape. Entering a nunnery would have increased admiration and silenced malicious gossips.[57]

Most of the Christian women captured by the Muslims were in all likelihood destined to serve in the houses and harems of their masters. An exception occurred in the case of Anne, who fell into the Saracens' hands after their conquest of Syracuse in 878. She was taken to Seville where her intellectual gifts and medical knowledge were utilized by a learned Muslim who wished to have clarifications about medical terms mentioned in a text written in Greek.[58]

There is also some rare information about Christians who managed to be redeemed and to return home. Accord to the Novalesa chronicler, this happened to a man captured during a Saracen raid in a valley of the western Alps, who was freed after working for thirty years in Muslim territory; thus, he could see again his old mother.[59]

On the other hand, the already mentioned Bishop of Vercelli, Peter, who was in captivity in Egypt, could go back to Italy with several other Christians thanks to the intercession of the Bolognese monk Bononius, who was living in that land and held in great esteem by the Muslims.[60]

A few references about the liberation of Christians through military action are available as well. In ca. 870 Emperor Louis II's troops managed to do so during an incursion in Calabria,[61] while a letter of Pope John VIII from 875 states that the pope freed about 600 of his coreligionists after defeating a Muslim fleet near Latium's coast.[62] In the expedition of 1087 against al-Mahdīya, the Pisans and their allies, emphasizes a Pisan author, liberated more than one hundred thousand persons.[63] Roger of Hauteville gained the same result with his conquest of Malta (ca. 1090); the account of the joy inspired by that event among the liberated and the liberators is extremely moving and pervaded by spirituality.

In accordance with the count's desires, they first released their Christian captives, a great many of which they held within the city... Seeing the

Christian captives as they left the city – tears of joy at their unanticipated liberation flowing from the depths of their hearts – carrying in their right hands crosses made of branches or reeds or whatever else could be found at hand, shouting *'Kyrie Eleison',* and bowing down at the count's feet, our men were themselves covered with tears, touched as they were by the emotion of such a pitiful sight.[64]

Despite having stayed among Allah's followers for many years and having had a Muslim husband and a son, the Christian mother of the Emir of Denia (Spain), Mujāhid, managed to go back to her coreligionists by taking advantage of her son's defeat by the Pisans in ca. 1015. The ship on which she was traveling was captured by the Pisans, and, although Mujāhid had offered to ransom all those who had been captured on that occasion, the woman preferred to remain 'among her people'.[65] The flight of a prisoner was fatal to the Saracens who had survived the elimination of their Garigliano base. Indeed, he went back to their hideout with some soldiers and killed all of them.[66]

The liberation of Christians occurred as a result of diplomatic relationships as well. Having established a peace treaty with Muslims of the Maghreb in 812, the Byzantine commander of Sicily requested the return of prisoners.[67] Wishing to maintain friendly relationships with the Christian community of his city and to create some with the pope, the emir of Bougie (Algeria) freed some Christians in ca. 1076.[68] On the other hand, in the ninth century, during the Muslim conquest of Sicily, the faithful of Christ freed some Muslims to prevent an attack by the Saracens. This also happened in Syracuse in 872/873.

This year a contingent of Muslims moved against Syracuse. The inhabitants of that city established a truce with them on condition that they free three hundred sixty Muslims whom the Syracusans had captured. When they were liberated, the troops withdrew.[69]

Except for the two Saracens who managed to flee and set a church of Turin on fire, narrative sources do not report Muslims escapes. Such escapes, however, could occur. According to a letter by Pope John VIII from 872/873, forty Muslims fled from some Byzantine ships and hid in Circeo's cape (ca. one hundred kilometers south of Rome), and the pontiff asked the Amalfitans to capture them.[70]

The detailed biography of Elias the Younger (ca. 823–ca. 903) is the only text to record most of the experiences that have just been mentioned. As a young boy, while he was in the countryside, Elias was captured by Saracen raiders, then bought by a Christian and taken on a ship to be conducted to

Africa.[71] Yet during the journey a Byzantine warship intercepted the Muslim vessel and freed Elias and the other prisoners.[72] Three years later the saint lost his freedom in the same way; he was again sold to a Christian and led to Africa where a local Christian bought him.

> An Agarenes' incursion more serious than the previous one occurred. The young man (Elias), who was far from the fortifications of his town ..., was captured by them, sold to a Christian again and brought to Africa. The Christian sold him there to another Christian, a very rich tanner.[73]

After a misadventure, due to the undesired attentions of his master's wife,[74] Elias managed to be redeemed thanks to his qualities. Having spent a few years in the Near East, he moved to Palermo (already under Muslim rule) where he met his mother.[75] He then moved to Taormina, still in Byzantine hands, without problems. From that moment onward he did not return to the 'House of Islam' anymore. According to the *Life of Saint Elias the Younger*, therefore, Christian slaves could be redeemed and travel freely in Muslim lands.

Notes

1 *Translatio Sancti Severini*, chapter 2, p. 453.
2 *Translatio Sancti Severini*, p. 457, note 1.
3 *Epistola Theodosii monachi*, p. 275.
4 Houben, 'Il saccheggio del monastero di S. Modesto in Benevento'.
5 BAS, vol. 1, pp. 396, 394, 428.
6 BAS, vol. 1, p. 370.
7 BAS, vol. 2, p. 34.
8 BAS, vol. 2, p. 70. The Normans of Dimas's castle were all executed. BAS, vol. 1, p. 458.
9 BAS, vol. 2, p. 86.
10 BAS, vol. 2, p. 50.
11 Leo III, *Epistolae*, number 6, p. 96; Liudprand of Cremona, *Antapodosis*, II, 54.
12 *Liber pontificalis*, vol. 2, p. 119.
13 *Cronicae Sancti Benedicti Casinensis*, II, 14.
14 *Chronicon Salernitanum*, chapter 83.
15 *Cronaca di Novalesa*, V, 1.
16 Thietmar of Merseburg, *Chronicon*, VII, 45.
17 Erchempert, *Piccola Storia dei Longobardi di Benevento / Ystoriola Longobardorum Beneventum*, chapter 29.
18 Moretus, 'Un opuscule du diacre Adalbert sur S. Martin de MonteMassico', chapter 7, p. 254.
19 John VIII, *Registrum*, number 22, p. 20.
20 *Cronaca di Novalesa*, V, 18.
21 BAS, vol. 1, p. 394.
22 *The Travels of Ibn Jubayr*, p. 351.
23 Erchempert, *Piccola Storia dei Longobardi di Benevento / Ystoriola Longobardorum Beneventum*, chapter 17.

122   *Prisoners*

24 *Das 'Itinerarium Bernardi Monachi'*, ed. J. Ackermann (Hanover, 2010), chapter 4, p. 117.
25 Auxilius, *In defensionem sacrae ordinationis pape Formosi libri duo*, in E. Dümmler, *Auxilius und Vulgarius. Quellen und Forschungen zur Geschichte des Papstthums im Anfange des 10. Jahrhunderts* (Leipzig, 1866), pp. 60–61.
26 Theophanes Continuatus, *Chronographia*, p. 306.
27 Andreas of Bergamo, *Historia*, chapter 17.
28 I. Dujcev, *Medioevo bizantino-slavo* (Rome, 1965), pp. 246–47.
29 *Annales Sangallenses maiores*, ed. I. von Arx, in MGH, *Scriptores*, vol. 1 (Hanover, 1826), p. 80.
30 *Vita Vitalis*, chapter 14; *Vita di s. Nicodemo di Kellàrana*, chapter 18; *Vita di san Nilo*, chapter 70.
31 BAS, vol. 1, p. 369.
32 V. Putzu, *Shabbetai Donnolo: un sapiente ebreo nella Puglia bizantina altomedievale* (Cassano delle Murge, Bari, 2004), pp. 47–48.
33 *Cronaca di Novalesa*, V, 9. The account is not clear and it is not possible to determine exactly where the chronicler's relative was liberated.
34 Geoffrey Malaterra, *De rebus gestis Rogerii*, III, 8.
35 Marinus II, *Epistolae et Privilegia*, in *Patrologia Latina*, vol. 133 (Paris, 1853), number 7, column 874b; *Registrum Petri Diaconi (Montecassino, Archivio dell'Abbazia, Reg. 3)*, eds. J.-M. Martin, P. Chastang, E. Cuozzo, L. Feller, G. Orofino, A. Thomas, M. Villani, 4 vols. (Rome, 2015), vol. 1, number 9, p. 74.
36 *Vita di san Nilo*, chapter 68.
37 Benedict IV, *Epistolae*, in *Patrologia Latina*, vol. 131 (Paris, 1853), number 3, columns 43–44.
38 *Chronica Monasterii Casinensis*, IV, 50, p. 516.
39 *Chronica Monasterii Casinensis*, III, 58.
40 BAS, vol. 2, p. 153.
41 BAS, vol. 1, p. 461 (the prisoners were later ransomed), vol. 2, pp. 157, 292.
42 BAS, vol. 2, p. 46. The same thing happened when the Normans conquered the island of Jerba. BAS, vol. 2, p. 157.
43 BAS, vol. 1, p. 463.
44 BAS, vol. 1, pp. 528–29.
45 *Chronicon Vulturnense*, vol. 2, pp. 27–29.
46 V. Brown, 'New Documents at Rieti for the Monasteries of San Benedetto *ad Xenodochium* and Santa Sofia in Ninth-Century Benevento', *Medieval Studies* 63 (2001), number 2, pp. 344–45. Other cases in *Codex Diplomaticus Cavensis*, vol. 1, numbers 75, 86, pp. 98, 110.
47 *Codex Diplomaticus Cavensis*, vol. 1, numbers 75 (brother), 86 (son), pp. 98, 110.
48 *Chronicon Sanctae Sophiae (cod. Vat. Lat. 4939)*, ed. J.M. Martin (Rome, 2000), III, 29. As for the first name, a free man named Egyptus is recorded in a 776-Beneventan charter. *Chronicon Sanctae Sophiae*, I, 1.
49 For example, see *Registrum Petri Diaconi*, II, numbers 172–73, pp. 527, 530, and *Codex Diplomaticus Cavensis*, vol. 1, numbers 5, 8, 20, 24. The last mention of this name, borne by an adult man, dates to 844. Persons named Saracen reappear in the eleventh century. It is unlikely that they were free Muslims who settled in those lands. Noteworthy is the fact that a Montecassino monk with that name is recorded in a charter of 1089. *Registrum Petri Diaconi*, III, number 557, p. 1525.
50 The letter, which is incomplete, was addressed to Archdeacon Leo, while Theodosius was still in prison in Palermo.
51 *The Epistle of the monk Theodosius*, p. 96.
52 *The Epistle of the monk Theodosius*, pp. 93-96.
53 *Historia et laudes SS. Sabae et Macarii*, chapter 6, p. 14.

54 Italian translation in *Regesti dei documenti dell'Italia meridionale*, p. 508, chapter 4.

55 *Fragmenta registri Stephani V. papae*, ed. E. Caspar, in MGH, *Epistolae*, vol. 7 (Berlin, 1928), number 15, p. 341.

56 Some members of the Orthodox Christian clergy could get married.

57 Italian translation in *Regesti dei documenti dell'Italia meridionale*, p. 507, chapter 2.

58 G. Mandalà, 'Tra minoranze e periferie. Prolegomeni a un'indagine sui cristiani arabizzati di Sicilia', in *'Guerra santa' e conquiste islamiche nel Mediterraneo (VII–XI secolo)*, eds. M. Di Branco and K. Wolf (Rome, 2014), p. 104.

59 *Cronaca di Novalesa*, II, 13.

60 *Vita et miracula sancti Bononii abbatis Locediensis*, chapters 7–8, p. 1028.

61 Andreas of Bergamo, *Historia*, chapter 17.

62 John VIII, *Registrum*, number 49, p. 303.

63 *Carmen in victoriam Pisanorum*, lines 265–66. According to the Norman chronicler Geoffrey Malaterra, that was one of the conditions the Pisans imposed to the Muslims. Geoffrey Malaterra, *De rebus gestis Rogerii*, IV, 3.

64 Geoffrey Malaterra, *The Deeds of Count Roger*, IV, 16.

65 T. Bruce, 'The politics of violence and trade: Denia and Pisa in the eleventh century', *Journal of Medieval History* 32, 2 (2006), p. 136.

66 *Chronica monasterii Casinensis*, II, 87.

67 Leo III, *Epistolae*, number 7, p. 98.

68 Gregory VII, *Registrum*, pp. 287–88.

69 BAS, vol. 1, p. 389.

70 John VIII, *Registrum*, p. 276, number 5.

71 *Vita di Sant'Elia il Giovane*, chapter 6.

72 *Vita di Sant'Elia il Giovane*, chapters 7–8.

73 *Vita di Sant'Elia il Giovane*, chapter 9.

74 This episode is reminiscent of the one regarding Joseph in the Bible.

75 It is not explained why the woman was in Palermo. *Vita di Sant'Elia il Giovane*, chapter 25.

10 'Going' to the other

Seeking shelter

Moving to Muslim territories was certainly an extreme decision for a Christian, because it necessitated leaving one's home, in most cases for good. At the same time, Islamic lands offered a refuge for those who wanted to avoid harsh punishments for their crimes, above all for the instigators of failed revolts, who were probably escaping the death penalty. This was the case for the Byzantine commander of Sicily, Elpidius, who fled to Africa in 782 after trying, without success, to become emperor.[1] Evidently believing it was impossible to remain on Christian soil after converting to Judaism, an Apulian priest and an archbishop of Bari also fled to the 'House of Islam' in the second half of the eleventh century.[2] The reverse sometimes occurred as well. Around 835, some Saracen warriors killed their commander, then 'moved to the Rūm', while, in 869, a follower of Allah fled to the Christians of Syracuse after murdering the Muslim governor of Sicily.[3]

Narrative sources of the Peninsula mention two examples of important persons who 'went to the Muslims' in order to find shelter from a powerful adversary. Having rebelled against Emperor Louis II, Count Ildepert was hosted in the emirate of Bari shortly after 860.[4] The son of the former king of Italy, Adalbert, moved to the Saracen base of Fraxinetum (Provence) after being deposed along with his father by the German ruler Otto in 961.[5] No comment is expressed about these episodes, probably because the authors believed that quoting these events sufficed to underline their gravity. In 876 Pope John VIII, on the other hand, accused some of his adversaries of having fled to the Saracens, probably in order to defame them.[6] Judicial proceedings against Christians guilty of having moved to Muslim lands are not available. We have some information, however, about a couple of proceedings that allow us to know other 'crimes' and the motives for making that choice. In 899, the prince of Salerno donated one of his slaves and the latter's relatives and properties to a church because he had gone to the Saracens and entered into a pact with them.[7] No further information is recorded and therefore we cannot determine if other punishments were inflicted on him. Considering his servile status, he likely made that decision to obtain freedom. Thanks to a confiscation of an estate in Benevento in 867, which was held illegally, we also know that a free man 'went to the Saracens'. In his case, he likely fled in order to avoid punishment.[8]

Fighting with the other

Among the various problems created by the growing presence of Muslims in southern Italy during the ninth century was the use of Saracen troops in conflicts among Christians. In this case, the precursor was again an officer of Byzantine Sicily. After his revolt against his emperor had failed in circa 827, Euphemius did not limit himself to fleeing to nearby northern Africa but sought military help against the imperial army. The Saracens agreed to provide it, but the plans of the rebel were foiled. Indeed, his allies were too powerful and acted autonomously, starting a series of campaigns to subjugate Sicily and disregarding the interests of the person who had invited them. This became clear as soon as the Muslims reached Sicily. Their commander told Euphemius and his men to step aside because there was no need for them.[9]

Perhaps aware of what had happened to Euphemius, the Christian leaders of southern Italy chose not to employ large contingents of Saracen soldiers and above all, not to turn to overly powerful Muslim overlords. The first to follow this model was the Duke of Naples, Andreas (834–839), who did so to fight the Lombards of Benevento who were besieging Naples. On this occasion there were no battles because the Beneventans retreated immediately after the arrival of the Saracens.[10] Subsequently, they took part in several clashes among southern Italian Christian potentates.

Following the saying 'one nail pushes out another', the prince of Salerno used Spanish Muslims to fight the Prince of Benevento's 'Libyans'. The Neapolitans and the Capuans used Saracen troops in battles against each other, the Beneventans utilized them against the Byzantines, and the Gaetans did the same to defend themselves against the Lombards.[11]

In the early 1060s, the Christian and Muslim citizens of Reggio Calabria attacked their neighbors to avoid being accused by the Normans of collaborating with the Sicilian Muslims.[12] During the final phases of the conquest of Sicily, Roger of Hauteville started to bestow lands on Saracen soldiers in exchange for their military service (even against their fellow Muslims). In 1079, he requested their help to suppress a revolt of Allah's followers.[13]

Averse to the reform party of his city and therefore nurturing no sympathy for Pope Gregory VII, the Milanese chronicler Landulf the Elder mentions the use of Muslim troops by the pope's supporters to show them in the most negative light possible. According to the Milanese writer, when Robert Guiscard went to Rome in 1084 to help the pontiff, who was besieged by Emperor Henry IV, he brought with him all the believers of Islam whom he could gather. Landulf not only records their otherness, but also emphasizes that they were well trained in committing misdeeds and homicides and that they put the city to fire and sword.[14] The existence of Muslim warriors in the Norman contingents is confirmed by Geoffrey Malaterra, who, in line with the new climate of collaboration with Allah's followers that had developed after the conquest of Sicily, made no comments on their use by Roger of Hauteville in the campaigns against his Christian adversaries in Apulia and Calabria.[15]

Almost as if they wanted to underline the futility of criticizing such practices and their widespread use, the ninth- and tenth-century chroniclers did not fault Christian leaders for having employed them. An anonymous Cassinese author harshly blames the prince of Salerno only because he utilized Montecassino's treasure to pay Muslim troops.

> On this occasion, Prince Siconolf took away an enormous treasure from the monastery of the most blessed Benedict... this was of no use to him and because of his action he killed his soul... those riches were of no utility, either to him or to his homeland. From that moment on, in fact, he gained no more victories.[16]

Erchempert became critical only when the hated Neapolitans used Muslim troops. Indeed, his account in which the Capuan Lombards employed Saracens, who had previously been utilized by the Neapolitans to pillage Neapolitan territory, reveals a malign satisfaction. The author, however, makes no comment about the use of Muslims to obtain that result.

> Having become much stronger, the people of Capua tore apart Naples and its surrounding lands by themselves, and with the help of the Saracens, destroying everything as if they were a fire. In this way, by Divine Justice, the man (the Bishop of Naples, Athanasius II), who had used Saracens to send untold numbers of Christians to the sword and to prison and had enriched himself with their wealth, was deservedly whipped, beaten and preyed-upon by those Saracens. And so, as Salomon says: 'who will cure the wizard once he is bitten by the serpent?'[17]

There are no accounts about Muslim mercenaries who passed to their employer's enemy because the latter paid better. As we have already seen, the overly sensitive Saracen leader Apolaffar abandoned the prince of Salerno and went into the service of the prince of Benevento because of a joke that had offended him. On one occasion, however, Allah's followers present in the opposing armies of Naples and Capua decided not to fight each other in battle.

> (The Bishop of Naples) Athanasius (II) gathered a large army of knights and foot-soldiers, formed of Greeks, Neapolitans and Ishmaelites, and he sent them to attack Capua. (The Count of Capua) Atenolf, who had troops sent by (the Prince of Benevento) Aio and also Saracens, met them... The Saracens from the opposite sides, however, gathered and did not help anyone.[18]

This episode suggests solidarity between the Muslims who refused to fight against their coreligionists in a battle between two Christian potentates. It also highlights how weak those who had hired them were. Saracens sometimes profited from such weakness, deciding not to serve their 'employers' anymore and instead creating independent dominions. This happened above all in the civil war between the Lombards of Benevento and Salerno in the 840s. Massar, probably a leader of the Muslim mercenaries, took control of Benevento for a brief period. On the other hand, the Emirate of Bari, which was occupied by the Prince of Benevento Radelchis's Saracen garrison of the city, lasted longer. Not having enough troops to recapture Bari, that Lombard ruler maintained friendly relations with those Muslims and requested their help to fight Salerno.[19] Islamic mercenaries constituted such a danger that both Beneventans and Salernitans agreed never to use them again when they signed a peace treaty in 849.[20] According to Liudprand of Cremona (ca. 920–972), the Muslims employed by the Byzantines presented a similar problem. Around 920, not having an army to send to Italy, Emperor Romanus Lecapenus gave a great sum of money to North African Muslims to put down a revolt against Constantinople in Apulia and Calabria. The Saracens then took advantage of the opportunity to establish a base near the Garigliano River and to ravage central Italy.[21] Because that settlement had been created about forty years earlier by Muslims sent there by the duke of Gaeta, it is probable, however, that this author provides that version of events to criticize the Byzantines. Induced by the same intent, an Oltralpine writer recounts how the Byzantines sent Allah's followers to Calabria against Otto II to halt the German ruler's expansionist policies in southern Italy.[22]

Reference to Christians fighting for Muslims can be found only in twelfth-century sources. The chronicler John narrates how in 881 some serfs of

St. Vincent at Volturno provided the Saracens with decisive help in destroy-
ing that abbey. In return for gifts and freedom, they had not only shown the
assailants how to get around the defenses of the monastery but had attacked
their masters together with the Muslims.[23] According to a text of the same
period, there was one other case of Christians providing military help to
the believers of Islam. At the beginning of the tenth century, the prince of
Capua and Benevento along with the Neapolitans and the Amalfitans besieged
the Muslims of Garigliano. The plan failed, however, because the Gaetans,
believing that those Saracens were useful to keep the expansion of Capua and
Benevento in check, attacked the besiegers.[24] Ibn 'al 'Atir (ca. 1160–ca. 1230)
reports that the Neapolitans helped the Saracens take Messina in 842/843.[25]
In 998 Allah's followers tried to conquer Bari along with the troops of an
Apulian who had rebelled against the Byzantines; the attempt, however, failed
because the rebels withdrew.[26] On the other hand, Roger of Hauteville feared
that, during his son Jordan's revolt, he might side with the Muslims.[27] This
circumstance indicates how in these years the danger that some Norman warriors, unwilling to obey a strong authority, could join the enemy was considered very great. A letter by Pope Leo III reports that in 813 the ambassadors
of North Africa's ruler, traveling to Sicily to establish a peace treaty with the
Byzantines and sailing on Venetian ships, destroyed two Spanish ships that
probably belonged to rival Muslims.[28] Unfortunately, the role of the Venetians
in this battle was not recorded.

In the eleventh century, the political fragmentation and factionalism among
Allah's followers in Sicily led to a change in roles. Around 1035 an emir
asked Constantinople for military help against his brother. The emperor gave
him the honorific title of patrician and a military contingent. The imperial
army landed in Sicily in 1037 yet withdrew soon after.[29] The Sicilian Saracens
renewed this request a few years later to confront an army of Muslims coming
from the Maghreb.[30] Toward 1061, after being defeated by a rival, the governor
of Catania, Betumen, fled to Roger of Hauteville in Calabria and asked for his
help. The Norman leader accepted the invitation but was never at Betumen's
service as the latter did not have his own troops; instead, Betumen was under
the command of Roger, to whom he supplied a few scouts.[31] The Norman
kings sometimes used Islamic auxiliaries in their campaigns in Africa,[32] but
not everyone accepted that Christians and Saracens could fight together.
According to 'Ibn 'al 'Atir, Roger II's offer of troops to some Tunisian emirs
to fight against their Moroccan rival was turned down because they wanted
only Muslim soldiers. Their adversary was a strict Islamist who condemned
any agreement with Christ's followers, and this probably influenced the decision of the Tunisian leaders who wanted to avoid being perceived as bad
Muslims by their subjects.[33]

Traitors

The most important person involved in treason to the Muslims was Pope Martin (649–653). In those years Allah's followers did not represent a threat to Italy but had conquered all the Near and Middle East, thus creating serious problems for the Byzantines. Constantinople's authorities accused the pontiff of having sent the Saracens letters, money, and a text about what they had to believe. The fact that Martin openly opposed the religious policy of the emperor leads one to hypothesize that the actions attributed to the pope were fabricated in order to discredit him.[34]

In the following centuries, examples of people who betrayed their coreligionists – for money, other compensations, or fear – can be found among both Christians and Muslims. As we have already seen, some serfs of St. Vincent at Volturno received gifts and freedom from Allah's followers to help them against their masters. Probably to defame some of his opponents, in 876 Pope John VIII emphasized that during their night flight from Rome they had left a city gate open to allow the Saracens to enter the city.[35] The 'thieves', who, paid by Ibrāhīm II, helped the emir to conquer Taormina were very likely Christians.[36] According to Elias Spelaeota's biography (ca. 860–ca. 960), a shepherd led some Muslims to the castle to which some monks and the local population had fled. The traitor is referred to as 'mercenary', a term indicating that he had received compensation for his action. He is also blamed for not having behaved as a true Christian.[37]

A Muslim writer narrates how this type of collaboration was obtained in a different manner. In 244 (857/858), having been captured by Islam's followers and sentenced to death, a Sicilian Christian told them how to take Castrogiovanni easily in return for his life.

> When winter came, he sent a contingent of soldiers; when they reached Castrogiovanni, they plundered and ruined that area. They returned bringing a man with them who was high-ranking among the Rūms. Al 'Abbas ordered him put to death, but he replied: 'Spare my life; I have good advice for you... I will make you the master of Castrogiovanni: and this will be the way. With such a winter and so much snow, the inhabitants believe that you will not attack them; therefore, they will not keep a close watch. If you send troops with me, I shall let you enter the city'.[38]

As the roles were reversed in the twelfth century, this kind of behavior can be found among the Saracens. King Roger II took possession of a castle in

Tunisia by bribing some Bedouins.[39] The Norman ruler was also able to be well informed about al-Mahdīya thanks to the presence of his spies (most likely Muslims) in that city.[40] In one case, at the beginning of the tenth century, a follower of Allah accepted Christian warriors to fight against his coreligionists not for compensation but to avenge an insult.[41]

For a similar reason – his chief took away a beautiful Christian prisoner from him – a Saracen from Fraxinetum explained to the Christians how to eliminate his companions.[42] On the other hand, a fight among Castronovo's Muslims allowed Roger of Hauteville to take possession of that town. Having been unjustly mistreated by the governor of Castronovo, a miller avenged himself by occupying the local fortress with his men and inviting the Norman leader to occupy the town.[43] Offers of collaboration to the other could sometimes be very dangerous. As already mentioned, a nephew of Roger of Hauteville was the victim of a double-crossing Muslim. Having gained the Norman's trust, the Saracen gave him false information, thus tricking him into an ambush in which the Christian lost his life.[44]

His constant changing of sides cost the life of a Muslim man who had sworn allegiance to Roger and had agreed to rule Catania on behalf of that Norman leader. When the Hauteville left Sicily, this Muslim was bribed by his coreligionist Benarvet, and he allowed the latter to enter the city at night. When the Normans besieged Catania, Benarvet decided to retire to Syracuse, but he first killed his unreliable ally, fearing that he might betray his people again.[45]

It, however, was not always the case that coreligionists betrayed each other. For example, at the beginning of the twelfth century, fearing to lose his job in the Muslim administration in Tunisia because of his lord's death, a Christian from Antioch, by name George, fled to the Norman court of Palermo, where he had a great career.[46] On the other hand, the inhabitants of the Calabrian city of Rossano violently rebelled against the Byzantine authorities' order concerning the war against Islam's followers. They did not side with the latter but set fire to the ships built both for defending Calabria and for attacking the Saracens in Sicily. The refusal to provide the crews for those ships, a task never previously performed by the Rossanesi, was the reason for that uprising. Nevertheless, the possibility should not be ruled out that they also feared that the Muslims could have assaulted their town if they had obeyed that order. Thanks to Saint Neilos's intervention, the Rossanesi were forgiven.[47] The same did not happen to the imperial commander of Taormina who was accused of high treason for having abandoned the city before its fall in 902; he was deposed and forced to become a monk.[48]

To collaborate with the other

Narrative works mainly focus on war episodes and deeds about saints and secular and Church leaders; they therefore lack information about those who held administrative functions and other jobs at the Muslim courts in Sicily. Some rare information suggests that Christian subjects were sometimes allowed to hold such positions. For example, a letter by Saint Neilos addressed to a Sicilian emir was translated by a secretary of that ruler who is referred to as a 'very good and most pious Christian'.[49] Although it was in theory forbidden by the Muslims, two followers of Christ, father and son, worked as court physicians in Palermo at the end of the tenth century. The fate of the second, by name John, highlights how obtaining a prestigious position that bestowed on him a social and economic status superior to that of many Muslims could be dangerous for a Christian. After having asked him and obtained a donation twice as large as the usual one, a Saracen officer asked John to convert to Islam. At the latter's refusal, the Muslim falsely accused him of insulting Mohammed before the emir of Palermo. Because the ruler refused to condemn his physician, the officer did not have any problem in stirring up the local Muslims to lynch John.[50]

At the beginning of that century, there was the rare case of a Muslim in the non-military service of a Christian. Having been captured by the men of the Marquise of Tuscany, Bertha, while he was at the command of a Muslim fleet coming from North Africa, a eunuch, by name 'Alī, obtained the trust of the Italian aristocrat and, after seven years of captivity, in 905/906 led a diplomatic mission of Bertha to the caliph of Baghdad al-Mü'ktafī (902–908). The marquise confided in 'Alī so much that she entrusted him with a secret message that he had to give the Muslim ruler verbally. It is unknown if she used some form of blackmail, but the eunuch tried to accomplish his mission; only his death during the return voyage prevented him from bringing back to Bertha the caliph's reply.[51]

During the Norman conquests of Sicily and a part of Tunisia, some local Muslim leaders decided to collaborate with the invaders. Not having many warriors, Roger entrusted the governance of Catania to a follower of Allah, who, having been later bribed by the Saracen enemies of the Norman leader, surrendered the city to them.[52] Muslim authors do not refrain from criticizing those who had agreed to rule in the name of Roger II. After describing the submission of the governor of Gabès to the Norman king in exchange for a command position, Ibn 'ab Dinar wonders whether people with such features were men or demons interested only in material benefits; he also asks God to keep him away from such evil temptations.[53] Taking advantage of his lord's absence, a Muslim of Gabès did the same thing, thus causing the revolt of the local citizens who tortured and castrated the traitor, who was also accused of having abused the city governor's women.[54]

To convert

Religious faith constituted an important part of a person's identity, but it could be used to emphasize the subordination of those belonging to a religious minority or a subjugated people. It should not surprise, therefore, that some persons decided to adopt the religion of their conquerors or masters in order not to be considered 'different' and therefore inferior. The available sources prevent any assessment about how many Sicilians embraced Islam. The presence of Christians on the island between the ninth and the eleventh centuries in both the main cities and small towns clearly proves that not all the inhabitants of the island had chosen that course.[55] According to Ibn Ḥawqal, Allah's followers of the Sicilian countryside spoke an incomprehensible Arabic and did not follow the practices of Islamic religion. Muslim men were married to Christian women and male sons of these unions followed their father's religion, while the daughters adopted their mother's faith.[56] If these remarks are worthy of trust, they suggest that in those places the acculturation to Islam of many Sicilians converted to the Muslim religion was incomplete, and that they created forms of coexistence with those who remained Christians.

Except for the term 'apostate' applied to a Muslim commander about whom there is no further information,[57] examples of Christians converted to Islam cannot be found in works by Christian authors. An allusion to the fact that this could happen can be found in the *Life of Saint Sabas* where it is stated that under those conditions the risk that one's soul could 'be penetrated' was very high.[58] A text probably inspired by these fears and by the necessity to model exemplary behavior is the one about the vicissitudes of two brothers. Having been captured with their father John after the Muslim conquest of Syracuse in 878, Peter and Antoninus were taken to northern Africa. The two young Sicilians received an Islamic education and, thanks to their intellectual talents, obtained relevant offices in the Muslim administration. It was discovered, however, that they secretly always followed the Christian faith and consequently were tortured and executed: their father met the same destiny.[59] Another work, on the other hand, underlines what happened to the apostates who collaborated with the Muslims. Indeed, God harshly punished the Archbishop of Bari, Ursus, who, after having been forced to abjure Christianity by violence, became the caliph of Cairo's adviser by suggesting to the Muslim ruler a way to obtain the conversion of the Christian prisoners detained in that Egyptian city.[60]

The existence of such a phenomenon clearly appears from the answers given by the Patriarch of Constantinople, Photios, to the queries by the Calabrian Archbishop Leo about how to treat the Christians who had been captured by Islam's followers. As far as the children converted to Islam were concerned, his advice was to forgive them if there had been coercion, since they were unable to withstand violence.

> It was decided to forgive the children disfigured by the Saracens' evil costumes and not to deny them holy communion, unless they had voluntarily committed the sin; in this case, they would undergo the standard punishment.[61]

According to the Koran, force cannot be used to convert anyone to Islam, but practice could be very different. As already seen, Christian authors recount how Emir Ibrāhīm II tried to do so with the bishop of Taormina and how a Muslim officer had the court physician John lynched because he refused his invitation to adhere to Islam. Muslim texts indicate that such information was not just invented by Christian authors. For example, the following happened during the clashes in 1160 between the Normans and the Almohad leader 'Abd al-Mu'min, a very radical Islamist. After his conquest of Tunis, recounts Ibn al Athir, 'Abd al-Mu'min ordered the killing of all the Christians and Jews who refused to convert to Islam. During the siege of al-Mahdīya, he offered to spare the lives of the Normans if they would become Muslims. They refused and afterwards convinced him to let them go back to Sicily, but the threat by the Norman king to execute Sicilian Saracens if his men had been killed probably motivated that decision.

> He proposed to embrace Islam to all Jews and Christians who were in the city: those who became Muslims were saved, while those who refused were killed.
>
> 'Abd al-Mu'min offered them to convert to Islam, but they refused. For several days, however, they kept seeking an agreement and soothing the caliph so much that he gave up ... let them prepare ships on which they left ... The prince of Sicily had threatened: 'If 'Abd al-Mu'min kills our people of al-Mahdīya, we will kill as many Muslims in the island of Sicily and we will take their women and goods'.[62]

Some information is also available about Muslims who converted to Christianity. In the peace agreement of 849 between Beneventans and Salernitans it was decided to expel all the Saracens from their lands, except those who had become Christians in the 820s and 830s, but it was specified that this applied to those who had not reconverted to Islam.[63] The baptism of Muslim infants—Patriarch Photios explains to the Calabrian Archbishop Leo—was licit if their mothers wished so (these women were probably Saracen slaves). He stresses that 'the Church allowed the baptism of infants regardless of the behavior that the baptized would have adopted when adult, particularly as a result of a barbaric education'. He recommends, however, that the parents provide a Christian education to their children.[64] According to a work on Saint Antoninus of Sorrento's miracles, a Muslim prisoner was baptized, but nothing is said about how this happened or if the Saracen was freed.[65] A Muslim physician who adhered to Christianity is mentioned around the mid-ninth century, probably in Rome. Unfortunately, nothing is known about him and so it cannot be determined whether he voluntarily moved to Christian lands or if he was a prisoner. Because he subsequently went back to the 'House of Islam' and abjured the Christian religion, the second hypothesis is more likely.[66]

Although characterized by semi-legendary features, more information is available about another learned man who lived two centuries later. Born in Tunisia, the man known as Constantine the African traveled for many years throughout the East to satisfy his great thirst for knowledge. Returning to his homeland, he aroused the suspicions of his fellow citizens and, to avoid being killed, went to southern Italy, where he was welcomed with full honors by Robert Guiscard. He entered Montecassino and enriched the monastery's library with translations of medical and scientific texts. In his case, however, it must be pointed out that the sources never mention that he was a Muslim converted to Christianity. Perhaps this was taken for granted, but the possibility should not be ignored that Constantine was a Christian born in the 'House of Islam'.[67]

Geoffrey Malaterra reports an example of remarkable bravery and loyalty displayed by Elias, a Saracen who had become Christian and had been in the service of Roger of Hauteville. Having fallen into the hands of his former coreligionists, he refused to abjure his new faith and demonstrated his attachment to it by 'ending his life laudably with martyrdom'.[68] On the other hand, in that period the Muslim governor of Castrogiovanni agreed to surrender to Roger of Hauteville and to be baptized with his family in return for an estate in Calabria and the confirmation that his marriage would be considered still valid even though his wife was a relative of his. He pretended to be captured by the Normans in order to avoid being killed by his fellow citizens.[69] The two Saracens who married two Christian women of the South of the Peninsula very likely converted to Christianity. In another case the adhesion of a follower of Allah to the new faith was so strong that he became a priest.[70] A Saracen apostate is also mentioned in a Muslim source. Among the Rūms captured on the island of Pantelleria in 833, the believers of Islam discovered a Muslim renegade who evidently was not able to hide his origins. They were all taken to northern Africa and beheaded.[71] According to the agreement about the mosque built in Reggio Calabria in 952/953, the Muslim prisoners converted to Christianity could take refuge in that building; it is unknown if their coreligionists punished them.[72]

Not everyone, however, perceived the Saracen warriors' conversion as a positive thing. After the conquest of Sicily, Roger forbade any effort to baptize the Saracens of his army who were besieging some of his Christian enemies, thus contravening the request that the pope had sent him some years before.[73] Such a measure was probably intended to avoid any discontent among his Muslim subjects and to ensure the presence of soldiers very eager to fight Roger's Christian enemies.

Marrying the other

Many Christian women captured by the Muslims were undoubtedly used as concubines. It is unknown whether some married their masters as sometimes happened in Spain. As already mentioned, in his unflattering description of the Sicilians, Ibn Ḥawqal records the interesting information that marriage between Muslim men and Christian women was permitted with rules about the religion according to which the children were to be educated. Even though the author does not specify this, most likely these women were free. Although they did not have the same status as the Muslims, some heirs of the conquered were nevertheless given some important rights.

The existence of this practice is confirmed by a Christian source: two hymns written in honor of John Terista, who was born in Sicily from the union of a Muslim man and a Christian woman. The importance of these texts lies in the evidence that the exceptions to the rule were not accepted when the religion of the male progeny was concerned. Indeed, John's decision to follow his mother's creed caused the opposition of the Muslims and the young man decided to leave the island in order to be baptized in Calabria.[74]

Notes

1 Theophanes, *Chronographia*, ed. C. De Boor (Bonn, 1839), AM 6273–74.
2 C. Colafemmina, 'Gli ambienti ebraici meridionali e le Crociate', in *Il Mezzogiorno normanno-svevo e le crociate* (Bari, 2002), pp. 399–404; B. Blumenkranz, 'La conver-

sion au Judaisme d'André, archeveque de Bari', *Journal of Jewish Studies*, 14 (1963), pp. 33-36.

3 BAS, vol. 1, p. 369; vol. 2, p. 14.

4 *Cronicae Sancti Benedicti Casinensis,* II, 17.

5 Liudprand of Cremona, *Historia Ottonis*, chapter 4.

6 John VIII, *Registrum*, number 9, pp. 326–29.

7 *Codex Diplomaticus Cavensis*, vol. 1, number 111, p. 140.

8 *Chronicon Sanctae Sophiae*, III, 21, pp. 512–13.

9 BAS, vol. 1, pp. 308, 366.

10 John the Deacon, *Gesta episcoporum Neapolitanorum*, chapter 57.

11 Erchempert, *Piccola Storia dei Longobardi di Benevento / Ystoriola Longobardorum Beneventum*, chapters 17, 73, 77.

12 Amatus of Montecassino, *Ystoire de li Normant*, V, 11.

13 Geoffrey Malaterra, *De rebus gestis Rogerii*, III, 20.

14 Landulf the Elder, *Historia Mediolanensis*, p. 100.

15 Geoffrey Malaterra, *De rebus gestis Rogerii*, IV, 17, 22, 26.

16 *Cronicae Sancti Benedicti Casinensis*, II, 7.

17 Erchempert, *Piccola Storia dei Longobardi di Benevento / Ystoriola Longobardorum Beneventum*, chapter 77. The use of Muslim soldiers by the Neapolitans is also mentioned in a Neapolitan source. *Vita s. Athanasii*, chapters 6–7, p. 135–36.

18 Erchempert, *Piccola Storia dei Longobardi di Benevento / Ystoriola Longobardorum Beneventum*, chapter 73.

19 Erchempert, *Piccola Storia dei Longobardi di Benevento / Ystoriola Longobardorum Beneventum*, chapter 16.

20 Martin, *Guerre, accords et frontières*, pp. 202, 212, chapters 3, 24.

21 Liudprand of Cremona, *Antapodosis*, II, 45.

22 *Annales Sangallenses maiores*, p. 80.

23 *Chronicon Vulturnense*, vol. 1, p. 364.

24 *Chronica Monasterii Casinensis*, I, 50.

25 BAS, vol. 1, p. 374.

26 Lupus Protospatarius, *Annales*, p. 56, year 998.

27 Geoffrey Malaterra, *De rebus gestis Rogerii*, III, 36.

28 Leo III, *Epistolae*, number 8, pp. 99–100.

29 V. Von Falkenhausen, *La dominazione bizantina nell'Italia meridionale dal IX all'XI secolo* (Bari, 1978), p. 73.

30 Neilos, *Vita di san Filareto di Seminara*, pp. 42–43.

31 The Muslim leader was not able to convince any of his subjects to side with him and was killed while he was trying to find some allies among them. Geoffrey Malaterra, *De rebus gestis Rogerii*, II, 3, 4, 16, 18, 22. The possibility that Malaterra minimized the assistance provided by Betumen should not be ruled out. Amatus of Montecassino, who reports that the Muslim leader asked Robert Guiscard for help, states only that on one occasion Betumen was at the head of the troops that occupied two Sicilian cities. Amatus of Montecassino, *Ystoire de li Normant*, V, 8, 22.

32 BAS, vol. 1, p. 479.

33 He was the Almohad leader 'Abd al-Mu'min (1094–1163), who conquered all the Maghreb and southern Spain.

34 This is mentioned in a letter by Pope Martin, copied in the ninth century by Anastasius Bibliothecarius, in which the pontiff underlines that those accusations were false. Anastasius Bibliothecarius, *Collectanea*, in *Patrologia Latina*, vol. 129 (Paris, 1853), column 587.

35 The pope added that this had not happened thanks to God's intervention. John VIII, *Registrum*, number 9, pp. 326–329.

36 *Translatio Sancti Severini*, chapter 2, p. 454.
37 *Vita S. Eliae Spelaeotae*, chapter 69.
38 BAS, vol. 1, p. 379.
39 BAS, vol. 2, p. 69
40 BAS, vol. 2, p. 75.
41 Liudprand, *Antapodosis*, II, 49–50.
42 *Cronaca della Novalesa*, V, 18.
43 Geoffrey Malaterra, *De rebus gestis Rogerii*, III, 12.
44 Geoffrey Malaterra, *De rebus gestis Rogerii*, II, 46.
45 Geoffrey Malaterra, *De rebus gestis Rogerii*, III, 30.
46 F. Delle Donne, 'Giorgio d'Antiochia', in *Dizionario biografico degli Italiani*, vol. 55 (Rome, 2000), pp. 347–50.
47 On that occasion, the Rossanesi also killed the captains of the ships. *Vita di san Nilo*, chapter 60.
48 Von Falkenhausen, *La dominazione bizantina nell'Italia meridionale*, p. 102.
49 *Vita di san Nilo*, chapter 70.
50 Mandalà, 'The Martyrdom of Yūḥannā, Physician of Ibn Abī 'l-Ḥusayn Ruler of the Island of Sicily', pp. 93–94.
51 *Book of Gifts and Rarities (Kitāb al-Hadāyā wa al-Tuḥaf): Selections Compiled in the Fifteenth Century from an Eleventh-Century Manuscript on Gifts and Treasures*, trans. G. al Ḥijjāwī al-Qaddūmī (Cambridge, MA, 1996), pp. 91–94.
52 Geoffrey Malaterra, *De rebus gestis Rogerii*, III, 30.
53 BAS, vol. 2, pp. 293–94.
54 BAS, vol. 2, p. 54.
55 For Christians in Val Demone and Petralia, see Geoffrey Malaterra, *De rebus gestis Rogerii*, II, 14, 20, 45; and Amatus of Montecassino, *Ystoire de li Normant*, V, 25.
56 Ibn Ḥawqal, *Kitab Surat al-Ard*, ed. J. H. Kramers, 2 vols. (Leiden, 1938–1939), vol. 1, p. 129.
57 *Annales Barenses*, p. 53, year 1003.
58 *Historia et laudes SS. Sabae et Macarii*, chapter 6, p. 14.
59 *Synaxarium Ecclesiae Constantinopolitanae, Propylaeum Ad AASS Novembris*, ed. H. Delehaye (Brussels, 1902), pp. 72–74.
60 Ursus was captured by the Muslims during his pilgrimage to the Holy Land. *Hystoria de via et recuperatione Antiochiae atque Ierusolymarum (olim Tudebodus imitatus et continuatus). I Normanni d'Italia alla prima Crociata in una cronaca cassinese*, ed. E. D'Angelo (Florence, 2009), pp. 105–8.
61 Italian translation in *Regesti dei documenti dell'Italia meridionale*, p. 508, chapter 5.
62 BAS, vol. 1, pp. 487, 490.
63 Martin, *Guerre, accords et frontières*, p. 212, chapter 24.
64 Italian translation in *Regesti dei documenti dell'Italia meridionale*, pp. 507–8, chapter 3.
65 *Vita Antonini abbatis Surrentini*, chapter 24.
66 John the Deacon, *Vita Sancti Gregorii Magni*, in *Patrologia Latina*, vol. 75 (Paris 1849), column 233.
67 V. Von Falkenhausen, 'Costantino l'Africano', in *Dizionario biografico degli Italiani*, vol. 30 (Rome, 1984), pp. 320-24.
68 Geoffrey Malaterra, *De rebus gestis*, III, 30.
69 Geoffrey Malaterra, *De rebus gestis*, IV, 6.
70 Orderic Vitalis, *Historia ecclesiastica*, ed. M. Chibnall (Oxford, 1969), vol. 4, 22; A. Guillou – K. Tchérémissinoff, 'Note sur la culture arabe e la culture slave dans le Katepanat d'Italie (Xe-XIe siècles)', *Mélanges de l'Ecole française de Rome. Moyen-Age, Temps modernes* 88, 2 (1976), p. 680; A. Guillou, 'Italie méridionale byzantine ou Byzantins en Italie méridionale?', *Byzantion* 44 (1974), p.154.

71 BAS, vol. 1, pp. 370–71.
72 BAS, vol. 1, p. 421.
73 Eadmer, *Vita Anselmi*, ed. R. W. Southern (London, 1962), p. 111; Gregory VII, *Registrum*, p. 272.
74 Peters, *Joannes Messor*, pp. 8–11; Acconcia Longo, 'S. Giovanni Terista', pp. 145–48.

11 Encounters

Truces, pacts, and diplomatic missions

In antiquity as in the Middle Ages, a way to ensure that the defeated would comply with treaties was hostage-giving, a practice also adopted by Christians and Saracens in Early Medieval Italy. On several occasions during the Muslim campaigns in Sicily, the faithful of Christ gave hostages to gain a truce. To end the attacks of the Emir of Bari, Sawdān, the Prince of Benevento, Adelchis (854–878), gave his daughter and other persons to the Muslim ruler. Although Emperor Louis II subsequently conquered the Apulian city, Sawdān did not harm the girl; rather, he seems to have preserved her as a bargaining chip. Indeed, as he was barricaded in a tower, surrounded by Christians, he succeeded in gaining the protection of the ruler of Benevento in exchange for the release of his still virgin daughter.[1] In the following centuries, it was the Muslims' turn to give hostages. To avoid the rebellion of subjugated regions, the Normans utilized hostage-taking in Sicily in the eleventh century.[2] The Norman kings preferred to give the government of conquered Tunisian cities to local people, but, to ensure their loyalty, they held hostage one of their relatives.[3] In one case, however, this hostage method failed. To ensure the governor of Sfax's obedience, King William held his father hostage but hanged him when the governor, at the instigation of his father, rebelled and killed all the Christians living in that city.[4]

There is also an example of a prisoner turned into a hostage. Around 1015 a fleet of Pisan and Genoese ships defeated Mujāhid, the emir of Denia (Spain); among those captured on that occasion was Alī, Mujāhid's young son. Almost everyone was ransomed, excepting the boy, who was most likely detained by the Pisans to deter his father from conducting raids in the upper Tyrrhenian Sea. Alī remained with the Christians for sixteen years, adapting to his new environment so well that he adopted his hosts' customs, language, and religion. The Pisans found him so valuable that they sent him to the German Emperor Henry II as a hostage. He, however, did not stay at the German court for long, as the sovereign returned him to the custody of a Pisan family. In 1031, Mujāhid finally managed to gain his son's release.[5]

A more usual practice to end hostilities or to gain non-aggression treaties was to give tribute. In addition to the hostages, the Prince of Benevento, Adelchis, paid Sawdān a sum of money. The abbot of Montecassino had to resort to the same method in order 'to mitigate the ferocity' of that emir of Bari.[6] Probably influenced by his hatred for the Neapolitans, is, on the other hand, the information reported by Erchempert that a Muslim leader had ordered his previous allies, the Neapolitans, to give him some girls, along with horses and weapons, to stop his assaults against Naples.[7] Closer to reality is the mention that, in the mid-tenth century, to persuade the Saracens to renounce their siege of the city, the Neapolitans accepted the Muslims' demand to hand over all their precious objects to their assailants.[8] In 991, on the occasion of a Saracen incursion into the surroundings of Amalfi, the duke of that city, fearing to provoke a violent reaction, rejected the advice of his fellow citizens, who were eager to fight the enemy, and instead offered the attacking Muslims gifts to persuade them to leave the area.[9]

Deeply affected by Muslim campaigns in Apulia in the 920s and probably fearing encirclement by an alliance between these adversaries and the Bulgarians, in 931/932 the Byzantines obtained a long truce by paying the Saracens a large amount of gold.[10] This practice was often adopted in Calabria in the tenth century and was still used around 1020.[11] In 942/943 some Sicilian Christian rebels used a monk for such a task,[12] while in mid-tenth century the inhabitants of a part of Byzantine southern Italy made a peace agreement with the Muslims in the same way on their own initiative.[13] At the beginning of the eleventh century Allah's followers besieged Salerno because its inhabitants refused to give them the customary tribute. Thankfully for the defenders, a group of Norman pilgrims defeated the assailants, thus ending that forced payment.[14] In turn, the Sicilian Muslims had to pay tributes to the Normans on several occasions to stop their attacks.[15]

Although it was a choice attributable to several reasons, according to a letter of Pope Leo III, already in 812 the Neapolitans showed their desire not to fight the Muslims when they refused to help the Byzantine commander of Sicily against them.[16] In the second half of the ninth century and at the beginning of the tenth, the need to keep the trade routes through the Tyrrhenian Sea free led the dukes of Naples, Amalfi, and Gaeta to establish non-aggression treaties with the Muslims. Thanks to these agreements, in 872 Amalfitan merchants could, for instance, trade in a city on the coast of northern Africa, while the Muslims were there equipping a fleet to attack Salerno.[17] In the case of the Neapolitans, they also provided logistical support to the Saracens. In a letter dating to 870, Emperor Louis II complained to the Byzantine Emperor Basil that Naples seemed to have become Palermo[18] or Africa.

> Indeed, the Neapolitans give the infidels weapons, food supplies, and other aids and lead them along the coasts of all our empire... so that Naples does not appear to be different from Palermo or Africa. And when our soldiers chase the Saracens, these, to escape from them, take refuge in Naples, and stay there hidden as long as they like, and then suddenly go back to their raids.[19]

The correspondence of Pope John VIII (872–882) shows how the pontiff condemned the agreements made between the Christians from southern Italy and the Muslims in extremely harsh terms. He sometimes excommunicated those who did not obey his injunctions, with, however, few results. For example, in 879 the pontiff reproached the duke of Amalfi for keeping his agreement with the faithful of Islam and breaking his oath to protect the Latium coast against their incursions. For this task, adds the pope, the Amalfitans had received a considerable sum of money, of which John VIII demanded restitution.[20] To persuade the Neapolitans to end their agreements with the Saracens, the pontiff did not hesitate to order the decapitation of Neapolitan soldiers who had been captured by his allies, to support financially the faction opposing the current duke of Naples, and to back his brother, the Bishop of Naples, Athanasius II (876-898), in acquiring the leadership of the duchy. To John VIII's great disappointment, the bishop-duke also established alliances with Allah's followers and employed them in his army.[21] These relationships with the Muslims guaranteed indispensable advantages to the Neapolitans. The destruction of the Muslim base on the Garigliano River in 915, however, changed the geopolitical situation of the area, and, in 936/940, the Neapolitans and their neighbors from Capua and Benevento swore to help each other against the Saracens.[22]

There is no information about the pacts between the Muslims and the city-states of the Tyrrhenian coast or how these were formed. The historian 'Ibn 'al 'Atir, however, mentions some details about an agreement concerning a mosque built in Reggio Calabria during a Muslim campaign in that area in 952/953. Since the faithful of Islam foretold that they could not hold the city for a long time, they wanted to protect the right to practice their own faith for those Saracens who would remain in Reggio Calabria. Christians were forbidden to enter the mosque even though Muslim prisoners (including those converted to Christianity) took refuge in that building. There were also threats of retaliation against churches in Sicily and Africa if the followers of Christ should damage the building. Though the mosque was, in fact, destroyed a few years later by a Byzantine officer, it is unknown whether there were reprisals.[23]

> 'Al Hasan returned to Reggio where he built a large mosque in the middle of the city. A minaret was erected in one of the corners. He established with the Rūms that the Muslims were allowed to keep this mosque open, to pray and listen to the mu'addin's call; no Christian would have entered it, even though some Muslim prisoners who professed their faith or who had converted to Christianity had taken refuge there. He also stated that if the Christians would take away one stone from that mosque, all their churches would have been destroyed in Sicily and Africa. These covenants were observed with submission and reverence.[24]

Information about diplomatic missions between Christians and Muslims is also available. In 813 Saracen ambassadors of northern Africa's ruler went to Sicily to make a peace treaty with the Byzantines.[25] Around 855, the emir of Bari sent a legate to Salerno, who was welcomed with all honors and hosted in the bishop's palace despite the strong opposition of the city's prelate.[26] In the tenth century the duke of Amalfi sent a precious gift to the caliph of Cairo's Jewish vizir, who was from Apulia, in order to maintain good relationships with the authorities of an area frequented by Amalfitan merchants.[27] At the beginning of his rule, the Duke of Venice, Peter II Orseolo (991–1008), sent legates to the most important Christian and Muslim rulers in order to establish friendly relationships with them.[28] Muslim and Christian sources both mention the existence of peace agreements between Roger of Hauteville and the governor of northwestern Africa. According to the biographer of the Norman leader, he refused the Pisans' offer to occupy a city that had been taken by the Tuscans, in order to preserve his friendship with the Muslim ruler of that region.[29]

The most famous and best documented diplomatic mission between Christians and Muslims was organized in 905/906 by the Marquise of Tuscany, Bertha, who sent gifts and a letter to the caliph of Baghdad. More precisely, one should talk about her attempt to enter into an agreement with the Muslim ruler; the caliph's reply never arrived because the messenger died on the return journey. Although the marquise's epistle does not clarify what her request was (it was reported verbally) and the gifts brought to the caliph were not comparable to the usual standards of his court, this exchange provides a fascinating glimpse through an unexpected window, allowing one to see the width of the marquise's ambitions and some features of that period's culture. Brought to Baghdad by a Muslim eunuch (we have already mentioned him), the missive was translated from Latin to Greek by a European Christian and then from Greek to Arabic by a Middle-Eastern Christian. Bertha wrote to the caliph that she had decided to contact him after discovering that he ruled over the governor of northwestern Africa and, exaggerating her power, invited the caliph to establish peaceful relations with her, perhaps hoping to create an alliance against the Byzantines.[30]

Trade

Commercial exchanges between Christians and Muslims took place as well, and slaves were the most precious commodity. Explaining which products came from the West, a Muslim geographer added that 'Slav, Rūm, and Lombard slaves are brought from the sea of the West'.[31] The biography of Elias the Younger (ca. 823–ca. 903) indicates that Christian subjects of the 'House of Islam' bought their coreligionists, who had been captured by the Saracens, and kept them as their slaves.[32] The account by the Novalesa's chronicler about his relative who had fallen into the hands of Allah's followers is rather obscure, but it suggests that even the inhabitants of Piedmont had sometimes been involved in the purchase of Christians captured by the Muslims.[33] The lack of comment by Elias's biographer could be interpreted as proof that it was not an unusual practice.

While considering possible exaggerations and the writers' desire to color some stories, these episodes are confirmed by archival sources. According to a document from 928, a Neapolitan bought two slaves named Rose and Leo from the Saracens. Their origin is not recorded, but their names suggest that they were Christians.[34] Around 867 two Gaetans (one of them a clerk) purchased some fellow citizens from the Muslims and freed them after receiving their estates as reward; the bishop of Gaeta unsuccessfully attempted to obtain the return of those lands to the legitimate owners.[35] In 873 Pope John VIII wrote to some Sardinian aristocrats, admonishing them not to sell Christian prisoners who had been freed from Allah's followers; these Christians probably had been liberated by Byzantine soldiers who later sold them to the Sardinians.[36] The believers of Islam did not obtain slaves only through their raids. According to Erchempert, the Byzantines sold Lombards to them.[37]

To demonstrate that this account was not a complete invention, there is a section of a peace treaty from 836 between the Principality of Benevento and the Duchy of Naples, which had become independent from Constantinople a few years earlier. This treaty prohibited the Neapolitans from purchasing Lombards and above all from selling them overseas, that is, to Muslims and Byzantines. The Beneventans, on the other hand, were forbidden to do the same with those who worked in the area owned by the Lombards and the Neapolitans.[38] These prohibitions were probably not very effective. The fines were not very high and those who had been forced to pay them had been able to recover their losses with some additional sales.

News about the slave trade had circulated before. In a letter to Pope Hadrian from 778, Charlemagne states that some Romans sold Christians to the Muslims. According to the pontiff, if this were true, it happened without his knowledge. Moreover, the pope added that it was the 'Greeks' who had bought slaves from the Lombards.[39] A reference to this practice is also present in one of Pope Hadrian's letters to Charlemagne from 783, in which the pontiff accused two of his adversaries of having sold some Ravennati to the 'pagans'.[40]

The Venetians played a significant role in this type of trade from the eighth century onward. The biographer of Pope Zachary (741–752) reports that the Venetians used to buy Christian slaves in Rome's market and then sell them to the Muslims in Africa. Since the pope could not allow baptized people to suffer such a fate, he bought those unfortunate individuals from the Venetians and freed them.[41] Trade relationships with the Muslims were so important to the Venetian economy that, by prohibiting the sale of slaves, timber, and weapons to the Saracens, Duke Peter IV Candiano (959–976) antagonized many members of the Venetian elite, who were neither persuaded by the ruler's moral scruples nor afraid of the Byzantine threat of burning the ships that traveled to Muslim territories carrying such goods. Most of the wealthy families refused to subscribe to the ban, and the duke, to reach a sufficient number of signatories, had to seek the support of the middle-low-ranking people. These prohibitions increased the opposition to Peter IV Candiano to such an extent that he was killed in a bloody rebellion. The permission to leave, granted to three ships directed to Libya and Tunisia with a load of wooden axles and other wooden objects (when the prohibition of trading with Muslims was issued), further emphasizes the importance of these activities to the Venetians.[42]

This, after all, was not the first time the Venetians had been forced to face the prohibition to travel to Muslim territories. According to the text that recounts the relocation of Saint Mark's relics from Alexandria to Venice in 827/828, at that time the Venetian duke forbade his subjects to undertake that kind of journey, in accordance with the orders of Constantinople. According to the anonymous author, the Venetian ships, however, did not go to the Egyptian city to transgress that order, but because a divine wind had pushed them there. Having solved the problem of the presence of his compatriots in a Muslim land through this narrative strategy, the writer, most likely a churchman, demonstrates that he shares the market-oriented mentality of his homeland. Indeed, he adds that those Venetians carried out business in Alexandria. Since they were there (allegedly not by their own will), it would have been a waste of time and money not to take advantage of their time in one of the most important Mediterranean trading centers.

> Therefore, after the Saracens had invaded the whole Egypt and Alexandria, Leo, who had become Roman emperor, sent orders to the various regions of his empire that no one was ever to approach the land of Egypt to trade. This order, sent out all around, was also referred to the Venetians, and Justinian, who was duke of Venice at that time, confirming his emperor's will, reiterated the same order to his citizens. But the Venetians, as usual, were searching for new markets; while some of them sailed offshore with loaded ships in order to go overseas, due to the divine will it happened that a favorable wind blew and they were almost involuntarily brought to Alexandria, a deed which they did not dare to do on their own initiative because of the orders of the rulers... The Venetians were busy in doing their business in that city.[43]

The reference to a 'ship of Venice with merchandise' at Cairo in 1026, the purchase of Egyptian aloe by Venetians in 1071, and the comment of a Jewish merchant about those traders' behavior in Alexandria that year represent further evidence of Venetians' trade activities in Egypt. The fact that some of them were killed by pirates on the Nile River around 1026 underlines how these locations could sometimes be very dangerous.[44] One cannot rule out that the four great Venetian ships carrying spices and sunk in an unknown place in 1017 were coming from Muslim territories.[45]

Amalfitans too played a significant role in these trade ventures. Merchants from that Campanian city are recorded on the coast of northern Africa and in Cairo in the ninth and tenth centuries.[46] Amalfi, says William of Apulia, 'is a very rich and populous city. None is richer in silver, clothes, and gold, which come from innumerable regions. Many sailors, able to open their ways through the sea and the sky, live in that city. Various goods from Alexandria and Antioch come there. Its inhabitants cross many seas. They know the Arabs, the Libyans, the Sicilians and the Africans and are well known throughout almost all the world, because they bring their goods and love to bring back those which they buy'.[47]

Amalfitans' presence in Egypt is further confirmed by a Near-Eastern text. According to this work, in 996, during a period of strong tension between Allah's followers and the Byzantines in the eastern Mediterranean, some inhabitants of Misr (Old Cairo) accused the Campanian merchants residing in that city of having set fire to some Muslim ships; to avenge that affront, they attacked the Amalfitans, pillaged their properties, and killed 160 of them. An officer of the caliph of Cairo ordered them to stop the killings and the looting, to return the stolen goods, and he harshly punished those responsible for the aggression, thus acknowledging the importance of the Amalfitan community to the city's economy.[48]

The persecutions against Christians by the Caliph of Cairo al-Hakim (996–1021) likely prevented the Amalfitan merchants from continuing their activities in Egypt in that period. The reference, however, to the arrival of an Amalfitan ship carrying honey and silk in that area around 1050 indicates that, after the 'storm', the Campanian merchants resumed their usual activities in the region.[49]

The Amalfitans traded in Muslim Spain as well. Having acknowledged their usefulness to commerce, in 942 some Cordoban merchants invited the Amalfitans to settle in their city, where they were put under the protection of the local authorities. The Amalfitans brought many precious goods with them, among which were brocades and purple clothes. The caliph of Cordoba was allowed to buy most of them at half price, probably as thanks for a friendly welcome. The Cordobans, emphasizes a Muslim author, praised the Amalfitans' activities and took great advantage of them.[50]

Pisa too had trade relationships with the Muslims in Sicily and Tunisia during the eleventh century. The Pisan expedition against al-Mahdīya in 1087 was not due exclusively to the Pisans' wish to fight the enemies of Christ. Indeed, on that occasion, the Pisans wanted to punish the Saracens of that area, who were guilty of damaging and offending the Pisans who went there to trade. For the same reason, a few years earlier, their ships carried out a symbolic raid against Palermo by breaking the chain located at the entrance of the city's harbor.[51] Since Calabria is very close to Sicily, that region suffered several attacks by Sicilian Muslims. The relationships between the inhabitants of those two areas, however, were not always of that sort. In fact, some merchants from Calabria profited from their proximity by trading on the island. For instance, in the tenth century, a Byzantine commander of that region speculated by selling foodstuffs at a high price to Allah's followers.

> He bought cheaply all the resources which the inhabitants (of Calabria) needed for living, and then sold them at a very high price to the Saracens, who, given the indigence and hunger in the cities, agreed to pay them with the gold they owned.[52]

The great production of raw silk in Calabria might be interpreted as a response to the high demand for that good by the Sicilian Muslims.[53]

Usually, the Saracens preferred to utilize Christian and Jewish merchants. Some of their coreligionists, however, also carried out such activities. Indeed, there is evidence of some Muslims attending Rome's markets around 800.[54]

Shortly after 1100, a monk recorded disapprovingly that the faithful of Islam were a constant presence in Pisa.[55] Ibn Ḥawqal praised the quality of the linen fabrics manufactured in Naples, claiming to have seen them personally in that city, a detail which suggests the presence of Muslim merchants there.[56] Although characterized by some exaggerations, the description by al-Turtusi attests the presence of Muslim merchants in a Lombard city as well.[57]

Muslim objects found or mentioned in Christian territories might have arrived in several ways and therefore cannot simply be interpreted as coming directly from Muslim lands. The fact that such objects have been found mostly in those areas just mentioned, however, suggests that these artifacts may corroborate the evidence recorded in the written sources. Muslim coins have been discovered in Venice and in various sites in the South of the Peninsula.[58] In this respect, it is worth recalling that some southern Italian cities produced Muslim gold coins in their mints because they were considered a particularly reliable currency. Early medieval Islamic ceramics have been found in Pisa.[59] Precious objects, probably produced in the 'House of Islam', are recorded in an Amalfitan testament from 1025.[60] Two crystal jugs bearing the name of al-'Azīz (975–996), the Caliph of Cairo, currently preserved in the treasury of St. Mark's Basilica (Venice), were probably bought by Venetian merchants after some Turkish mercenaries looted the caliph's palace in 1062.[61] Finally, one may not exclude that the bag of pepper mentioned in a mid-ninth-century Venetian document was purchased in Muslim lands.[62]

Notes

1 Erchempert, *Piccola Storia dei Longobardi di Benevento / Ystoriola Longobardorum Beneventum*, chapter 29; *Chronicon Salernitanum*, chapter 108.
2 *Chronica Monasterii Casinensis*, p. 378; William of Apulia, *La Geste de Robert Guiscard*, III, line 340.
3 BAS, vol. 2, p. 210.
4 BAS, vol. 2, p. 210.
5 M. J. Rubiera Mata, *La taifa de Denia* (Alicante, 1985), pp. 67–70, 95–98.
6 *Chronica monasterii Casinensis*, I, 35, pp. 96–97.
7 Erchempert, *Piccola Storia dei Longobardi di Benevento / Ystoriola Longobardorum Beneventum*, chapter 49.
8 A Neapolitan source mentions this. *Ex miraculis Sancti Agrippini*, chapter 11, pp. 464–65.
9 *Sermo de virtute Costantii*, chapter 10, p. 1017.
10 A. Metcalfe, *The Muslims of Medieval Italy* (Edinburgh, 2009), p. 49.
11 A. Cilento, *Potere e monachesimo: ceti dirigenti e mondo monastico nella Calabria bizantina: secoli IX–XI* (Florence, 2000), pp. 23–24. According to the Anglo-Norman chronicler Orderic Vitalis, under Pope Benedict VIII (1012–1024), North-African Muslims went to Apulia and Calabria every year and required a tribute from the peoples of those regions. Orderic Vitalis, *Historia ecclesiastica*, vol. 3, p. 56.
12 The source is not clear, and therefore one cannot understand exactly who those Christians were. BAS, vol. 1, pp. 416, 419.

13 Theophanes Continuatus, *Chronographia*, VI, 30, pp. 453–54.
14 Amatus of Montecassino, *Ystoire de li Normant*, I, 17.
15 Geoffrey Malaterra, *De rebus gestis Rogerii*, II, 45, IV, 16.
16 Leo III, *Epistolae*, number 6, pp. 96–97.
17 *Chronicon Salernitanum*, chapter 110.
18 In this period, Palermo was under Muslim rule.
19 *Chronicon Salernitanum*, chapter 107.
20 John VIII, *Registrum*, p. 194, number 217.
21 P. Bertolini, 'Atanasio', in *Dizionario biografico degli Italiani*, vol. 4 (Rome, 1962), pp. 510–18.
22 Martin, *Guerre, accords et frontières*, p. 218, chapter 2.
23 BAS, vol. 1, p. 291.
24 BAS, vol. 1, p. 421.
25 Leo III, *Epistolae*, number 8, pp. 99–100.
26 *Chronicon Salernitanum*, chapter 99.
27 R. Bonfil, *History and Folklore in a Medieval Jewish Chronicle: The Family Chronicle of Aḥima'az ben Paltiel* (Leiden, 2009), chapter 48.
28 John the Deacon, *Istoria Veneticorum*, IV, 31.
29 Geoffrey Malaterra, *De rebus gestis Rogerii*, IV, 3.
30 *Book of Gifts and Rarities*, pp. 91–94.
31 *I Cammini dell'Occidente. Il Mediterraneo tra i secoli IX e X. Ibn Khurdâdhbah, al-Muqaddasî, Ibn Hawqal*, Italian translation by A. Vanoli (Padua, 2001), p. 3.
32 *Vita di Sant'Elia il Giovane*, chapter 9.
33 *Cronaca di Novalesa*, V, 9.
34 *Regii Neapolitani Archivi Monumenta* (Naples, 1845), vol. 1, 1, number 13.
35 *Codex Diplomaticus Cajetanus*, vol. 1 (Montecassino, 1887), number 13.
36 McCormick, *Origins of the European Economy*, p. 948, number 625.
37 Erchempert, *Piccola Storia dei Longobardi di Benevento / Ystoriola Longobardorum Beneventum*, chapter 81.
38 Martin, *Guerre, accords et frontières*, pp. 188–89, chapters 3–4.
39 It seems that the Lombards did so out of hunger. *Codex Carolinus*, ed. W. Gundlach, MGH, *Epistolae*, vol. 3 (Berlin, 1892), number 59.
40 *Codex Carolinus*, number 75.
41 *Liber pontificalis*, vol. 1, p. 433.
42 That exception was made because of the merchants' 'poverty'. They, however, were forbidden to carry other types of timber. *Documenti relativi alla storia di Venezia anteriori al Mille*, ed. R. Cessi, 2 vols. (Padua, 1942–1943), vol. 2, numbers 41 and 49.
43 *Translatio Marci Evangelistae Venetias*, chapters 8–9.
44 *Vita s. Symeonis auctore Eberwino abbate S. Martinis Treveris*, in *Acta Sanctorum, Junii* (Antwerp, 1695), p. 91, chapters 10–11; D. Jacoby, 'Venetian commercial expansion in the Eastern Mediterranean, 8th–11th centuries', in *Byzantine Trade, 4th–12th Centuries: the Archaeology of Local, Regional, International Exchange*, ed. M. Mundell Mango (Farnham, 2009), pp. 383–84.
45 Thietmar of Merseburg, *Chronicon*, VII, 76.
46 *Chronicon Salernitanum*, chapter 110; *Codex Diplomaticus Cavensis*, vol. 2, number 300. In reality, in the latter source it is stated that an Amalfitan was at Cairo without saying why.
47 William of Apulia, *La Geste de Robert Guiscard*, III, lines 477–85.
48 C. Cahen, 'Un texte peu connu relatif au commerce oriental d'Amalfi au XIe siècle', *Archivio Storico per le Province Napoletane* 34 (1953–1954), pp. 3–8.
49 B. Figliuolo, 'Amalfi e il Levante nel Medioevo', in *I Comuni italiani nel regno crociato di Gerusalemme*, eds. G. Airaldi - B. Kedar (Genoa, 1986), pp. 584–85.
50 P. Skinner, *Medieval Amalfi and its Diaspora: 800–1250* (Oxford, 2013), p. 236.

51 Geoffrey Malaterra, *De rebus gestis Rogerii*, IV, 3, II, 34.
52 The emperor deposed him for having done that. John Scylitzes, *Synopsis historiarum*, ed. H. Thurn (Berlin-New York, 1972), p. 265.
53 Feniello, *Sotto il segno del leone*, p. 167.
54 McCormick, *Origins of the European Economy*, p. 885, number 232.
55 Donizo, *Vita di Matilde di Canossa*, I, lines. 1370–72, pp. 120–21.
56 BAS, vol. 1, pp. 24–25.
57 Mandalà, 'La Longobardia, i Longobardi e Pavia', p. 356.
58 McCormick, *Origins of the European Economy*, pp. 832–33; S. Gelichi, 'La storia di una nuova città attraverso l'archeologia: Venezia nell'alto Medioevo', in *Three Empires, Three Cities. Identity, Material Culture and Legitimacy in Venice, Ravenna and Rome, 750–1000*, ed. V. West-Harling (Turnhout, 2015), pp. 85–86.
59 G. Berti, S. Menchelli, 'Pisa: Ceramiche da cucina, da dispensa, da trasporto, dei secoli X–XV', *Archeologia Medievale* 25 (1998), pp. 330–33: K. R. Mathews, 'Plunder of war or objects of trade? The reuse and reception of Andalusi objects in medieval Pisa', *Journal of Medieval Iberian Studies*, 4 (2012), pp. 249–52.
60 Feniello, *Sotto il segno del leone*, pp. 152–53.
61 Jacoby, 'Venetian commercial expansion in the Eastern Mediterranean, 8th–11th centuries', p. 383.
62 *S. Lorenzo (853–1199)*, ed. F. Gaeta (Venice, 1959), number 1.

Conclusions

In Italy, during the first centuries of the Middle Ages, the clashes between Muslims and Christians were undoubtedly numerous and caused great human loss and destruction. It is therefore not surprising that the majority of the texts from that period, both Christian and Muslim, describe adversaries negatively. After all, what can one expect from descriptions of enemies who pillaged the authors' country and either killed or enslaved relatives and friends? It is from this point of view that these accounts must be understood. For this reason, it is necessary to give due consideration to the existence of a few nuances in these texts and to try to contextualize the most negative images of the 'other'. Moreover, several Christian authors do not depict the Muslims as evil incarnate and as the worst enemies of their compatriots. Actually, some Muslims proved to have humanitarian principles, that, on the contrary, several Christian rulers lacked. The latter were also guilty of having created the very conditions for the Saracens' victories. The presence of strong criticism directed towards those who had relationships with the Muslims that were not exclusively based on either rejection or elimination is proof of the existence among the Christians of different ways of dealing with the followers of Islam. When the roles were reversed, the same motifs characterized Muslim texts about this period. If one considers these negative descriptions and violent behaviors as innate qualities of either the Muslims or the Christians and subsequently portrays this period as exclusively marked by a clash of civilizations, one will reach a misleading interpretation influenced by motivations that have nothing to do with history. At the same time, such texts cannot be labeled as exaggerations or complete inventions. One should not conclude that there were no differences between Muslims or Christians either. The available sources do not allow us to reconstruct the interactions between them accurately, but the windows they open to that period indicate that, first and foremost, in early medieval Italy there was not a perpetual state of belligerence between the faithful of the two religions. Alongside ambassadors and a few pilgrims and travelers, there were both Christians and Muslims who sought to profit from the economic opportunities offered in the Mediterranean area. Information circulated with commodities, thus permitting the 'other' to become a little better known and, sometimes, appreciated. Obviously, relationships were not always harmonious. In moments of tension, there were those who, because of envy or hatred, underlined the differences or, as was the case with the Amalfitans in Egypt, painted everyone with the same brush, scapegoating them. That same episode, however, also shows that not everybody shared those attitudes and that the Muslim authorities strongly condemned them.

Appendix

Primary sources

Works composed by the vanquished and by subjects ruled by the 'other' are not available. All the sources about Christians and Muslims in early medieval Italy were therefore produced in areas that suffered the attacks of the other. The letter by the Syracusan monk Theodosius about the Muslim conquest of his city (878) and his subsequent captivity in Palermo and the account about the killing of the Christian physician John in Palermo at the end of the tenth century are relevant exceptions.

For ninth-century southern Italy there are some chronicles written by authors who lived in that period: the anonymous *Cronicae Sancti Benedicti Casinensis* (*Chronicles of Saint Benedict of Cassino*) and the *Ystoriola Longobardorum Beneventum degentium* (*Little History of the Lombards of Benevento*) by the Cassinese monk Erchempert. Important for that epoch and rich in details is also the *Chronicon Salernitanum* (*Salernitan Chronicle*), composed by an unknown author around 970. The chronicle by Andreas of Bergamo (second half of the ninth century) reports relevant information about Louis II's campaigns in the South. Brief annals in Greek, the *Annales Barenses* (*Annals of Bari*) and the *Annales* by Lupus Protospatarius contain useful chronological data for the ninth through the eleventh centuries.

Even though they are focused on a specific period and areas, the biographies of the Calabrian and Sicilian saints (the latter fled to the Italian peninsula) contain relevant information about Sicily and especially Calabria. Most of these works were written by their disciples a few years after the death of their masters, who are: Elias the Younger (ca. 823–ca. 903), Elias Spelaeota (ca. 860–ca. 960), Sabas (ca. 910–ca. 991), Neilos of Rossano (ca. 910–ca. 1004), Gregory of Cassano (ca. 930–ca. 1002), Luke of Demenna (tenth century), Vitalis of Castronovo (tenth century), Nicodemus of Kellarana (tenth/ eleventh century), John Terista (tenth/eleventh century), and Philaretos of Seminara (d. 1076). Texts on the saints' miracles and their relics, which contain information about the Saracens in the ninth and the tenth centuries, were written in Campania as well. The most relevant accounts are those concerning Saint Severinus (Naples), Saint Agrippinus and Saint Januarius (Naples), Saint Euphebius (Naples), Saint Constantius (Capri), Saint Antoninus (Sorrento), and Saint Martin of Monte Massico (northwestern Campania).

The main source for the Norman conquest of Sicily is the chronicle by the Norman Geoffrey Malaterra, who moved to southern Italy and described Roger of Hauteville's campaigns. Some information about these events can be found in the biography of Robert Guiscard by William of Apulia and in the *Ystoire de li Normant* (*History of the Normans*) by the Cassinese monk Amatus.

For central Italy in the ninth and tenth centuries there are the chronicle of Benedict of St. Andreas of Soratte (end of the tenth century), the text of the destruction of the abbey of Farfa by Abbot Hugh (ca. 972–1038), and the biographies of Pope Sergius II (844–847) and Pope Leo IV (847–855).

For the northern part of the Peninsula there are the works by Liudprand of Cremona (ca. 920–972), the chronicle of the abbey of Novalesa (composed around the mid-eleventh century), and a Pisan text on the expedition against al-Mahdīya (1087). The *Istoria Veneticorum* (*History of the Venetians*) by John the Deacon (beginning of the eleventh century) reports some data about the Muslim raids in the Adriatic Sea and the clashes between the Venetians and Allah's followers in the ninth and at the beginning of the eleventh centuries. The text about the transfer of Saint Mark's relics from Alexandria to Venice in ca. 828 focuses on just a single episode but contains precious information.

Except for a letter of Emperor Louis II to the Byzantine Emperor Basil in ca. 870, that of the Syracusan monk Theodosius, that of the Patriarch of Constantinople Photios to the Calabrian archbishop Leo, and that of the Marquise of Tuscany Bertha to a caliph in 905/906, the epistles referring to the faithful of Islam are those of the pontiffs, especially those of Pope John VIII (872–882).

As for the archival sources, only donations and sales of properties in the territories under Christian rule are available and therefore contain very little information useful for this study.

Besides the already noted lack of archival sources in Islamic Sicily, no historical Muslim work written in the early Middle Ages has survived. Indeed, the information about that period is present in texts written by authors who lived two or three centuries after that epoch and probably are summaries of works that went missing; in most cases they are just lists of events, seldom reporting detailed descriptions. The most important of these accounts is a history of the world titled *al-Kāmil fī l-ta'rīkh* (*The Perfect History*, i.e., *The Complete History*) by 'Alī ibn al-Athīr (ca. 1160–ca. 1230) who lived in the Middle East. Some information about the faithful of Islam and the Christians of Italy in that period is also contained in geographical works. The most relevant of them is the *Kitāb al-masālik wa l-mamālik* (*Book of Routes and Realms*) by the Iraqi traveler and geographer Ibn Ḥawqal who visited Sicily around 973. Homesickness for his native land and resentment for Christians are sometimes present in some of the brief texts in verse by Ibn Ḥamdîs, who was born in Sicily around 1056, moved to Andalusia in 1078 because of the Norman conquest of the island, and then to the Maghreb. A detailed description of the conditions of the Sicilian Muslims under the Normans' rule in the late twelfth century is recorded in the Spanish writer Ibn Jubayr's account of his travel to Mecca, because between late 1184 and the beginning of the following year he had to stay in Sicily for a few weeks after the ship that was taking him home sunk.

Timeline

827. The followers of Allah begin the conquest of Sicily.

827/828. Venetian merchants steal the relics of Saint Mark in Alexandria and take them to Venice.

846. Muslim attack upon Rome. The basilicas of Saint Peter and of Saint Paul are pillaged.

840s. The Saracens create the emirates of Taranto and Bari.

871. Emperor Louis II conquers Bari, thus ending the Muslim rule over that city.

872. The faithful of Islam besiege Salerno without success.

875. The Saracens pillage and burn Comacchio.

878. The followers of Allah conquer Syracuse.

881. The Muslims destroy the monastery of Saint Vincent at Volturno.

883. The Saracens plunder and burn Montecassino.

902. The faithful of Islam take Taormina. Emir Ibrāhīm II dies during the siege of Cosenza.

906. The followers of Allah destroy the abbey of Novalesa.

915. Elimination of the Muslim base near the Garigliano River.

934/935. The Saracens pillage Genoa.

973. Destruction of the Muslim base of Fraxinetum.

982. The faithful of Allah defeat Emperor Otto II in Calabria.

1002. The Venetians end the Muslim siege of Bari.

1015/1016. A fleet of Pisan and Genoese ships defeat the Emir of Denia (Spain) Mujāhid.

1041–1042. Campaign of the Byzantine general Maniakes in Sicily.
1061. First expedition of Roger of Hauteville in Sicily.
1072. The Normans conquer Palermo.
1087. The Pisans and their allies attack al-Mahdīya.
1091. Completion of the Norman conquest of Sicily.

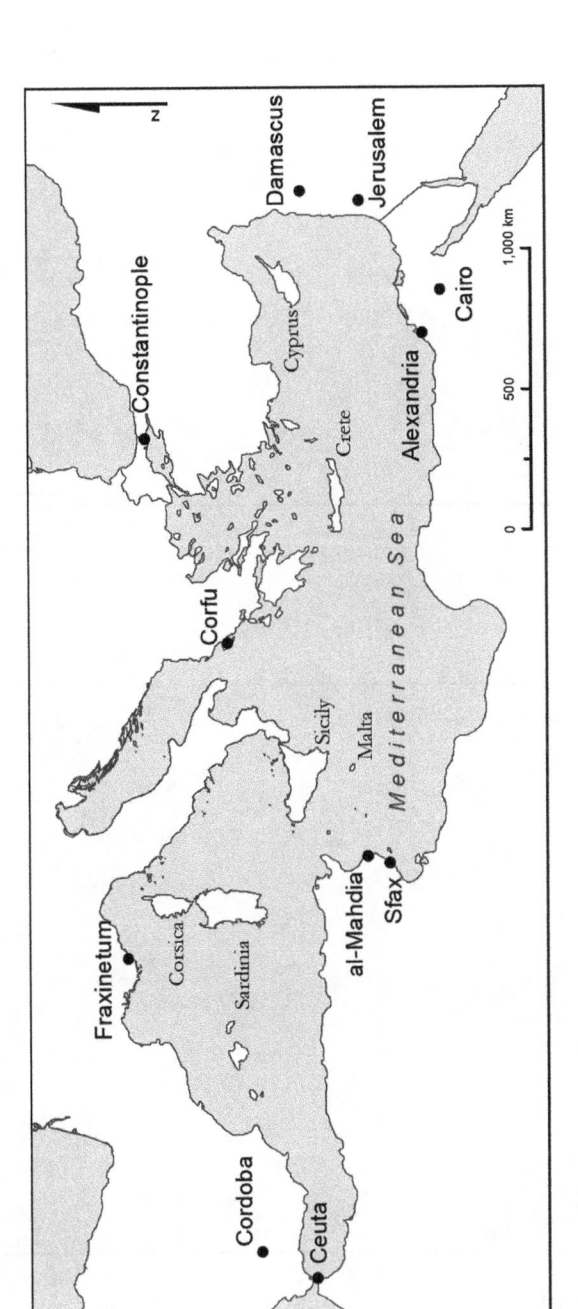

Map 1 The Mediterranean Area.

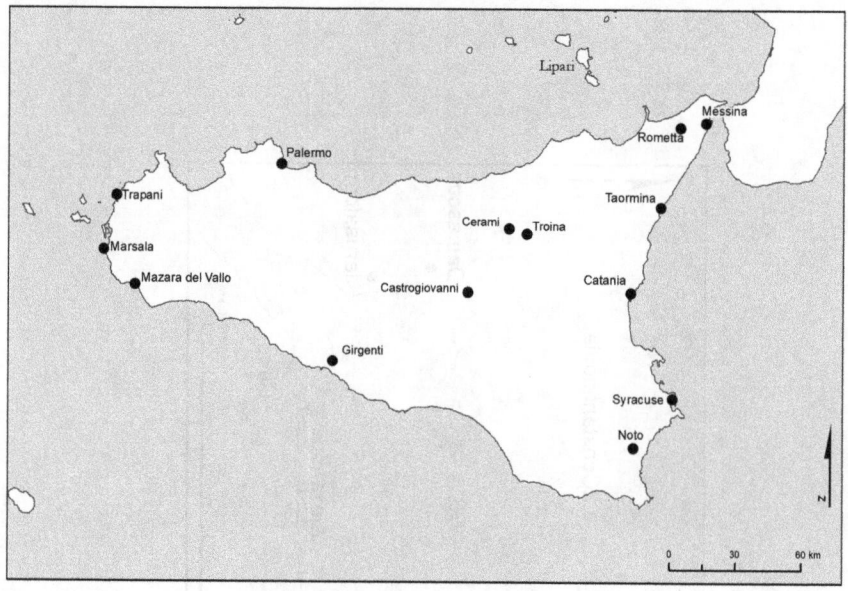

Map 2 Sicily.

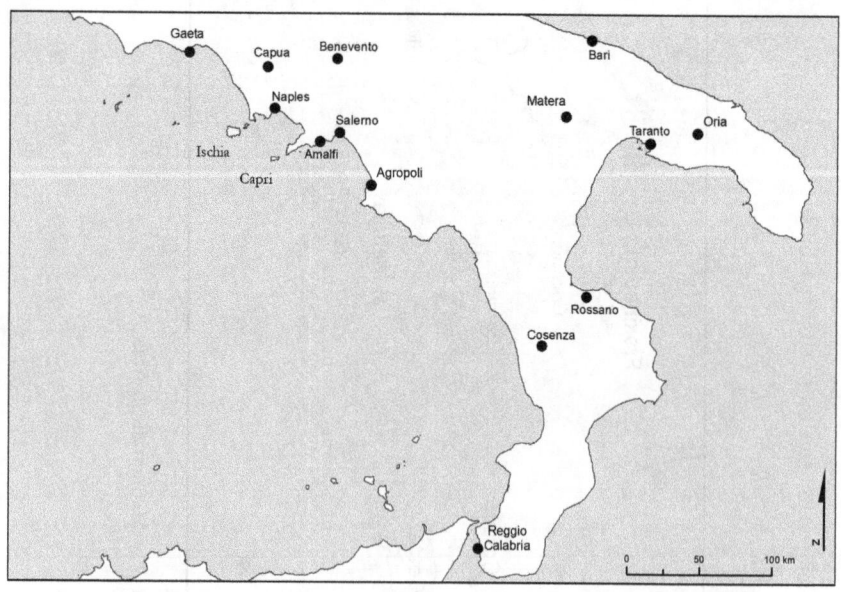

Map 3 Southern Italy.

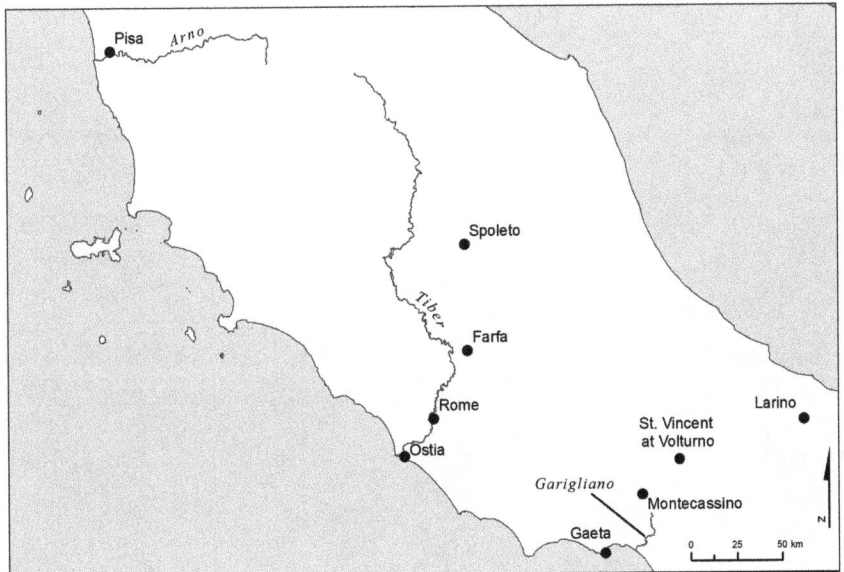

Map 4 Central Italy.

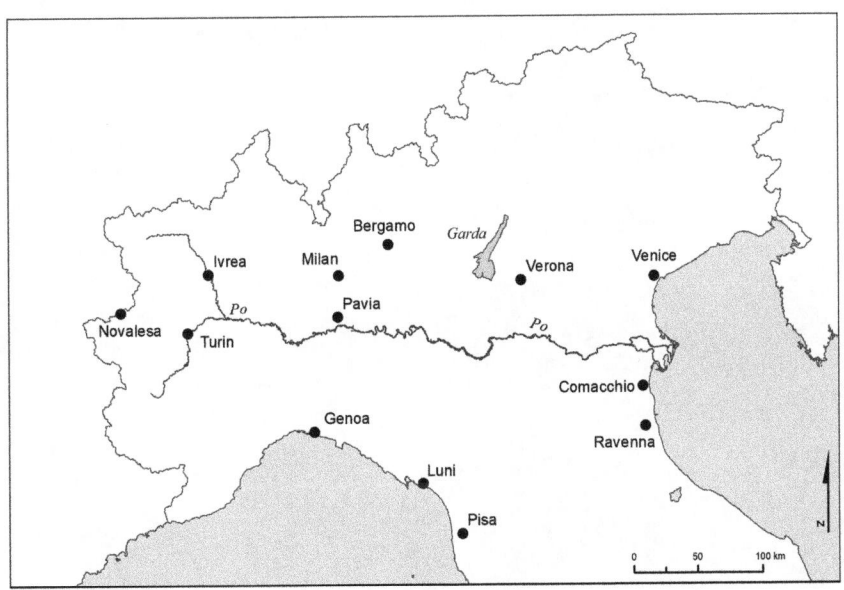

Map 5 Northern Italy.

Bibliography

Primary sources

Acta Fortunati, Caii, et Anthae, in *Acta Sanctorum, Augusti*, XXVIII (Antwerp, 1743), p. 168.

Agnellus of Ravenna, *The Book of Pontiffs of the Church of Ravenna*, trans. D. Mauskopf Deliyannis (Washington, DC, 2004).

Amatus of Montecassino, *Ystoire de li Normant*, ed. V. de Bartholomeis (Rome, 1935). Another edition in Amatus of Montecassino, *Ystoire de li Normant*, ed. M. Guéret-Laferté (Paris, 2011).

Anastasius Bibliothecarius, *Collectanea*, in *Patrologia Latina*, vol. 129 (Paris, 1853), columns 553–704.

Andreas of Bergamo, *Historia*, in *Italian Carolingian Historical and Poetic Texts*, edition and English translation by L. A. Berto (Pisa, 2016), pp. 66–95.

Annales Barenses, ed. G. Pertz, in MGH, *Scriptores*, vol. 5 (Hanover, 1844), pp. 52–56.

Annales Fuldenses, eds. G. Pertz and F. Kurze, MGH, *Scriptores rerum Germanicarum in usum scholarum separatim editi* (Hanover, 1891).

Gli Annales Pisani di Bernardo Marangone, ed. M. L. Gentile, *Rerum Italicarum Scriptores*, 6/2 (Bologna, 1937).

Les Annales de Saint Bertin, eds. F. Grat, J. Vielliard, S. Clémencet (Paris, 1964).

Annales Sangallenses maiores, ed. I. von Arx, in MGH, *Scriptores*, vol. 1 (Hanover, 1826), pp. 73–85.

The Annals of St Bertin, trans. J. Nelson (Manchester, 1991).

Arab Historians of the Crusades, trans. F. Gabrieli (Berkeley, 1969).

Arnulf of Milan, *Liber gestorum recentium*, ed. I. Scaravelli (Bologna, 1996).

Auxilius, *In defensionem sacrae ordinationis pape Formosi libri duo*, in E. Dümmler, *Auxilius und Vulgarius. Quellen und Forschungen zur Geschichte des Papstthums im Anfange des 10. Jahrhunderts* (Leipzig, 1866), pp. 59–95.

Becker, G., *Catalogi bibliothecarum antiqui* (Bonn, 1885).

Benedict IV, *Epistolae*, in *Patrologia Latina*, vol. 131 (Paris, 1853), columns 39–44.

Benedict of St. Andreas, *Chronicon*, in *Il Chronicon di Benedetto, monaco di S. Andrea del Soratte e il Libellus de imperatoria potestate in urbe Roma*, ed. G. Zucchetti (Rome, 1920), pp. 3–187.

Benedizione del vessillo di Sant'Eusebio a Vercelli (964), in *Le carte dello Archivio capitolare di Vercelli*, eds. D. Arnoldi, G. C. Faccio, F. Gabotto, G. Rocchi (Pinerolo, 1912), p. 353.

Benzo of Alba, *Ad Heinricum IV. imperatorem libri VII*, ed. H. Seyffert, MGH, *Scriptores rerum Germanicarum in usum scholarum separati editi*, vol. 65 (Hanover, 1996).

Bonfil, R., *History and Folklore in a Medieval Jewish Chronicle: The Family Chronicle of Aḥima'az ben Paltiel* (Leiden, 2009).

Book of Gifts and Rarities (Kitāb al-Hadāyā wa al-Tuḥaf): Selections Compiled in the Fifteenth Century from an Eleventh-Century Manuscript on Gifts and Treasures, trans. G. al Ḥijjāwī al-Qaddūmī (Cambridge, MA, 1996).

Brown, V., 'New Documents at Rieti for the Monasteries of San Benedetto *ad Xenodochium* and Santa Sofia in Ninth-Century Benevento', *Medieval Studies* 63 (2001), pp. 337–52.

I Cammini dell'Occidente. Il Mediterraneo tra i secoli IX e X. Ibn Khurdâdhbah, al-Muqaddasî, Ibn Hawqal, Italian translation by A. Vanoli (Padua, 2001).

Capitularia regum Francorum, eds. A. Boretius, V. Krause, MHG, *Leges sectio* 3, 2 vols. (Hanover, 1883–1897).

Carmen in victoriam Pisanorum, in G. Scalia, 'Il carme pisano sull'impresa contro i Saraceni del 1087', in *Studi di filologia romanza offerti a Silvio Pellegrini* (Padua, 1971), pp. 597–625.

Chronica Monasterii Casinensis, ed. H. Hoffmann, MGH, *Scriptores*, vol. 34 (Hanover, 1980).

Chronicon Salernitanum: A critical edition with Studies on Literary and Historical Sources and on Language, ed. U. Westerbergh (Stockholm, 1956).

Chronicon Sanctae Sophiae (cod. Vat. Lat. 4939), ed. J.-M. Martin (Rome, 2000).

Chronicon Vulturnense del Monaco Giovanni, ed. V. Federici, 4 vols. (Rome, 1925–1940).

Codex Carolinus, ed. W. Gundlach, MGH, *Epistolae*, vol. 3 (Berlin, 1892).

Codex Diplomaticus Cajetanus (Montecassino, 1887).

Codex Diplomaticus Cavensis, vol. 1, eds. M. Morcaldi - M. Schiani - S. De Stefano (Naples, 1873).

Codex Diplomaticus Cavensis, vol. 2, eds. M. Morcaldi - M. Schiani - S. De Stefano (Naples, 1875).

Constantinus Porphyrogenitus, *De administrando imperio*, eds. G. Moravcsik - J. H. Jenkins (Washington, DC, 1967).

Cronaca Cassanese del X secolo, ed. V. Saletta (Rome, 1966).

Cronaca di Novalesa, ed. G. C. Alessio (Turin, 1982).

The 'Cronaca di Partenope': An Introduction to and Critical Edition of the First Vernacular History of Naples (c. 1350), ed. S. Kelly (Leiden, 2011).

Cronicae Sancti Benedicti Casinensis, ed. L. A. Berto (Florence, 2006).

Destructio monasterii Farfensis edita a domno Hugone abbate, in *Il Chronicon Farfense di Gregorio di Catino: precedono la 'Constructio Farfensis' e gli scritti di Ugo di Farfa*, ed. U. Balzani (Rome, 1903), vol. 1, pp. 27–51.

Dialogi de miraculis sancti Benedicti auctore Desiderio, eds. G. Schwartz – A. Hofmeister, in MGH, *Scriptores*, 30/2 (Hanover, 1934), pp. 1111–51.

Documenti latini e greci del conte Ruggero I di Calabria e Sicilia, ed. J. Becker (Rome, 2013).

Documenti relativi alla storia di Venezia anteriori al Mille, ed. R. Cessi, 2 vols. (Padua, 1942–1943).

Donizo, *Vita di Matilde di Canossa*, ed. P. Golinelli (Milan, 2008).

Eadmer, *Vita Anselmi*, ed. R. W. Southern (London, 1962).

The Epistle of the monk Theodosius to the Archdeacon Leo concerning the capture of Syracuse, in F. M. Crawford, *The Rulers of the South*, 2 vols. (London, 1901), pp. 79–98.

Epistola Theodosii monachi ad Leonem Archidiaconum de expugnatione Syracusarum, in *Vitae Sanctorum Siculorum*, ed. O. Caietani, vol. 2 (Palermo, 1657), pp. 272–77.

The '*Epistolae vagantes*' *of Gregory VII*, ed. H. E. J. Cowdrey (Oxford, 1972).

Erchempert, *Piccola Storia dei Longobardi di Benevento / Ystoriola Longobardorum Beneventum degentium*, ed. L. A. Berto (Naples, 2013).

Fragmenta registri Stephani V. papae, ed. E. Caspar, in MGH, *Epistolae*, vol. 7 (Berlin, 1928), pp. 334–53.

Geoffrey Malaterra, *The Deeds of Count Roger of Calabria and Sicily and of his Brother Duke Robert Guiscard*, trans. K. B. Wolf (Ann Arbor, 2005).

Geoffrey Malaterra, *De rebus gestis Rogerii Calabriae et Siciliae Comitis et Roberti Guiscardi ducis fratris eius*, ed. E. Pontieri, *Rerum Italicarum Scriptores, Series Secunda*, vol. 5, 1 (Bologna, 1925–1928).

Gregory VII, *Registrum*, ed. E. Caspar, MGH, *Epistolae selectae in usum scholarum*, 2 vols. (Berlin, 1920–1923).

Hadrian II, *Epistolae*, ed. E. Perels, in MGH, *Epistolae*, vol. 6 (Berlin, 1925), pp. 691–765.

Historia Langobardorum codicis Gothani, in *Italian Carolingian Historical and Poetic Texts*, edition and English translation by L. A. Berto (Pisa, 2016), pp. 50–63.

Historia et laudes SS. Sabae et Macarii iuniorum e Sicilia auctore Oreste Patriarcha Hierosolymitano, ed. G. Cozza-Luzi (Rome, 1893).

Hystoria de via et recuperatione Antiochiae atque Ierusolymarum (olim Tudebodus imitatus et continuatus). I Normanni d'Italia alla prima Crociata in una cronaca cassinese, ed. E. D'Angelo (Florence, 2009).

Ibn Ḥamdîs, *Il Canzoniere*, Italian translation by C. Schiaparelli (Palermo, 1998).

Ibn Ḥawqal, *Kitab Surat al-Ard*, ed. J. H. Kramers, 2 vols. (Leiden, 1938–1939).

Das 'Itinerarium Bernardi Monachi', ed. J. Ackermann (Hanover, 2010).

John the Deacon, *Gesta episcoporum Neapolitanorum*, in *Storia dei vescovi napoletani (I secolo −876) / Gesta Episcoporum Neapolitanorum*, ed. L. A. Berto (Pisa, 2018), pp. 72–111.

John the Deacon, *Istoria Veneticorum*, ed. L. A. Berto (Bologna, 1999).

John the Deacon, *Vita Sancti Gregorii Magni*, in *Patrologia Latina*, vol. 75 (Paris, 1849), columns 59–242.

John VIII, *Registrum*, ed. E. Caspar, in MGH, *Epistolae*, vol. 7 (Berlin, 1928), pp. 1–272.

John Scylitzes, *Synopsis historiarum*, ed. H. Thurn (Berlin-New York, 1972).

Landulf the Elder, *Historia Mediolanensis*, eds. L. C. Bethmann – W. Wattenbach, in MGH, *Scriptores*, vol. 8 (Hanover, 1848), pp. 32–100.

Leo III, *Epistolae*, ed. K. Hampe, in MGH, *Epistolae*, vol. 5 (Berlin, 1899), pp. 85–104.

Leo IV, *Epistolae Selecta*, ed. A. de Hirsch-Gereuth, in MGH, *Epistolae*, vol. 5 (Berlin, 1899), pp. 585–612.

Liber pontificalis, ed. L. Duchesne, 2 vols. (Paris, 1886–1892).

The Life of Saint Neilos of Rossano, edited and translated by R. L. Capra, I. A. Murzaku, D. J. Milewski (Harvard, MA, 2018).

Liudprand of Cremona, *Antapodosis*, in Id., *Opera omnia*, ed. P. Chiesa, *Corpus Christianorum, Continuatio Mediaevalis*, vol. 156 (Turnhout, 1998), pp. 3–150.

Liudprand of Cremona, *Historia Ottonis*, in Id., *Opera omnia*, ed. P. Chiesa, *Corpus Christianorum, Continuatio Mediaevalis*, vol. 156 (Turnhout, 1998), pp. 169–83.

Liudprand of Cremona, *Relatio de legatione Constantinopolitana*, in Id., *Opera omnia*, ed. P. Chiesa, *Corpus Christianorum, Continuatio Mediaevalis*, vol. 156 (Turnhout, 1998), pp. 187–218.

Liudprand of Cremona, *Retribution*, in *The Complete Works of Liudprand of Cremona*, trans. P. Squatriti (Washington, DC, 2007), pp. 41–202.

Lupus Protospatarius, *Annales*, ed. G. Pertz, in MGH. *Scriptores*, vol. 5 (Hanover, 1844), pp. 52–63.

Mandalà, G., 'The Martyrdom of Yūḥannā, Physician of Ibn Abī 'l-Ḥusayn Ruler of the Island of Sicily: Editio Princeps and Historical Commentary', *Journal of Transcultural Medieval Studies* 3 (2016), pp. 33–118.

Marinus II, *Epistolae et Privilegia*, in *Patrologia Latina*, vol. 133 (Paris, 1853), columns 863–78.

Martin, J.-M., *Guerre, accords et frontières en Italie méridionale pendant le Haut Moyen Âge. 'Pacta de Liburia, Divisio Principatus Beneventani' et autres actes* (Rome, 2005).

Miracula S. Euphebii episcopi Neapolitani, in *Acta Sanctorum, Mai*, V (Antwerp, 1685), pp. 236–38.

Miracula sancti Felicis Nolani, in Peter the Subdeacon, *L'opera agiografica*, ed. E. D'Angelo (Florence, 2002), pp. 209–13.

Ex miraculis Sancti Agrippini, in MGH, *Scriptores rerum Langobardicarum et Italicarum saec. VI–IX* (Hanover, 1876), pp. 463–65.

Moretus, H., 'Un opuscule du diacre Adalbert sur S. Martin de MonteMassico', *Analecta Bollandiana* 25 (1906), pp. 243–58.

Neapolitanorum victoria ficta, ed. G. Waitz, in MGH, *Scriptores rerum Langobardicarum et Italicarum saec. VI–IX* (Hanover, 1878), pp. 465–66.

Neilos, *Vita di san Filareto di Seminara*, ed. U. Martino (Reggio Calabria, 2014, second edition).

Nicholas, *Epistolae*, ed. E. Perels, in MGH, *Epistolae*, vol. 6 (Berlin, 1925), pp. 257–690.

Orderic Vitalis, *Historia ecclesiastica*, vols. 3, 4, ed. M. Chibnall (Oxford, 1969).

Passio s. Bertharii abbatis Cassinensis, in *Acta Sanctorum, Octobris*, IX (Paris – Rome, 1869), pp. 670–82.

Passio Sancti Herasmi, in D. Lohrmann, 'Die Jugendwerke des Johannes von Gaeta', *Quellen und Forschungen aus italienischen Archiven und Bibliotheken* 47 (1967), pp. 376–81.

Paul the Deacon, *Historia Langobardorum*, eds. L. Bethmann – G. Waitz, in MGH, *Scriptores rerum Langobardicarum et Italicarum saec. VI–IX* (Hanover, 1878), pp. 12–187.

Peter the Deacon, *Ortus et vita iustorum cenobii Casinensis*, ed. R. H. Rodgers (Los Angeles, 1972).

Peter the Deacon, *Vita, translatio, et miracula S. Martini abbatis*, in *Acta Sanctorum, Octobris*, X (Bruxelles, 1861), pp. 835–40.

Peters, A., *Joannes Messor, seine Lebensbeschreibung und ihre Entstehung*, Diss. (Bonn, 1955).

Radoynus, *Vita S. Pardi episcopi*, in *Acta Sanctorum, Mai*, VI (Antwerp, 1688), pp. 371–73.

Regesti dei documenti dell'Italia meridionale (570-899), eds. J. M. Martin, E. Cuozzo, S. Gasparri, M. Villani (Rome, 2002).

Regii Neapolitani Archivi Monumenta (Naples, 1845).

Registrum Petri Diaconi (Montecassino, Archivio dell'Abbazia, Reg. 3), eds. J.-M. Martin, P. Chastang, E. Cuozzo, L. Feller, G. Orofino, A. Thomas, M. Villani, 4 vols. (Rome, 2015).

Rythmus de captivitate Lhuduici imperatoris, in *Italian Carolingian Historical and Poetic Texts*, edition and English translation by L. A. Berto (Pisa, 2016), pp. 108–11.

S. Lorenzo (853–1199), ed. F. Gaeta (Venice, 1959).

Schreiner, P., *Die byzantinischen Kleinchroniken* (Vienna, 1975).

Sermo de transito Sancti Constantii, ed. A. Hofmeister, in MGH, *Scriptores*, vol. 30, 2 (Leipzig, 1934), pp. 1019–22.

Sermo de virtute Sancti Constantii, ed. A. Hofmeister, in MGH, *Scriptores*, vol. 30, 2 (Leipzig, 1934), pp. 1017–19.

Synaxaria Selecta [50], in *Synaxarium Ecclesiae Constantinopolitanae*, in *Acta Sanctorum, Nov.* XIX (online edition), pp. 237–39.

Synaxarium Ecclesiae Constantinopolitanae, Propylaeum Ad AASS Novembris, ed. H. Delehaye (Brussels, 1902).

Stasolla, M. G., 'Arabi e Sardegna nella storiografia araba del medioevo', *Studi Maghrebini* 14 (1982), pp. 163–202.

Theophanes, *Chronographia*, ed. C. De Boor (Bonn, 1839).

Theophanes Continuatus, *Chronographia*, in *Theophanes Continuatus, Joannes Cameniata, Symeon magister, Georgius Monachus*, ed. J. Bekker (Bonn, 1838).

Thietmar of Merseburg, *Chronicon*, ed. R. Holtzmann, MGH, *Scriptores rerum Germanicarum in usum scholarum*, n. s. 9 (Berlin, 1935).

Translatio corporis sancti Bartholomei apostoli Beneventum et miracula, in Anastasius Bibliothecarius, *Sermo Theodori Studitae de sancto Bartholomeo*, ed. U. Westerbergh (Stockholm, 1963), pp. 8–12.

Translatio corporis sancti Bartholomei in Gallias, in Anastasius Bibliothecarius, *Sermo Theodori Studitae de sancto Bartholomeo*, ed. U. Westerbergh (Stockholm, 1963), pp. 3–8.

Translatio Marci Evangelistae Venetias [BHL 5283–5284], in E. Colombi, *Storie di cronache e reliquie nella 'Venetia' altomedievale* (Trieste, 2012), pp. 17–63.

Translatio S. Fortunatae et sociorum, ed. O. Holder Hegger, in MGH, *Scriptores*, vol. 15, 1 (Hanover, 1887), p. 473.

Translatio S. Ianuarii et sociorum, ed. O. Holder Hegger, in MGH, *Scriptores*, vol. 15, 1 (Hanover, 1887), p. 473.

Translatio sancti Severini auctore Iohanne Diacono, ed. G. Waitz, in MGH, *Scriptores rerum Langobardicarum et Italicarum saec. VI–IX* (Hanover, 1878), pp. 452–59.

The Travels of Ibn Jubayr, trans. R. Broadhurst (London, 1952; Reprint, Noida, 2001).

Vehse, O., 'Das Bündnis gegen die Sarazenen vom Jahre 915', *Quellen und Forschungen aus italienischen Archiven und Bibliotechen* 19 (1927), pp. 181–204.

Vita Antonini abbatis Surrentini, in *Acta Sanctorum, Februarii*, II (Venice, 1785), pp. 787–94.

Vita e fatti del nostro padre Bartolomeo, in G. Zaccagni, 'Il Bios di san Bartolomeo da Simeri', *Rivista di studi bizantini e neoellenici*, n.s. 33 (1996), pp. 229–74.

Vita et miracula sancti Bononii abbatis Locediensis, eds. G. Schwartz - A. Hofmeister, in MGH, *Scriptores*, vol. 30, 2 (Leipzig, 1934), pp. 1023–33.

Vita et Miracula Sancti Fantini, in *Acta Sanctorum, Iulii*, V (Antwerp, 1727), pp. 556–67.

Vita s. Athanasii, in *Vita et Translatio s. Athanasii Neapolitani episcopi (BHL 735 e 737) sec. IX*, ed. A. Vuolo (Rome, 2001), pp. 113–43.

Vita di Sant'Elia il Giovane, ed. G. Rossi Taibbi (Palermo, 1962).

Vita S. Eliae Spelaeotae, in *Acta Sanctorum, Septembris*, III (Venice, 1761), pp. 843–88.

Vita di San Giovanni Terista, ed. S. Borsari, *Archivio Storico per la Calabria e la Lucania* 22 (1953), pp. 135–51.

Vita S. Gregorii abbatis Porcetensis posterior, ed. O. Holder-Egger, in MGH, *Scriptores*, vol. 15, 2 (Hanover, 1888), pp. 1191–99.

Vita S. Gregorii abbatis Porcetensis prior, ed. O. Holder-Egger, in MGH, *Scriptores*, vol. 15, 2 (Hanover, 1888), pp. 1187–90.

La Vita di san Leone Luca di Corleone, ed. M. Stelladoro (Badia Greca di Grottaferrata, 1995).

Vita di s. Luca vescovo di Isola Capo Rizzuto, ed. G. Schirò (Palermo, 1954).

Vita s. Lucae abbatis Armenti, in *Acta Sanctorum, Octobris*, VI (Paris-Rome, 1868), pp. 337–41.

Vita di s. Nicodemo di Kellarana, ed. M. Arco Magri (Rome, 1969).

Vita di san Nilo fondatore e patrono di Grottaferrata, ed. G. Giovannelli (Badia di Grottaferrata, 1973).

Vita s. Symeonis auctore Eberwino abbate S. Martinis Treveris, in *Acta Sanctorum, Junii*, I (Antwerp, 1695), pp. 89–95.

Vita S. Venerii, in *Acta Sanctorum, Septembris*, IV (Antwerp, 1763), pp. 115–19.

Vita Vitalis, in *Acta Sanctorum, Martii*, II (Antwerp, 1668), pp. 26–34.

Vita Walfredi und Kloster Monteverdi: Toskanisches Mönchtum Zwischen Langobardischer und Fränkischer Herrschaft, ed. K. Schmid (Tübingen, 1991).

Vuolo, A., *Una testimonianza agiografica napoletana: il 'Libellus miraculorum s. Agnelli' (sec. X)* (Naples-Rome, 1987).

William of Apulia, *La Geste de Robert Guiscard*, ed. M. Mathieu (Palermo, 1961).

Secondary sources

Acconcia Longo, A., 'S. Giovanni Terista nell'agiografia e nell'innografia', in *Calabria bizantina. Civiltà bizantina nei territori di Gerace e Stilo* (Soveria Mannelli, Catanzaro, 1998), pp. 121–43.

Arthur, P., 'Saraceni, schiavi e il Salento', in *III Congresso Nazionale di Archeologia Medievale* (Florence, 2004), pp. 443–45.

Berti, G., S. Menchelli, 'Pisa: Ceramiche da cucina, da dispensa, da trasporto, dei secoli X–XV', *Archeologia Medievale* 25 (1998), pp. 307–33.

Bertolini, P., 'Atanasio', in *Dizionario biografico degli Italiani*, vol. 4 (Rome, 1962), pp. 510–18.

Blumenkranz, B., 'La conversion au Judaisme d'André, archeveque de Bari', *Journal of Jewish Studies*, 14 (1963), pp. 33–36.

Borruso, A., 'Some Arab-Muslim perceptions of religion and medieval culture in Sicily', in *Muslim Perceptions of Other Religions: A Historical Survey Overview* (New York, 1999), pp. 136–42.

Bruce, T., 'The politics of violence and trade: Denia and Pisa in the eleventh century', *Journal of Medieval History* 32, 2 (2006), pp. 127–42.

Cahen, C., 'Un texte peu connu relatif au commerce oriental d'Amalfi au XIe siècle', *Archivio Storico per le Province Napoletane* 34 (1953–1954), pp. 3–8.

Cilento, A., *Potere e monachesimo: ceti dirigenti e mondo monastico nella Calabria bizantina: secoli IX–XI* (Florence, 2000).

Colafemmina, C., 'Gli ambienti ebraici meridionali e le Crociate', in *Il Mezzogiorno normanno-svevo e le crociate* (Bari, 2002), pp. 397–406.

Delle Donne, F., 'Giorgio d'Antiochia', in *Dizionario biografico degli Italiani*, vol. 55 (Rome, 2000), pp. 347–50.

Dujcev, I., *Medioevo bizantino-slavo* (Rome, 1965).

Erdmann, C., *The origin of the idea of crusade*, trans. M. W. Baldwin and W. Goffart (Princeton, 1977).

Feniello, A., *Sotto il segno del leone. Storia dell'Italia musulmana* (Rome-Bari, 2011).

Figliuolo, B., 'Amalfi e il Levante nel Medioevo', in *I Comuni italiani nel regno crociato di Gerusalemme*, eds. G. Airaldi - B. Kedar (Genoa, 1986), pp. 571–664.

Flori, J., *La guerre sainte: la formation de l'idée de croisade dans l'Occident chrétien* (Paris, 2001).

Gelichi, S., 'La storia di una nuova città attraverso l'archeologia: Venezia nell'alto Medioevo', in *Three Empires, Three Cities. Identity, Material Culture and Legitimacy in Venice, Ravenna and Rome, 750–1000*, ed. V. West-Harling (Turnhout, 2015), pp. 51–98.

Guillou, A., 'Italie méridionale byzantine ou Byzantins en Italie méridionale?', *Byzantion* 44 (1974), pp. 152–90.

Guillou, A. – K. Tchérémissinoff, 'Note sur la culture arabe e la culture slave dans le Katepanat d'Italie (Xe-XIe siècles)', *Mélanges de l'Ecole française de Rome. Moyen-Age, Temps modernes* 88, 2 (1976), pp. 677–92.

Houben, H., 'Il saccheggio del monastero di S. Modesto in Benevento: un ignoto episodio delle incursioni arabe nel Mediterraneo', in Id. *Medioevo monastico meridionale* (Naples, 1987), pp. 55–65.

Jacoby, D., 'Venetian commercial expansion in the Eastern Mediterranean, 8th–11th centuries', in *Byzantine Trade, 4th–12th Centuries: the Archaeology of Local, Regional, International Exchange*, ed. M. Mundell Mango (Farnham, 2009), pp. 371–91.

Joannou, P., 'La personalità storica di Luca di Bova attraverso i suoi scritti inediti', *Archivio Storico per la Calabria e la Lucania*, 29 (1960), pp. 175–237.

Kedar, B. Z., *Crusade and Mission: European Approaches Toward the Muslims* (Princeton, 1984).

König, D. G., *Arabic-Islamic Views of the Latin West. Tracing the Emergence of Medieval Europe* (Oxford, 2015).

Luzzi, A., 'La vita di san Nilo da Rossano tra genere letterario e biografia storica', in *Les vies des saints à Byzance. Genre littéraire ou biographie historique?* eds. P. Odorico - P. A. Agapitos (Paris, 2004), pp. 175–89.

Mango, C., 'On re-reading the Life of St. Gregory the Decapolite', *Byzantina* 13 (1985), pp. 633–46.

McCormick, M., *Origins of the European Economy: Communications and Commerce AD 300–900* (Cambridge, 2002).

Mandalà, G., 'La Longobardia, i Longobardi e Pavia nei geografi arabo-islamici del Medioevo', *Aevum* 88 (2014), pp. 331–86.

Mandalà, G., 'Tra minoranze e periferie. Prolegomeni a un'indagine sui cristiani arabizzati di Sicilia', in *'Guerra santa' e conquiste islamiche nel Mediterraneo (VII-XI secolo)*, eds. M. Di Branco and K. Wolf (Rome, 2014), pp. 95–124.

Marazzi, F., 'Le 'città nuove' pontificie e l'insediamento laziale nel IX secolo', in *La storia dell'alto Medioevo italiano (VI-X secolo) alla luce dell'archeologia*, eds. R. Francovich - G. Noyé (Florence, 1994), pp. 251–77.

Mathews, K. R., 'Plunder of war or objects of trade? The reuse and reception of Andalusi objects in medieval Pisa', *Journal of Medieval Iberian Studies*, 4 (2012), pp. 233–58.

Metcalfe, A., *The Muslims of Medieval Italy* (Edinburgh, 2009).

Putzu, V., *Shabbetai Donnolo: un sapiente ebreo nella Puglia bizantina altomedievale* (Cassano delle Murge, Bari, 2004).

Rubiera Mata, J., *La taifa de Denia* (Alicante, 1985).

Settia, A. A., 'I Saraceni sulle Alpi: una storia da riscrivere', *Studi storici* 28 (1987), pp. 127–43.

Settia, A. A., *Castelli e villaggi nell'Italia padana: Popolamento, potere e sicurezza fra IX e XIII secolo* (Naples, 1984).

Settia, A. A., 'L'alto medioevo ad Alba. Problemi e ipotesi, in *Studi per una storia d'Alba*, V. *Alba medievale. Dall'alto medioevo alla fine della dominazione angioina: VI–XIV secolo*, ed. R. Comba (Alba, 2010), pp. 1–29 (digital version available in www. retimedievali.it).

Skinner, P., *Medieval Amalfi and its Diaspora: 800–1250* (Oxford, 2013).

Von Falkenhausen, V., *La dominazione bizantina nell'Italia meridionale dal IX all'XI secolo* (Bari, 1978).

Von Falkenhausen, V., 'Costantino l'Africano', in *Dizionario biografico degli Italiani*, vol. 30 (Rome, 1984), pp. 320–24.

Von Falkenhausen, V., 'La Vita di s. Nilo come fonte storica', in *Atti del Congresso internazionale su S. Nilo di Rossano* (Rossano-Grottaferrata, 1989), pp. 271–305.

Further readings

General history

In English: A. Ahamad, *A History of Islamic Sicily* (Edinburgh, 1975); A. Metcalfe, *The Muslims of Medieval Italy* (Edinburgh, 2009); L. C. Chiarelli, *A History of Muslim Sicily* (Venera, Malta, 2011); S. Davis-Secord, *Where Three Worlds Met: Sicily in the Early Medieval Mediterranean* (Ithaca, 2017), pp. 111–212.

In Italian: F. Gabrieli, 'Storia, cultura e civiltà degli Arabi in Italia', in *Gli Arabi in Italia*, eds. F. Gabrieli - U. Scerrato (Milan, 1979), pp. 109–48; F. Maurici, *Breve storia degli arabi in Sicilia* (Palermo, 2006); A. Feniello, *Sotto il segno del leone. Storia dell'Italia musulmana* (Rome-Bari, 2011); M. Di Branco, *915: La battaglia del Garigliano. Cristiani e musulmani nell'Italia medievale* (Bologna, 2019).

Southern Italy in the ninth and tenth century

B. Kreutz, *Before the Normans. Southern Italy in the Ninth and Tenth Centuries* (Philadelphia, 1991); *Les dynamiques de l'islamisation en Méditerranée centrale et en Sicile: nouvelles propositions et découvertes récentes*, eds. L. Arcifa, A. Bagnera, E. Pezzini, A. Nef, F. Ardizzone (Bari, 2014); *La Sicilia del IX secolo tra bizantini e musulmani*, eds. S. Modeo, M. Congiu, L. Santagati (Caltanissetta, 2013); M. Di Branco, K. Wolf, 'Terra di conquista? I musulmani in Italia meridionale nell'epoca aghlabita (184/800–269/909)', in *'Guerra santa' e conquiste islamiche nel Mediterraneo (VII-XI secolo)* (Rome, 2014), pp. 125–66; M. Di Branco, K. Wolf, 'Hindered Passages. The Failed Muslim Conquest of Southern Italy', *Journal of Transcultural Medieval Studies* 1 (2014), pp. 51–74; G. Musca, *L'emirato di Bari. 847–871* (Bari 1967, second edition); N. Cilento, 'Le incursioni saraceniche nell'Italia meridionale', in Id., *Italia meridionale longobarda* (Milan – Naples, 1971, second edition), pp. 135–66; F. Marazzi, '*Ita ut facta esse videatur Neapolis Panormus vel Africa*. Geopolitica della presenza islamica nei domini di Napoli, Gaeta, Salerno e Benevento nel IX secolo' *Schede Medievali*, 45 (2007), pp. 159–202; K. Wolf, 'Gli hjpati di Gaeta, papa Giovanni VIII e i Saraceni: tra dinamiche locali e transregionali', *Bullettino dell'Istituto storico italiano per il medio evo*, 116 (2014), pp. 25–60; D. Alvermann, 'La battaglia di Ottone II contro i Saraceni nel 982', *Archivio storico della Calabria e della Lucania*, 62 (1995), pp. 115–30; L. A. Berto, 'The Muslims as Others in the Chronicles of Early Medieval Southern Italy', *Viator. Medieval and Renaissance Studies*, 45, 3 (2014), pp. 1–24; L. A. Berto, 'The others and their stories: Byzantines, Franks, Lombards, and Muslims in ninth-century Neapolitan narrative texts', *Medieval History Journal*, 19, 1 (2016), pp. 34–56; A. Galdi – E. Susi, 'Santi, navi e Saraceni. Immagini e pratiche del mare tra agiografia e storia dalle coste campane a quelle dell'Alto Tirreno (secoli VI-XI)', in *Dio, il mare e gli uomini, Quaderni di storia religiosa*, 15 (Verona, 2008), pp. 53–102; L. A. Berto, 'Riscrivere e colmare i vuoti della storia dei musulmani e dei cristiani nell'alto Medioevo italiano nei testi narrativi medievali', *Mediterranean Chronicle* 8 (2018), pp. 259–84.

Normans and Muslims in the eleventh century

A. Nef, *Conquérir et gouverner la Sicile islamique aux XIe et XIIe siècles* (Rome, 2011); U. Rizzitano, 'Ruggero il gran conte e gli arabi di Sicilia', in *Ruggero il Gran Conte e l'inizio dello Stato normanno* (Rome, 1977), pp. 189–212; S. Tramontana, 'Ruggero I e la Sicilia musulmana', in *Il Mezzogiorno normanno-svevo e le crociate* (Bari, 2002), pp. 49–64; M.-A. Lucas-Avenel, 'L'immagine dei saraceni nelle cronache 'normanne' dell'XI secolo', in *Mezzogiorno e Mediterraneo. Territori, strutture, relazioni tra Antichità e Medioevo*, eds. G. Coppola, E. D'Angelo, R. Paone (Naples, 2006), pp. 233–46; K. B. Wolf, *Making History. The Normans and their Historians in Eleventh Century Italy* (Philadelphia, 1995); T. Smit, 'Pagans and Infidels, Saracens and Sicilians: Identifying Muslims in the Eleventh-Century Chronicles of Norman Italy', *The Haskins Society Journal* 21 (2009), pp. 67–86. M. T. Mansouri, 'Roger Ier le Normand dans les sources arabes', in *Ruggero I, Serlone e l'insediamento normanno in Sicilia*, eds. I. Giannetto, M. Ragusa, S. Tramontana (Troina, 2001), pp. 125–34.

Central and Northern Italy

L. Balletto, 'Le incursioni saracene del secolo X nell'area subalpina', *Rivista di storia, arte e archeologia per le province di Alessandria e di Asti*, 100 (1991), pp. 9–26; C. Bocca – M. Centini, *Saraceni nelle Alpi: storia, miti e tradizioni di una invasione medievale nelle regioni alpine occidentali* (Ivrea, 2006); A. A. Settia, *Barbari e infedeli nell'alto Medioevo italiano: storia e miti storiografici* (Spoleto, 2011); M. Nallino, 'Il mondo arabo e Venezia fino alle crociate', in *La Venezia del Mille* (Florence, 1965), pp. 161–81; L. A. Berto, 'I Musulmani nelle cronache dell'Italia centro-settentrionale altomedievale (secoli VIII-XI)', *Mediterranean Chronicle* 6 (2016), pp. 57–95; L. A. Berto, 'I musulmani nell'agiografia altomedievale della Toscana e dell'Italia settentrionale', *Hagiographica* 25 (2018), pp. 99–112.

Index